Knowing and Acting:
Inquiry, Ideology and Educational Studies

The Wisconsin Series of Teacher Education

General Editor: Professor Carl A. Grant, School of Education, University of Wisconsin-Madison, Madison. Wisconsin, 53706 USA

Contradictions in Teacher Education and Society: A Critical Analysis
Mark B. Ginsburg, University of Pittsburgh, USA

Knowing and Acting: Inquiry, Ideology and Educational Studies
Landon E. Beyer, Cornell College, Iowa, USA

The Wisconsin Series of Teacher Education

Knowing and Acting: Inquiry, Ideology and Educational Studies

Landon E. Beyer
Cornell College, Iowa

(22) The Falmer Press
(A member of the Taylor & Francis Group)
London • New York • Philadelphia

USA   The Falmer Press, Taylor & Francis Inc., 242 Cherry Street, Philadelphia, PA 19106-1906

UK   The Falmer Press, Falmer House, Barcombe, Lewes, East Sussex, BN8 5DL

First published 1988

Library of Congress Cataloging in Publication Data

Beyer, Landon E., 1949–
  Knowing and acting.

  (Wisconsin series of teacher education; 2)
  Bibliography: p.
  Includes index
  1. Teachers—Training of. 2. Education—Humanistic.
3. Teaching. I. Title. II. Series.
LB1715.B49 1988 370.11′2 88-3918
ISBN 1-85000-348-3
ISBN 1-85000-349-1 (pbk.)

Jacket design by Caroline Archer

Typeset in 11/13 Bembo by
Mathematical Composition Setters Ltd, Ivy Street, Salisbury

Printed in Great Britain by Taylor & Francis (Printers) Ltd, Basingstoke

Contents

Acknowledgments   vii

Series Editor's Introduction   ix

Chapter 1: Liberal versus Applied Studies: The Plight of
              Educational Inquiry   1
                  Liberal Studies and the Domain of Education
                  Education Views the Liberal Disciplines
                  Summary and Conclusions

Chapter 2: Knowledge, Ideology, and Inquiry   47
                  Liberal Studies and the Domain of Knowledge
                  Epistemology, History, and Social Context
                  Knowledge and Ideology: Toward Participatory
                  Communities

Chapter 3: Educational Studies and Ideology   93
                  Education and Social Context
                  Beyond Reproduction: Reconstructing
                  Educational Inquiry

Chapter 4: Education, Moral Action and the Practice of
              Possibility   135
                  Moral Principles and Normative Judgments
                  Schooling and the Culture of Democracy

Chapter 5: Beyond Training: Teacher Education as Praxis   173
                  The Nature of Teacher Preparation
                  Against Technicism: The Role of Educational
                  Foundations
                  Critical Reflection, Praxis, and Field Experience
                  The Institutional Contexts of Teacher Education

Contents

Chapter 6:   Critical Scholarship and the Practice of Teacher
             Education   209
                 The Practice of Teacher Education and Liberal
                 Inquiry
                 Implementing Educational Reform: Praxis, Politics
                 and Renewal

Index   245

Acknowledgments

Any author owes more to those who influence his/her work that can be recounted in a short space. Partly because of our tendencies towards individualization and privatization, moreover — tendencies that are in fact the subject of critique here — we often assume an isolation of educational work that is as inaccurate as it is politically deforming. In any case, I want to formally thank at least some of the people whose support, questioning, and friendship have influenced this book.

Michael W. Apple, Carl Grant, Susan Laird, Jo Anne Pagano, and Philip H. Steedman all read drafts of this manuscript and often made detailed, helpful suggestions for their revision; I gratefully acknowledge their diligent work in this regard, and request their forgiveness for occasionally disregarding their thoughtful advice. I also want to acknowledge the assistance of those people whose ideas, work, and affect on my own thinking (directly and indirectly) have been especially important in thinking through the issues with which this monograph deals: Mimi Bloch, Linda Dybas, Walter Feinberg, Madeleine Grumet, Glen Hudak, Herbert M. Kliebard, Patti Lather, Daniel P. Liston, Jane Roland Martin, John Pickles, William F. Pinar, Robert E. Rouse, Paula Salvio, George M. A. Stanic, Jeanne Sullivan, Geoffrey Tabakin, Joel Taxel, Kenneth Teitelbaum, James A. Whitson, George H. Wood, and Kenneth M. Zeichner.

This book attempts to develop a portion of the groundwork for altering some of the harmful intellectual and social hierarchies that are injurious for educational and everyday life. This requires more than intellectual work, obviously, as we restructure our relations and activities with those involved in cultural, social, familial, and political practice. Happily, I have already benefitted in many ways from what this democratization of day to day life might portend. While her formal title is that of 'secretary,' Diane Harrington provides daily evidence of the extent to which collaboration, friendship, and intellectual and moral support can intermingle in ways that go beyond the bureaucratic definitions that attempt to shape consciousness. Without her conscientious work, critical eye, and unfailing diligence this book would have stalled at chapter one. Similarly, Noelle Hawk and Ann Alfirevic provided models of student assistance.

Last, I wish to acknowledge the contributions to the four teachers to whom this book is dedicated, without whose encouragement and help many more things would remain beyond my grasp.

Series Editor's Introduction

Knowing and Acting: Inquiry, Ideology, and Educational Studies is an outstanding contribution to the educational literature at a critical time in the history of teacher education. Educators engaged in program improvement, the reform effort, and current discussions of 'liberal' versus 'professional' activities should read *Knowing and Acting*. This book aids in our response to the current debates over the value of the liberal arts and its relation to teacher education. Professor Beyer, in situating the debate epistemologically, historically and institutionally, demonstrates the problematic consequences of much of this debate for teacher educators. Liberal studies has been separated from applied studies, 'educational foundations' from 'teacher education'. Beyer, like Dewey, reconceptualizes the debate so that it is not a question of either-or; instead of liberal or applied studies, Beyer argues that education offers a unique opportunity for the integration of theory and practice or the development of praxis.

Professor Beyer argues that teacher education as praxis encourages linking the practice of teaching to an analysis of the sociological and ideological role of schooling within a normative framework. The study of education becomes a unique opportunity to make use of theoretical analyses of everyday life. Students would be in a field in which questions of knowledge, politics and ethics interpenetrate practice.

Beyer supports his argument through an analysis of changes in epistemology and the historical and institutional structure of educational studies and teacher education. His review of recent epistemological analyses provides both a critique of positivism and an analysis of how positivism contributes to our current conception of education. By critiquing positivism and arguing in support of an epistemology that connects action to knowledge, teacher preparation becomes a union of reflective inquiry and practical action that would define teacher preparation as praxis.

Teacher education programs represent then a way to lead students to learn that knowledge is created in the practice of teaching. Teacher education students learn that knowing and acting must be combined if they (and their pupils) are to become critical thinkers in control of their lives, and people who promote social change through educational transformation.

What such a teacher education program will look like is described in Chapter 6, where Professor Beyer explains the educational reforms he has been involved in. He allows the reader a close-up view of the frustrations, failures and successes involved in implementing critical scholarship in educational studies programs.

Professor Beyer's proposal to reform teacher education conflicts with other more well known proposals such as The Holmes Group report, *Tomorrow's Teachers*. He questions many of its recommendations, including its reliance on developing a 'science of education', and the need to remove educational studies from the other 'academic majors' at the undergraduate level. Besides asking, 'where is the research to back up its claims?' (p. 237), the author's argument points out the narrowness and futility of believing that more of liberal arts per se will lead to the successful preparation of the reflective and socially engaged teachers that are needed.

I believe readers of *Knowing and Acting* will find this book so rich and informative that they will spontaneously recommend it to their colleagues.

Carl A. Grant
University of Wisconsin-Madison

Dedication

To four teachers who made a difference:

Bob Murphy, my fifth grade teacher who allowed me to feel good about, and begin to believe in, myself;

Steve Fortney, who in high school opened my eyes to the wonders and possibilities of poetry and philosophy;

Don Crawford, whose commitment to philosophical clarity was matched by his sensitivity to the arts, as he taught my first undergraduate course in aesthetics; and

Mike Apple, who first helped me consider the importance of educational work.

1
Liberal versus Applied Studies: The Plight of Educational Inquiry

There is perhaps no educational question more often discussed than the proper relationship between theory and practice. In both teaching and research activities, this relationship frequently becomes a fundamental pivot upon which turn a host of allied problems and issues; in some form or another the problem of how to conceptualize theory and practice, and their possible relations, must be resolved in order for discussion to proceed on other matters, or for action to be taken in specific contexts. Failure to openly discuss this issue frequently leads to miscommunication and a resultant mismatch in expectations. For instance, student teachers are sometimes impatient with 'theoretical' or 'abstract' questions which, at least initially, may be regarded as having no clear relevance for the activities of teaching. Likewise, teachers may find it difficult to question, for instance, the ethical and political views which underlie their classroom interactions. At the same time, educational theorists sometimes engage in complex arguments and inquiries using language that is unfamiliar and intimidating. These inquiries sometimes seem to be pursued for their own internal elegance and rigor, quite apart from their significance in helping solve real, human and social problems. In short, 'practice' is often taken to refer to the behaviors of people in a relatively controlled and stable institutional situation, while 'theory' is presumed to represent the kind of wide ranging questioning, analyzing, and debating that characterize what academics do in colleges and universities. Now clearly these categories, and their presumed antagonisms, serve a normative or affiliative purpose: for academics, the use of forms of reasoning, analytical styles, and modes of discourse identifies their work as part of a larger scholarly tradition, and also highlights their special purpose — the creation of new knowledge through intellectual investigation. Discussion of appropriate 'practice' offers teachers (members of a beleagured and, for the most part, unappreciated vocation) the possibility of aligning with a particular set of norms and perceptions that culminate in a notion of 'professionalism'. Within this perspective, 'theory' is removed from activities rooted in the 'real world of the public schools', regarded as someone else's domain, and treated with indifference or suspicion.[1] Dewey hinted at these tensions when he observed:

> We are met ... with the belief that instruction in theory is merely theoretical, abstruse, remote, and therefore relatively useless to the teacher as a teacher, unless the student is at once set upon the work of teaching; that only 'practice' can give a motive to a professional learning, and supply material for educational courses.[2]

Such is the state of affairs, over eighty years after Dewey's remarks, that confronts those involved in contemporary education. These assumptions permit educationalists to speak of the 'useful' in contrast to the 'theoretical' in education.[3]

To understand the etiology and meaning of this central educational dichotomy, we must explore the conceptual, historical, and institutional nature of larger divisions that buttress it. For the dichotomy between theory and practice is a reflection of deeper, more long standing divisions that have grown out of traditions in epistemology, the historical genesis of higher education, and the development of professional areas of study. These in turn have often enhanced, and been sustained by, social and political divisions having to do with ideological issues.

One of the strands in the entanglement of issues surrounding the separation of educational theory from practice is the relationship between the liberal arts and sciences, on the one hand, and the domain of applied, professional, useful, or vocational areas within which schools and departments of education are normally located, on the other. The former disciplines are regarded as theoretical and foundational in their central activities, while educational studies, teacher preparation, a variety of courses in instructional methodology and those devoted to actual work in schools (consider the puzzling nature of the expression, 'practice teaching'), are considered practical in orientation. Hence the larger distinction between liberal and applied studies forms the backdrop against which the dichotomy between theory and practice in education must be seen. Within this division between liberal and applied studies, education is often seen as a derivative area, a weak sibling if you will, with aims and purposes that are fundamentally different from liberal studies. The further separation of 'educational foundations' from 'teacher education' is a reflection of this deeper schism between liberal and applied studies, with foundations having a liberal sheen and teacher education carrying professional overtones. This chapter will examine the basic division between liberal and applied studies by looking first at some of the historical and philosophical justifications for it that have been made by advocates of liberal learning; we will then consider this division as it has been exacerbated by some writings in education generally, and teacher preparation in particular.

Liberal Studies and the Domain of Education

The Culture and History of the University

It is initially important to see how the history of liberal disciplines has been linked with the history of higher education. For the disparity between allegedly 'pure' disciplinary inquiry and more applied or derivative branches has been fostered by cultural characteristics of the university itself. The history of the university and its cultural affinities thus form an important element in the web of understandings that has served to separate the liberal from the applied, the true disciplines from their applications in fields like education.[4]

Learning in the Middle Ages was largely comprised of the seven liberal arts — namely, grammar, rhetoric, logic, geometry, arithmetic, astronomy, and music.[5] To be educated was to become acquainted with the major ideas in each of these domains, and especially with the classical literature on each subject. While education in Law, Medicine, and Theology was also pursued by certain universities and colleges, their place within the university was frequently the subject of debate and criticism, especially as students began to pursue a course of study aimed at these professions:

> ... in the twelfth and thirteenth centuries ... the cathedral, monastic, and urban schools evolved into universities, with a faculty of the *arts liberales* surmounted by higher faculties of law, medicine, or theology. Undergraduates at that time, as now, sought to focus all their efforts on those liberal arts, such as

logic, that were part of or would lead them to the lucrative, professional arts. In response, instructors such as John of Garland and John of Salisbury railed against this trend, saying that true arts that 'are called "liberal" ... liberate us from cares incompatible with wisdom. They often even free us from worry about [material] necessities, so that the mind may have still greater liberty to apply itself to philosophy'.[6]

From its beginning concerned with the seven subject areas thought to comprise liberal education, the classical university has often struggled against the admission and legitimation of professional or applied fields, as the latter have been conceived as diluting or misshaping the central, scholastic and liberal mission of the university.

In part a legacy of this era, one traditional goal of the modern university was to provide 'permanent institutions of learning' geared toward 'the training of scholars and the maintenance of the tradition of learning and investigation'.[7] The very term 'university' means an association of scholars leading a common life of learning. Given this tradition, the university can be understood as a 'repository of our heritage,' and a transmitter of this heritage to succeeding generations of students.[8] As Cardinal Newman put it in his classic work, *The Idea of a University*:

> [The] process of training, by which the intellect, instead of being formed or sacrificed to some particular or accidental purpose, some specific trade or profession, or study or science, is disciplined for its own sake, for the perception of its own proper object, and for its own highest culture, is called Liberal Education ... to set forth the right standard, and to train according to it, and to help forward all students towards it according to their various capacities, this I conceive to be the business of a University.[9]

In offering a general or liberal education that centered on disciplined, intrinsically valued inquiry, the university was responsible for protecting and disseminating those forms of knowledge thought central to the Western tradition, and for expanding the minds of those under its tutelage. As such, the university could in good conscience include relatively small numbers of faculty and students within an 'ivory tower'; from such a lofty perspective, the surrounding societal landscape was largely obscured and irrelevant. This exclusionary tradition is reflected in the elitist nature of some undergraduate liberal arts institutions and in some liberal arts disciplines within larger universities.[10]

Though this image of the university as an elite association of scholars guarding and transmitting our cultural heritage continues, its historical dominance was undercut by changes initiated in the German system of higher education. Beginning in the nineteenth century, the university was 'to establish on impregnable bases the new sciences — chemistry, biology, medicine...'[11] Initially a part of philosophy, the advancing interest in the natural sciences and their social usefulness provided an important impetus for expanded university research activities. It is important to see that this commitment to research was undertaken largely for instrumental reasons — that is, for the larger social, economic, and cultural attainments it would procure. The modern American university began to take on 'the immense responsibility of creating new knowledge, both for the preservation of the nation ... and for the health and sanity of our national culture.'[12] When Yale University added the Sheffield Scientific School to its educational offerings in 1844, as an illustrative case in point, the medieval lineage of the university was to be permanently disrupted, along with the general destiny of American higher education.[13]

Yet the place of professional schools within the dominant cultural traits of the university was not clear. As we have already seen, even the inclusion of professional study in Medicine, Law, and Theology in the Middle Ages gave rise to criticism and concern on the part of liberal arts faculty who feared the tendencies toward intellectual narrowness of professional study. The further expansion of professional fields increased the criticism directed at the expanding university, as it might continue to encroach upon or undermine the central, liberating disciplines. One way to resolve this tension between liberal and professional studies was to focus not on the question of whether to include particular subject areas, but on their relationship to the central purposes of a liberal education. This was the position taken by Cardinal Newman when he said that in arguing against professional knowledge he was not 'disrespectful towards particular studies, or arts, or vocations ...' Instead, Newman continues:

> I do but say that there will be this distinction as regards [an instructor of professional subjects] ... that out of a University he is in danger of being absorbed and narrowed by his pursuit, and of giving lectures which are nothing more than a lawyer, physician, geologist, or political economist; whereas in a University he will just know where he and his science stand, he has come to it, as it were, from a height, he has taken a survey of all

knowledge, he is kept from extravagence by the very rivalry of other studies, he has gained from them a special illumination and largeness of mind and freedom and self-possession, and he treats his own in consequence with a philosophy and a resource, which belongs not to the study itself, but to his liberal education. [14]

One way to contain the advances of professional study was for the university to provide an intellectual and social boundary within which the potential excesses of professional instruction could be contained. The liberal disciplines could provide an intellectual ordering of academic pursuits within which the illiberal tendencies of professional occupations might be checked. The sciences, for example, can be included within the confines of the university if they are pursued for their value in promoting liberal education. Yet this is not always the case; 'Baconian Philosophy, by using its physical sciences in the service of man, does thereby transfer them from the order of Liberal Pursuit to ... the distinct class of the Useful.' [15] To be truly liberal, an area of study must serve no end beyond the pursuit of knowledge itself; thus the inclusion of professional fields by universities must be closely guarded by the community of the learned whose commitment is to the intrinsic value of knowledge and learning, apart from their individual or social utility.

While the university that incorporates professional studies into its curriculum may in this way safeguard its liberal tradition, smaller liberal arts colleges in the US have a different view of non-liberal studies. For the special role of these colleges is not the acceptance of professionally oriented fields of study that have liberal aspects (in addition to social and vocational utility). Rather, liberal arts colleges incorporate only those subjects that are truly liberal — thus identifying more closely with the medieval lineage of the *arts liberales*. In an address commemorating the one hundredth anniversary of the founding of Allegheny College on 23 June, 1915, Alexander Meiklejohn (President of Amherst College) pointed out a special problem confronting colleges like Allegheny and Amherst:

the one confusion which does today threaten our understanding of the function of the college is that which identifies it with the professional school, which declares that there is no genuine education which is not really professional, which characterizes the belief in a 'liberal education', separate from and independent of vocational and professional study, as an idle creation of dream and fancy.[16]

The growing demand for well trained professionals in the decades just before and after the turn of the century is alarming for those, like Meiklejohn, committed to liberal colleges and their special mission. Even in the days of liberal colonial colleges that graduated men for the clergy it is not that they were operating as professional schools, training prospective members of a vocation. The purpose of these institutions 'was to educate ministers — but in what sense? Our opponents have interpreted the purpose as that of educating men to be ministers. The real purpose was that of educating ministers to be men'.[17] Educating people rather than training employees for the twentieth century was especially difficult, given the increased emphasis on professionalism during this era.

The theme of 'educating people' rather than 'training for a profession' runs through much of the writing on the mission and value of a liberal education. Professional schools may be content to train students narrowly for a specific vocation. But the liberal college must be devoted to the general study of ideas and the pursuit of intellectual, human development: 'in the activities common to all men the guidance by ideas is quite as essential as in the case of those which different groups of men carry on in differentiation from one another'.[18] Liberal and professional studies can be distinguished by virtue of the former's interest in more general or universal ideas, while the latter are content to focus more specifically on particular abilities and skills required for an occupation. 'We pledge ourselves forever,' Meiklejohn concludes his comments to those celebrating the centennial of Allegheny College, 'to the study of human living in order that living may be better done. We have not yet forgotten that fundamentally the proper study of mankind is Man.'[19]

Contrary to such sentiments favoring the exclusion of professional study, however, the further development of the twentieth century university as an institution with a more popular appeal no doubt contributed to, and reflected, changed social and economic expectations.[20] Such changed expectations mediated the former emphases on disinterested inquiry and the intrinsic value of liberal studies that guarded liberal learning from the dangers of utilitarianism. Jacques Barzun captures the extent to which the modern university is woven into the social fabric:

[T]he American university has upheaved itself to 'catch up' and 'modernize', words that mean: has ceased to be a sheltered spot

for study only; has come into the market place and answered the
cries for help uttered by government, industry and the general
public; has busily pursued the enthusiasm of ... both private
patrons and big foundations. ... Today, the word 'multiversity'
has gained currency as a description of the changed reality.[21]

As an entity firmly committed to the generation of new socially and
economically useful knowledge through research, the multiversity
fosters an assemblage of self-enclosed specialties. Such a commitment in
many ways contradicts the older tradition of the university as an
association of scholars whose communal mission was the honoring and
transmission of the best of our cultural heritage. With the increased
competition for federal government and private foundation grants, the
contemporary situation is one in which 'the "independent" university is
a myth, or rather a memory'.[22]

Another aspect of the culture of the modern university is evident,
one that is especially relevant for understanding the division between
'pure' and 'applied' areas of study. The creation of land-grant universities demonstrates how political issues shape the current cultural
milieu. In many ways this development was meant to challenge, or at
least broaden, the elitist and separatist nature of the older tradition of
liberal and classical studies. As one scholar reports, 'the most important
idea in the genesis of the land-grant colleges and state universities was
that of democracy'.[23] Accelerating with the Morrill Act of 1862, many
universities became committed to such innovative ideas as, 'education
for the working man, practical education in the pursuits and professions
of practical life, experimentation and research, the college reaching into
the community through institutes and lyceums, [and] opportunities to
study in almost any subject ...'[24] By enlarging their programs, universities were to add the practical sciences to their subject areas, a
movement that promoted what one writer referred to as an 'equality of
studies', and more broad-based curricula.[25] This expansion of studies
was a direct violation of the older, more exclusionary traditions of
liberal arts colleges and universities. It is within such a climate of
expansion that professional schools were seen as a legitimate component of university life.

The culture of the modern university, then, revolves around at least
three historic and contemporary impulses: (i) the safeguarding and
dissemination of our cultural heritage; (ii) an emphasis on inaugurating
educational programs that foster the development of research based,
increasingly technological knowledge, with greater social and eco-

nomic payoffs; and (iii) provision of programs for future professionals through the practical sciences.[26] These three strands continue to thrive, to varying extents, in the modern, complex multiversity, even though the assumptions on which they are based may represent conflicting political and social aspirations. How have these conflicting aspirations affected the place of teacher education, as an applied area of study, with the university?

Programs of professional preparation, it has been alleged, generally fail to contribute to the preservation of the Western tradition and the dispassionate search for truth embodied by liberal education. Concerned with occupational preparation rather than 'the expansion of the mind' presumably fostered by more humanistic studies, teacher training is one of the areas that is perceived as anomalous within that aspect of university culture devoted to liberal studies. DeVane has claimed that:

> [V]ocational training programs (agriculture, business, education, journalism, and nursing) are not educational programs and their net effect is to dilute the quality of the university ... their effect upon the student confined to their care is to narrow the mind and spirit to an early practicality and specialization instead of liberating the individual.[27]

Vocational training programs like those in education do not, on this view, contribute any humanizing or liberating qualities to students. Simply put, vocationally oriented teacher training is not educative.[28] Such a view is lent support by some conceptions of teacher preparation found in the extant literature. B. O. Smith, for example, mourns the passing of those institutions most closely tied to vocational training in education — the normal schools. These schools, he says:

> [w]ere devoted solely to the preparation of teachers and more nearly met other criteria of professional institutions than the pedagogical colleges today.
>
> How was the further development of normal schools aborted? It began in the middle of the last century with the movement that ultimately took the training of teachers into the universities ... [the essential functions of normal schools] were to be seriously eroded as pedagogical education came under the pervasive influence of the norms and folkways of the academic community.
>
> In their early days, normal schools prepared elementary teachers and were not affiliated with institutions of higher learning.[29]

Teacher training within a normal school atmosphere is to be recommended, on this view, precisely because it is non-academic and non-liberal. Clearly such an orientation places teacher preparation at odds with the traditional role of liberal education. In agreeing with commentators like DeVane in the passage cited above, vocational training advocates like Smith not only accept, but intentionally harden, the division between liberal studies and professional training.

Teacher training programs also presumably fail to contribute to the development of new, technicized knowledge (the second trait of university culture discussed above). As one of the professional schools operating within its dominant cultural expectations, teacher training does not seem to qualify as an area devoted to the advancement of new knowledge from which will spring technical advances, new discoveries, and the production of socially or economically useful goods. Instead of technical advance and commodity production, teacher training aims at the enhancement of employment-related skills, proficiencies, and competencies.

There are important institutional consequences to the view that teacher training neither serves as a cultural repository nor as a catalyst for technical knowledge. One of the important side effects is that curricula for future teachers are often segregated from scholarly disciplines and areas of study, and valued chiefly for their potential in securing employment for graduates. As a species of specialized job preparation, teacher training aims at inculcating those skills, techniques, and attitudes that receive credibility by virtue of their immediate applicability in today's classroom — at least as this may be perceived by those who design and implement such programs. Competency examinations, the mastery of techniques of teaching, professional socialization, and anecdotal 'tricks of the trade' — all removed from any larger ideational or social context — are thus thought vital for teacher training. The certification of competence for vocational possibilities, rather than the expansion of the mind, the disinterested pursuit of knowledge, or the production of new technologies and commodities, seems to characterize such programs of teacher training. As illiberal and lacking in obvious, direct social and economic payoff, education as a field seems uncomfortably placed within this aspect of higher education. Yet what of the legitimacy of teacher preparation as one of the practical studies sanctioned by the land grant and other democratically minded reform movements?

This third cultural force that exerts pressure on the modern university is often considered ill-placed within, or conceptually distinct from, the more scholastic, elitist strain of the university's culture, as we have already seen. Yet certain professional programs do tend to be respected for their contribution to the growing technicism of the university, and/or pragmatically accommodated for their power in securing external financial resources. Professional preparation is seen as legitimate primarily in those areas most conducive to the proliferation of technical knowledge — especially given the appearance of strong financial incentives for pursuing such knowledge. Consequently, professional Schools of Business, Engineering, Medicine, and Management, which contribute more or less directly to the proliferation of technical, administrative skills and procedures, or to the short or long term production of consumer goods and services that offer enhanced economic possibilities, are compatible with the pursuits sanctioned by the multiversity. As components of university culture, these Schools contribute more obviously to the use of educational institutions as agents of technical and economic advancement.[30] Even though such professional schools are strategically accommodated within the multiversity, their inclusion does not stem from their liberalizing influence on students. Rather, it is their economic and social utility that is most responsible for their acceptance. Yet Schools of Education — unlike other professional areas more directly linked to the production of consumer goods and the transmission of various technical and administrative skills — offer little in the way of such utility. Because of these trends, professional Schools of Education can not promise to elevate the status of the multiversity — as they offer illiberal and non-utilitarian programs.

Beyond these historic and cultural causes for the demarcation and subordination of education, other, more conceptually oriented divisions have served to distinguish liberal from applied domains. By defining certain pursuits as 'liberal,' to be pursued for their intrinsic value, other areas of inquiry have been partitioned off as more applied, professional, or vocational ones. The notion that education is a derivative field, relying on the methods and insights of more liberal disciplines for its legitimacy, is one of the assumptions that has served to perpetuate an intellectually inferior role for educational studies. This conceptual distinction deserves clarification.

The Disciplines and Conceptions of Knowledge

Discipline based inquiry is often thought to be characterized by a commitment to a methodology. This methodology reflects an area's basic tenets and processes, the characteristic questions and puzzles with which researchers grapple, and an accepted language in which both problems and results are expressed. Biology, for example, may be thought of as that domain committed to the empirical observation and examination, study, and structural analysis of living organisms; particular examples might involve procedures and methods designed to investigate an animal's reproductive cycle, its immunological responses to foreign substances, or its potential in a variety of genetic engineering experiments. Again, philosophy is often conceived as the discipline dedicated to clarifying concepts, ideas, and actions, evaluating our conduct as human beings, understanding the value and nature of art, and so on. Sociology, to take a third example, may be considered the discipline committed to understanding social processes, norms, and interactions, the creation and integration of social institutions, the ways in which people are initiated into social roles and expectations, and the like. Each of these disciplines is thought to incorporate a specific, differentiated methodology and form of analysis in arriving at its truths: biology utilizes the scientific method as it seeks to confirm or falsify hypotheses that can further knowledge about a particular organism or process; philosophy employs the tools of conceptual or ordinary language analysis, deductive and inductive logic, and the use of counter-examples and thought experiments in substantiating claims to truth; while sociology uses a variety of empirical procedures (e.g. statistical analysis related to status attainment or the differences between ascribed and achieved attributes) in its search for genuine social knowledge. As such, these disciplines constitute a collection of relatively independent domains that, while perhaps sharing certain affinities or interests — sociological investigations and social philosophy provide one such example — are seen as discrete areas with special methodologies and characteristic concerns and questions.

This conceptual differentiation is extended within the culture of the university. As institutions of higher education have sponsored the growth of increasingly isolated and specialized sub-disciplines, especially via research activities, these have flowered in the specialized soil provided by the disciplines. As research and scholarship have become more and more narrowly defined, with an assemblage of professional journals devoted exclusively to the dissemination of rather esoteric and isolated findings, the separation of domains becomes intensified. The conceptual differentiation among disciplinary foci and the increased fragmentation within disciplines through ever more specialized research have worked together to make cross-disciplinary understanding difficult, both conceptually and psychologically; the separation of people and scholarship militates against such understanding. Thus the modern university fosters research and teaching quite far removed from the notion of a community of scholars who share a set of convictions and a commitment to mutual understanding.

The role of education within this context is again frequently anomalous. As an applied area, it does not embody any particular methodology, internal structure, or set of problems analogous to disciplines like biology, philosophy, or sociology. Instead, it selectively adopts and incorporates a variety of methodologies in its inquiries — from philosophy, history, sociology, the natural sciences, and so on. Whether the study of education utilizes the statistical and laboratory methods associated with the natural sciences, the tools of conceptual analysis associated with philosophy, or the ethnographic techniques found in sociological and anthropological research, it cannot claim, so this line of argument goes, any special methodology uniquely its own. Further, to the extent that education is focused on the study of schools, its center is a particular institution rather than a set of problems, questions, and methods. Teacher training, as the most vocational of the areas within educational studies, is the furthest removed, on this account, from the disciplines. For as we have already seen, the preparation of teachers is committed to a kind of vocational training rather than to the dispassionate search for truth, the expansion of the mind, or the elevation of the intellect and powers of reason; nor does it utilize a particular methodology to solve unique problems in the pursuing of knowledge.

In addition to considerations regarding a field's ability to incorporate a particular methodology that is used to analyze and resolve a discrete set of problems, there are intellectual traditions that make the position of educational studies distinct from the disciplines. The epistemological and ontological status of liberal and practical areas of investigation are essentially dissimiliar. This difference in status forms the center of the intellectual distinction between liberal and applied studies.

The conceptual lineage of the liberal arts and sciences can be traced in some ways to the writings of Plato in fifth century BC Athens. His views on the role of reason, the rightful pursuit of knowledge, and the obstacles to its attainment are especially relevant for this discussion. Basic to these views is the conviction, represented perhaps most cogently and poetically in the *Republic*, that the world of 'becoming' (dominated by objects, images, and shadows that are unreliable sources of understanding) needs to be differentiated from the world of 'Being,' where genuine knowledge and wisdom may be discovered.[31] This fundamental distinction is a key to understanding several related dualisms and for seeing the alleged disparity between liberal and applied fields of study.

For Plato, the physical world is composed of transitory, changeable, and often deceptive events and objects. Knowledge that is possible through the perception of physical events is unreliable — a straight stick in water appears to be crooked when we know water has no such powers; we may be deceived into mistaking a human-created bird call the real thing; we are apt to be swayed by a variety of inducements to see physical attractiveness in people as a substitute for deeper, more long lasting beauty and loveliness. The contemporary images of television, while historically post dating Plato's writings, illustrate nicely the dangers in mistaking images for real things, manipulated opinion from genuine knowledge and wisdom. All physical occurrences, by their very nature, Plato tells us, provide these dangers and are therefore always suspect as sources of secure knowledge. The world of becoming is, in short, never complete or stable.

As opposed to such images in the world of physical reality, the realm of Being is capable of providing us with permanent, transcendent realities. The highest sort of knowledge is to be found in the Forms, those other worldly, archetypal, eternal entities that provide earthly objects with the meager sort of reality they enjoy. For Plato, a Form exists for every physical object and quality, though in its pure, unmediated and whole manifestation — unlike those incomplete and putrified imitations which comprise our earthly, physical reality. The former are only available through mental calculation and deliberation; they can be pursued only through the mind's eye, and not through observing the elements of the physical universe. The task of the philosopher, then, is to discover these pure, uncontaminated Forms, through the use of reason, insight, and concerted attention to higher order intellectual activity.[32]

One of the consequences of this Platonic conception of true knowledge is a celebration of thought, calculation, and contemplation — activities of the mind — at the expense of activities of the body. The latter are not to be pursued with an eye to genuine knowledge since the objects of their activities are themselves subordinate sources of understanding. The life of the mind is to be honored over independent, self-serving activities of the body.[33] The entrenchment of a mind/body dualism in most Western secular thought (and a soul/body dualism in most theological doctrines) is one effect of this view. It is the mind and its proper development that is crucial for true knowledge. In addition, the proper objects of study are those other-worldly embodiments of perfection, compared with which our everyday realities are but pale reflections. Clearly the facts of social interaction, day to day activities, mundane but incessant decisions, and so on, are unavoidable. But an involvement in such activities, though necessary, will not of itself lead to wisdom and knowledge. Neither is the calculation of personal reward or advancement the proper path to genuine knowledge. The best rulers are those least interested in politics and social gain.

Yet another consequence of the epistemological tradition founded by Plato has a direct bearing on our conception of the liberal disciplines and the status of education. As Socrates demonstrated in the conduct of his own life, the pursuit of knowledge is to be undertaken because of the excellence or perfection of the Forms themselves or for the intrinsic qualities of wisdom, and not for any private gain they might afford the philosopher. Socrates was unconcerned with bodily beauty, private monetary gain, the approval of the masses, and the like; his death sentence on charges of 'misleading the youth of Athens' and failing to pay proper homage to the gods testifies to his lack of concern for worldly approbation and private advantage. His search was for the perfection to be found in knowledge itself, in genuine Being, which can only be pursued when one abandons concerns about private gain, personal success, and social approval.

It is but a short step from this view of the pursuit of knowledge as disinterested and intrinsic to the view that the liberal arts as the study of the disciplines should not be concerned with immediate success in a professional field, the attainment of specific skills required to accomplish a particular end, and the training of the senses so as to maximize our ability to comply with a narrowly circumscribed set of vocational assumptions. This distinction can be clearly seen, in fact, in the very teachings of Socrates himself. Never satisfied with immediate proficiency in a specific skill or technique, Socrates was intent on helping others see the principles, ideas, and higher order realities that lie behind the immediate and concrete of daily life. As a guide for the liberal disciplines, Plato's epistemology does not lend itself to the sort of emphasis on professional preparation, skilled competence in responding to immediate pressures and demands, and the general propensity to engage in isolated matters of the moment that seem to characterize professional areas like education. The legacy of Plato's thought thus appears to further that separation of liberal disciplines and applied fields at the same time that the lack of a unique methodology and set of problems for education separates the latter from liberal fields of study.

We are left, in sum, with a view of the disciplines and the classical university as concerned with: the pursuit and transmission of genuine, certain knowledge and truth, which is largely a matter of properly guiding mental capacities; the discovery of essentially non-physical, non-material realities; the intrinsic value of knowledge rather than the private gain or social approval it may bring; and the development of new knowledge sanctioned by disciplinary boundaries and methodologies. The contemporary university, while embodying some of these classical notions, has also included within its domain a commitment to research that significantly contributes to our social, economic, and cultural well-being. Educational studies faces a rather formidable opposition, concerned as it allegedly is with narrowly defined competence, the training of skills (especially those with a physical orientation), and socially and vocationally defined patterns of success, while disregarding the generation of new knowledge or technical advances. Moreover, unlike certain professionally preparatory units of the contemporary multiversity, education seems unable to promise much in the way of technological discovery or the development of administrative prowess.

Beyond these tensions between the liberal disciplines and the practical or applied fields of study, there has been a rather sustained attempt by educationists themselves to separate education from the disciplines associated with liberal study. The educational side of this dualism has been promoted both by some concerned with the foundational aspects of education (especially the philosophy of education) and by those concerned primarily with the preparation of teachers. It is to these aspects of the current disparity between liberal and professional studies that we now turn.

Education Views the Liberal Disciplines

Educational Foundations and School Practice

Perhaps because of the epistemological primacy often afforded philosophy as a discipline, those concerned with the philosophy of education have often been at the center of the issues surrounding the relationships between theory and practice. That is, philosophy as a discipline has been conceived as a centerpiece in the liberal arts tradition of the university, uniquely committed to a search for truth by employing particular methodologies and approaches, and fundamentally dedicated to the expansion of the mind as opposed to the training of people for specific occupations. Since education has been conceived as a professional or applied domain, the rupture between liberal and practical studies may be further drawn out by looking at issues associated with the philosophy of education.

A perennial question with both conceptual and practical faces arising in educational studies is where philosophy of education should be taught, and to what it should owe its primary allegiance. The issue of whether faculty in the Department of Philosophy or in the School/ Department of Education should offer such a course is frequently a matter of some debate and contention. Should this course be designed and taught by someone with a background and degree in philosophy, who presumably has an interest in educational issues, or should it be offered by a member of the education faculty who presumably has some interest and ability in philosophy? While this may be depicted as a narrow personnel question, it is not unusual for large amounts of intellectual capital and interpersonal good will to be expended on its resolution. The very distinction between liberal study and professional preparation is typically assumed and asserted in the process of resolving this question.

The central question involved here concerns the value and role of philosophy within the study and practice of education. This issue is raised head on by Jerome A. Popp in a recent article about the difference between practical and theoretical inquiry:

> Practical inquiry is aimed at the direction or guidance of action; its linguistic outputs are thus prescriptions. Theoretical inquiry is descriptive and its conclusions are asserted. 'Prescriptions are, thus, the fundamental units of practical thinking just as propositions are the fundamental units of theoretical thinking'.[34]

Since practical inquiry is devoted to solving immediate problems faced by people in concrete settings, its concern is with responding to and overcoming those problems. Philosophy, according to Popp, is a kind of theoretical activity, concerned with developing statements or claims that can be verified. As such, philosophy is not directly relevant to the queries of practical inquiry. It may extend knowledge, clarify meanings, articulate alternatives, and so on, and these may in the long run have a beneficial effect on teachers and others. Yet the point of doing philosophy is to extend knowledge and open up new avenues for research, and not to solve immediate problems at hand. Practical inquiry, on the other hand, is dedicated to the immediate resolution of just such a problematic situation. Thus, on this view, 'significant theoretical questions are inquiry expanding questions, while significant practical questions are inquiry extinguishing questions ... successful theoretical inquiry makes work for itself, while practical investigations, if successful, become unnecessary.'[35] Since practical inquiry aims at the resolution of a specific problematic situation, the realization of that aim signals an end to the inquiry. Philosophy of education, as a theoretical activity containing its own internal standards and methods, may only affect practical decisions in an indirect way, as a possible side effect.

This point is extended in the work of Israel Scheffler, among others. For example, in considering the relationship between teaching and theoretical inquiry, Scheffler says that they are 'two different activities ... The results of inquiry may be in improving the practice of teaching, but the goals of inquiry are nevertheless distinct from the goals of teaching'. Moreover, the activities of people engaged in achieving these goals, Scheffler tells us, are distinctive:

> inquiry normally ranges far from the practical, everyday world
> to which its results may one day be applied. It is because of this
> abstraction from the practical world that scientific inquiry is
> able to provide compact and comprehensive principles explain-
> ing what goes on in that world.[36]

Teachers and researchers entertain fundamentally different sorts of questions, apply divergent kinds of analysis, and must not be seen as engaged in similar pursuits — even if there may be a 'sympathetic interest' between these individuals. At most the researcher may take the concrete situations faced by teachers as a beginning point for his/her own research; yet the relevance, application, or utility of the eventual results of such research is not the subject of concern for the researcher as he/she engages in inquiry.

A somewhat less rigid separation of theoretical analysis and practical action has been offered by some British philosophers of education, especially in the writings of Richard Peters and Paul Hirst.[37] They argue, for instance, that 'philosophy, in brief, is concerned with questions about the analysis of concepts and with questions about the grounds of knowledge, belief, actions, and activities.'[38] Yet, these authors contend, two things are important about the sort of conceptual analysis engaged in by philosophers of education that work against the tendency toward abstraction suggested by Scheffler. First, the choice of which concepts to analyze is based on the assumption that something important is at stake in their clarification. For example, that Hirst and Peters are interested in the analysis of the concept of 'punishment' is a sign that something of importance hinges on our becoming clear about this concept (that might be brought out by looking, for example, at the ethical and political notions of freedom, autonomy, and democracy that stand behind it) that makes the analysis compelling. The work of conceptual analysis is not engaged in arbitrarily or haphazardly, without regard for some larger pattern of justification and belief. Second, the philosopher of education is necessarily concerned with several areas of philosophy; indeed the philosopher of education,

> can seldom turn to just one branch of philosophy. If he is interested, for instance, in problems of teaching and learning from a theoretical point of view ... he will be drawn into philosophical psychology ... He may also be led into the philosophy of history, mathematics and science in order to get clearer about what is distinctive of these particular forms of thinking. [And since he will also be interested in questions of what ought to be done] ... he will have also to study ethics and social philosophy in order to arrive at clearer answers to questions about what should be put on the curriculum, about teaching methods, and about how children should be treated.[39]

Clearly such interests and concerns militate against the view of philosophy as the abstract, armchair speculation of disinterested theorists who casually inquire into the meaning of isolated concepts.

Yet in another sense the separation of philosophy from practical inquiry is still maintained in the writings of these British philosophers of education. For the philosopher of education is characteristically concerned with the clarification and justification of concepts, and not their practical implementation or use in some institutional setting. To accomplish the latter, the work of philosophers must be integrated with that of others. As Peters expresses this in *Ethics and Education*:

> when it comes to the formulation of particular principles for implementation in particular schools the contribution of philosophy, in terms of abstract analysis and justification of principles, must be put together with that of psychologists, sociologists, and teachers, who have practical experiences of the particularities in questions. Philosophy contributes to practical wisdom but is not a substitute for it.[40]

Even though philosophical analysis in education may be concerned with concepts that have a bearing on practice, and may be integrated with other branches of philosophy and other disciplines as well, its characteristic ways of proceeding must be integrated with other more practical realms if it is to become personally useful to the teacher.

Reconnecting the links between theory and practice and making good the belief that philosophical analysis can prove insightful for educational activity, were the underlying purposes of the 80th year-book of the National Society for the Study of Education, *Philosophy and Education*. These were implicit aims of the volume's editor, Jonas Soltis, when he says, for example, that this anthology seeks to 'help the readers readjust their conceptions of what philosophy of education is and to come to see the many ways in which philosophy and education are connected'.[41] This notion is further elaborated when Soltis stipulates that the several authors in the volume were asked 'to demonstrate a philosophical perspective and the clarification that could be provided by locating an educational topic in the subareas of philosophy'.[42] Rather than attempting to explicate the traditional 'isms' in philosophical discourse — idealism, pragmatism, Deweyism, Marxism, and so on — Soltis divided this volume into philosophic subareas that could then provide insight into specific educational dilemmas or problems. In the process the relevance, value, and applicability of philosophic analysis could be displayed for the educator, to whom the book is addressed. Even Harry Broudy, who is clearly less than enthusiastic about this conceptual and organizational transformation of philosophical analysis,[43] admits that the division into subareas 'is designed to provide them [school people] with another way to conceive of philosophy of education and to match their concerns to its literature'.[44] Let us examine some general tendencies adopted to accomplish the overall purpose of the volume by looking at Chapter VII by Robert Ennis, 'Rational Thinking and Educational Practice'.

The underlying intention of this chapter is 'to speak to a diverse audience because ... there is a widespread and increasing belief among educators and the public that schools at all levels should promote high quality thinking, and that the study and discussion of educational theory and practice would profit from higher quality thinking'.[45] By equipping teachers with the skills and tendencies requisite for higher quality thinking they can realize a heightened decision making process, which will in turn elevate educational activity.

One of the examples Ennis provides to illustrate his conception of rational thinking involves a newspaper editorial about segregation, 'Jim

Crow, Long Outlawed, Still Hangs on in Chicago'. The author raises the question of whether the use of the term 'segregation' in the editorial is consistent with how that term was employed by the Supreme Court in the Brown case. Ennis develops three hypotheses in analyzing this question, concluding that whichever of the three one adopts, the logical fallacy of equivocation seems in danger of having been committed. Or, at least, the fallacy of 'impact equivocation' (using words such that the impact they are likely to have on a given audience will be to equivocate between one usage and another) is likely to occur as a result of reading the newspaper editorial.

After listing the twenty-two components of his rational thinking model, Ennis remarks, 'I invite you to reread the treatment of the "segregation" example and identify examples of each of these aspects. This is a long list. It suggests that in any real case one must exercise many aspects of rational thinking at one time. These aspects do not operate separately. A rational thinker must do many things at once'.[46]

The chapter by Ennis, and the others in this volume, utilize distinct subareas from philosophy. Yet each conceives of the impact of philosophic work in a similar manner. The authors seek to document the value and importance of some aspect of their respective specialty for the province of education. Each author points to ideas and practices that might illuminate and transform aspects of education. Yet in thinking about the tensions between liberal and applied studies, theory and practice, philosophy and schooling, it is important to note the tacit view of education contained in this volume, in addition to the ideas the authors explicitly promote. Such tacit views tell us much about the current plight of educational studies.

How we draw the boundaries around schools as places where educational exchanges take place is an exceedingly important question, yet one which is not systematically addressed by most of the authors in *Philosophy and Education*.[47] Schools, for the most part, are conceived as the arena where certain activities manifest themselves — activities which are susceptible to philosophically sensitive prescriptions, such as those related to rational thinking. They tend to be seen as 'background information': places where our best philosophic visions may be implanted as an important corrective. Within this conception, classrooms are seen as fixtures where changes in forms of reasoning may, if carefully analyzed and fully understood, provide the sort of assistance that will improve the quality of our educational endeavors. Schools are seen as 'black boxes' into which the sophistication of logical analysis can be instituted so as to improve practice. If we assume that schools are relatively autonomous institutions, concerned, say, with the dissemination of 'knowledge' — whether this be of a scientific, aesthetic, or logical sort — or the socialization that accompanies group interaction, we miss something important not only about education, but the role of philosophic inquiry into it as well. And this has consequences for our understanding of the linkage between theory and practice.

In order to realize the commitment to this linkage as detailed in the introduction to *Philosophy and Education*, the authors necessarily had to assume certain traits of educational phenomena as given, unimportant, or beyond the ken of their analyses. This is of course fully understandable. Yet what seems to have been almost uniformly accepted *a priori* is what kind of places schools *are*, what they 'teach' (tacitly or overtly), why they do these things, who benefits from their doing them, and so on. The problem of linking theory and practice, accordingly, is understood as largely resolvable by revitalizing the way teachers and others think about issues involving a variety of philosophic subareas. It seems fair to see this volume as regarding the matching of educational concerns and philosophical literature, the linking of theory and practice, as an essentially intellectual one, to be dealt with by application of the appropriate form of philosophic discourse and analysis. The links between theory and practice can effectively be established, on this view, by helping rational thinkers (teachers), who exist within and help support meritocratic institutions (schools), respond more carefully and thoughtfully to conceptual analysis (philosophy) and thus improve and enhance the quality of life within that institution (practice).

The chapters in *Philosophy and Education* take for granted the context for the injection of their philosophic ideas, as if that context is of secondary interest or significance. Not only do the educational implications of the resultant philosophic inquiry suffer due to this, but so too does the nature of philosophical work itself. Since the context for the analysis is not fully articulated, the sort of philosophic work that might actually unify theory and practice is also unrealized.[48]

Notice, as a part of the analysis that results, something else about this way of connecting theory and practice. It is assumed that philosophical analyses can be undertaken which will be useful in reorienting the work of teachers. Yet little is said about the conditions of teachers' work, the constraints imposed by the workplace itself, the dominant values, beliefs, and assumptions that inhere in that workplace, and so on, as these influence the significance of the ideas in this volume. The ability of philosophy to significantly alter and improve teaching and educational practice is to a large extent assumed; while this may require that teachers consider how the ideas from various philosophic subareas could alter current practice, little is said about how the latter might affect the legitimacy of the ideas addressed by the authors.

This is not to deny the value or importance of the ideas contained in the chapters of this yearbook. Many of the authors convey important insights from their areas of interest and suggest how these insights might reorient educational practice. Yet in avoiding a closer look at the practices of teachers, the material nature of the setting of teaching, as well as a more contextual analysis of the ideas, norms, and values sanctioned by schools as institutions, an important segment of educational studies is missing. As an attempt to link theory and practice, then, this volume is in the end a bit too one-sided, emphasizing the importance of philosophic insight and downplaying the significance of those contexts wherein this insight is to be transformative. Philosophically interesting and important distinctions, though of course valuable and worth doing, are not always useful. Yet one need not pay full attention to this question of usefulness if, as these authors do, we assume that well developed, articulate and cogent analysis provides its own context of use. If the central purpose of philosophy is reflection (even when this involves a reflection on practice), we should not be surprised that the contexts for this reflection on action — in this case, those provided by schools — should remain undervalued even in a work dedicated to relating philosophy to education.[49]

At the same time, we should recognize how this effort to specify the integration of theory and practice diverges from a good deal of writing in this area. Indeed, some commentators on *Philosophy and Education* have chastised it for too close an affiliation between philosophy as a discipline and the domain of education. For example, one reviewer of this work argues for the continued and expanded autonomy of theory if it is to be of practical value. 'Theorizing in general, and philosophical inquiry into education in particular, must be autonomous from particular problems if it is to provide the insight and understanding necessary for the solutions of such problems.'[50] What is suggested here is a paradox: for educational theory to be practically efficacious, it must not take its problems from questions and issues of practice. Instead, educational theory must remain within its parent, 'academic' (sometimes called 'proper') discipline of philosophy.

Even for ideas and readings in the philosophy of education that intentionally aim to overcome the separation of theory and practice (with the reservations noted above), the debate that springs from such readings frequently concerns the status of domains on each side of this separation. Since philosophy as a discipline so clearly belongs in the tradition of liberal studies, geared towards the justification of knowledge and the certification of truth, it is not difficult to understand why some commentators emphasize the importance of autonomous inquiry based in the allegedly parent discipline. The further separation of liberal and applied domains is encouraged by identifying educational foundations as a discrete component of the study of education, isolated from the practices of schools.

Teacher Training and Professionalism

The literature on teacher preparation, as perhaps the most applied wing of educational studies, further promotes the demarcation of theory and practice. We may identify three representative examples which demonstrate the vocational nature of many programs of teacher preparation and which contribute to the isolation of the foundations of education from teacher training. First, in *A Design for a School of Pedagogy*, B. Othanel Smith concludes that 'academic pedagogical knowledge ... seldom yields teaching prescriptions ...' and that 'theory has value in the art of teaching only if "theory" is used to mean empirical clinical knowledge. Since this form of knowledge is not called theory in either pedagogy or other sciences, the appeal to theory as practical knowledge in classroom teaching is bootless'.[51] Given that the main goal of teacher training is to equip people to perform whatever teaching strategies and methodologies are extant in the profession, direct knowledge of such strategies, whether through clinical observation or direct instruction, is much to be preferred, on Smith's view, to 'non-empirical' theoretical knowledge. 'Academic pedagogical activities', moreover, are not conceived of as valuable for the practice of teaching since they are less than immediately directive in terms of teaching strategies and behaviors. Thus, Smith reports, 'teachers are correct when they assert that what they learn in the so-called foundations of education is not helpful in managing the classroom and carrying on instructional activities'.[52] While such foundational courses may have a limited value in determining questions of policy, academic pedagogical knowledge (of which the foundations are a central part) is 'not appropriate for the development of skills for either classroom or interaction with peers and laypersons'.[53] The foundations are discredited by Smith for their lack of direct utility for clinical experiences and corresponding teacher behaviors.

Second, there is an increasing emphasis on field-based experience in teacher preparation programs. In many programs students now participate in 'early field experiences', so that student teaching is no longer the first and only time they work in the field; the feeling seems to be that the more time spent in the field the better. Despite the ambiguity of research undertaken on field-based experiences,[54] studies seem to consistently indicate that student teaching and other forms of field-based teacher education contribute to the development of 'utilitarian teaching perspectives'.[55] Student teachers tend to accept the practices they observe in their field placements as the upper and outer limits of what is possible. Katz refers to this condition as one of 'excessive realism'.[56] The school serves as a model for practice and is not itself an object for scrutiny and analysis. Within such a perspective the foundations of education may be seen as at best an obligatory prelude, at worst an unfortunate intrusion, into field work, the latter of which is ostensibly of greater value and import.

Third, yet another popular orientation to preservice teacher training is the 'personalized' approach based on the work of Frances Fuller and her colleagues at the University of Texas.[57] The essence of this approach is that the content of teacher education curricula be matched to the level of concerns that students are experiencing at a particular point in time. Given the largely survival-oriented skills articulated by Katz as being of special concern to beginning teachers, as well as Fuller's own corroborating studies of teacher development, this would mean that the curriculum for teacher preparation would be constructed primarily with a view toward helping student teachers survive more comfortably within a context that is largely taken for granted.

While these three approaches to teacher preparation are by no means identical, they do share an important, orienting perspective. All tend to see teacher preparation as existing to help students take on currently dominant teacher roles, expectations, and characteristics. Teacher preparation within this perspective is aimed at equipping students with the skills, dispositions, and competencies necessary for the perpetuation of school practice in its present form. Since educational foundations allegedly fail to help students cope with the day-to-day encounters of school practice, they are seen as dysfunctional, extraneous, and irrelevant.[58]

Within this vocational orientation, there is a tendency to assume a taken-for-granted posture with respect to both current school practice and educational programs that serve to train people to occupy the necessary occupational roles. The work of preservice teachers is, accordingly, often delimited to replicating current practice, or modifying such practice within certain prescribed limits, with the result that teaching is seen as problematic only within a technical and ameliorative perspective. Since the aim of these teacher training efforts is to acquaint students with current practice, and perhaps increase their proficiency at such practice, provide necessary 'survival skills', or ease the transition into established roles, activities and solutions to problems tend to be circumscribed by what we might call an 'internal' perspective on teaching. The domain of teacher preparation within this perspective is defined by and limited to classroom phenomena and processes abstracted from wider, more encompassing contexts. Teacher training, accordingly, is often felt to primarily involve isolated practice, dominated by concerns for such matters as increasing student achievement, maintaining discipline and order in classrooms, or providing 'meaningful learning experiences'. Conceived in these terms, more intellectually engaging issues and problems, the generation of knowledge and the search for truth as advocated in liberal inquiry, seem extraneous and non-practical indeed.

The irrelevance of normative questions of the sort that often typify liberal inquiry is baldly asserted by Smith:

> The preservice student should not be exposed to theories and practices derived from ideologies and philosophies about the way schools *should* be. The rule should be to teach, and to teach thoroughly, the knowledge and skills that equip beginning teachers to work successfully in today's classroom.[59]

As perhaps the clearest statement of a vocational approach to teacher preparation, Smith's views exemplify the posture commonly assumed by those involved in teacher training. Such teacher preparation programs characteristically present curriculum knowledge as a predefined set of 'worthwhile' activities to be mastered. This externalized or objectivist conception of knowledge characterizes US teacher education and, as a result, prospective teachers come to believe that knowledge is something that is detached from the human interactions through which it was constituted and by which it is maintained.[60]

The dominant culture of teacher preparation is one emphasizing the following traits: vocational training, the replication of current school practices, field-based experience aimed at promoting survival skills, technical proficiency, utilitarian approaches to curriculum and teaching, and the measurement of competencies that are specific, often behaviorally organized, and systematic. Within this culture the sort of questioning, analyzing, and reflection often touted by spokespersons for the liberal arts are all but absent. Instead, a largely technical, quantifiable, specific training in discrete skill areas is mandated. Accordingly, 'theory' is either rejected outright as irrelevant (as in the case of B. O. Smith) or accepted grudgingly provided it does not intrude too closely on the territory of application or practice. Once more we see how educationists, like the liberal arts proponents discussed above, have widened the gulf between theory and practice.[61]

An interesting paradox is worth noting here that provides insight into the dichotomization of theory and practice in education. Recall that the essays in the Soltis volume outlined above tend to highlight the importance of philosophic analysis for changes in the practice of education; these philosophers of education, to generalize, tend to downplay the import of the context of teaching, as this may diminish the significance of such a reflection-based discipline. At the same time, the vocational nature of teacher training efforts, in focusing on the particular and immediate context of teaching, tend to discount the sort of theoretical work undertaken by foundational scholars such as those concerned with the philosophy of education. As the former group undervalues the significance of the context of schooling and teaching, latter proponents focus only on such a context. Each sees its interests in precisely those areas the other advocates deny, implicitly or otherwise.

If teacher training efforts have accentuated the non-theoretical, vocationally preparatory nature of the preparation of teachers, the contemporary movement for reform of teacher education has promoted the technical nature of the training required for prospective teachers. And insofar as an emphasis on technical approaches to teacher preparation further removes educational studies from the liberal arts, the gap between pure and applied fields becomes increasingly taken for granted. It is important, then, in terms of understanding the current predicament of educational studies, to see how reform efforts in teacher education are being conceptualized more and more in technical, managerial, and procedural terms almost exclusively.

Echoing many of the sentiments of the much discussed *A Nation At Risk*,[62] the Carnegie Forum on Education and the Economy makes numerous recommendations for improving teaching and the quality of programs for preparing future teachers. It begins its summary in terms reminiscent of the earlier report by the National Commission on Excellence in Education:

America's ability to compete in world markets is eroding. The productivity growth of our competitors outdistances our own. The capacity of our economy to provide a high standard of living for all our people is increasingly in doubt ...

As in past economic and social crisis, Americans turn to education. They rightly demand an improved supply of young people with the knowledge, the spirit, the stamina and the skills to make the nation once again fully competitive ... There is a new consensus on the urgency of making our schools once again the engines of progress, productivity and prosperity ... success depends on achieving far more demanding educational standards than we have ever attempted to reach before ... [and] the key to success lies in creating a profession equal to the task ...[63]

Here the linkages among social prosperity, economic productivity, competitiveness and educational 'excellence',[64] and reforms in teacher education are quite openly stated. To accomplish these larger goals, the Carnegie task force offers several recommendations. For our purposes, some of the more interesting of these proposals include: creating a national certification board, establishing a multi-layered teaching force, requiring an undergraduate degree 'in the arts and sciences' as a prerequisite to a Master of Teaching degree, and emphasizing student performance coupled with higher 'teacher productivity'.[65] The use of economic language in this report — the concern with productivity, high unemployment, supply and demand considerations regarding teachers, performance and accountability measures, and so on — is hardly an accident. Included on the Carnegie Forum Advisory Council are the former head of Bell Telephone, a Vice President of IBM, an Executive Vice President of an investment firm and the Chief Executive Officer of American Can Company.[66] The intent of this report is to transform the craft of teaching in a way that harkens back to another Carnegie Foundation campaign — the improvement of the medical profession brought about through the efforts of Abraham Flexner and others.

In discussing the role of their proposed National Board for Professional Teaching Standards, the Carnegie Task Force on Teaching as a Profession says the Board should 'judge the quality of candidates' general education, their mastery of the subjects they will teach, their knowledge of good teaching practices in general and their mastery of techniques required to teach specific subjects'.[67] Further, this Board will work with teacher preparation institutions and faculty to help students understand the processes of assessment that will be used to judge their teaching ability, and help evaluate their readiness to be examined and certified by the Board. A more rigorous, extensive program of testing and assessment is a central feature of the Carnegie Foundation plan.

In discussing the means by which to help students meet these new standards, the Carnegie report makes several suggestions for programs of teacher preparation. They say that since four years is inadequate to produce a professionally prepared teacher, 'the undergraduate years should be wholly devoted to a broad liberal education and a thorough grounding in the subjects to be taught. The professional education of teachers should therefore take place at the graduate level'.[68] This report does suggest, though, that some provision could be made at the undergraduate level 'for students with an early interest in teaching', to gain exposure 'to the underlying theory, research, and history of education'.[69]

The term 'competency' is often used in the Carnegie report as it stresses the recommendation that a new Master of Teaching degree become adopted as a prerequisite for Board certification. This program is designed to 'prepare candidates to take maximum advantage of the research on teaching and the accumulated knowledge of exceptional teachers. It would develop their instructional and management skills, cultivate the habit of reflecting on their own practice of teaching, and lay a strong base for continuing professional development'.[70] A technical, skill development, and assessment model of teacher preparation is given center stage in the ideas of this group. Even when the report mentions the importance of 'reflection on practice' — which we might suppose would include some relating of ideas from foundational studies in education to the work of teaching — the grounds or bases for such reflection are not clarified. And since this report does sanction the provision of foundational courses at the undergraduate level, before 'professional' study begins, the isolation of theory and practice appears to be reinforced. As well, the report says that what is essential in the Master of Teaching program is a strong element of field-based preparation, offering opportunities for reflection that are integrated with the professional coursework of the program. This reflection would presumably be guided by 'Lead Teachers', who have received an 'Advanced Teacher's Certificate' (in addition to the initial 'Teacher's Certificate') from the National Board for Professional Teaching Standards.

The report stresses a technical approach to teaching through a separation of theoretical from professional coursework, a focus on activities enhancing classroom management and instructional technique, a commitment to the central importance of skill development, and an emphasis on field-based experience guided by Lead Teachers. Such emphases are extended in the report's discussion of incentives and productivity in the teaching profession. In language that smacks of the earlier emphasis on scientific management of schools and curricula,[71] the Carnegie report says,

> ... resources are never unlimited, so we turn out to be interested in the best possible performance at the lowest possible cost ... we believe improvements are not likely to be made until the structure of incentives for teachers and other school employees is redesigned to reward them for student accomplishment.
>
> But the issue is not just performance. The rate at which student performance must improve exceeds by far the rate at which school revenues can reasonably be expected to rise, even at the most optimistic levels.[72]

The relationship between student achievement and revenue expended on schools is taken for granted by the members of this group, as a part of the 'common sense' of education. The problem is that added expenditures will not keep pace with the increases necessary in student achievement. Again we see the utilization of technical, business-oriented language in the discussion of educational quality. The authors also say that for those facing pressure to improve schools, 'there is an important parallel here to the challenge faced by American business and industry'. The key to this parallel in challenges faced by both economic and educational institutions lies in the concept of productivity:

> ... American business exposed to foreign competition [must] improve productivity. That pressure shows some promise of leading to a sweeping reassessment of long-standing production methods, the introduction of new technologies, innovative labor-management practices, improved forms of organization, and the introduction of new management methods — all in the search for quality and efficiency. American schools also need to produce a higher quality product with greater efficiency, but are not subject to market forces.[73]

The equivocation between business interests and educational excellence is here starkly and bluntly put. Like industrialists, educational managers and workers must emphasize increased productivity, the maintenance of a higher quality 'product', and gains in efficiency, through the adoption of new management systems, better incentives, and the use of new technologies. The report specifically cites 'market methods' that could be used to develop the incentives needed for increased productivity: developing specialty schools that offer open enrollment opportunities, offering teaching services to other staff, and contracting with businesses to provide needed services. Utilizing the lenses provided by contemporary corporate America, the Carnegie Forum on Education and the Economy envisions an educational arena allied with the values, principles, procedures, and aims of our economic apparatus. What is good for General Motors, the authors seem to be reminding us, is not only good for the U.S. generally, but for our system of schooling in particular. Hardly a new idea, this report surfaces at a time when economic problems beset large segments of American society, so that school improvement and business enhancement appear conjoined.[74]

There are several critical issues related to this perspective, having to do with its social, political, and ideological ramifications. We will deal with these issues more directly in succeeding chapters of this book. For now, we should note how the tendencies to equate business interests with educational improvements, and the very language with which this equivocation is generated, have consequences for the separation of educational studies from the search for truth and knowledge, and their intrinsic value, that are embedded in the liberal disciplines. In accepting parallels between business and education, we implicitly adopt a system of beliefs, expectations, and aims that are hardly centered on the pursuit of knowledge for its own sake. Far from promoting teacher preparation and the practice of teaching as the pursuit and transmission of genuine knowledge, this report instructs us to use essentially technical, business-oriented activities to reinvigorate education and teaching. The result is a system of teacher preparation emphasizing economic concepts and discourse, market inducements, and principles of management quite far removed from that disinterested pursuit of knowledge advocated by Plato and sanctioned by the earlier traditions of the university and the liberal arts college. Indeed, this approach to education and the preparation of teachers is best suited to that aspect of the culture of the contemporary university devoted to the production of new commodities through specialized research and development activities. As research in scientific and engineering schools may generate new technologies, the schools of education will assist in the development of better 'products' of a sort as well. Such language and ways of thinking about education aggravate the separation of teacher preparation, and educational studies generally, from the liberal disciplines.

A Call for Change in Teacher Education, by the National Commission for Excellence in Teacher Education, seems to contradict in some ways the ideas put forth by the Carnegie Commission. For example, this reform proposal assumes that, 'teachers are professionals, not merely technicians. They do not simply follow directions in a teacher's manual or obey instructions from principals or supervisors ... teachers continually make complex decisions about the curriculum, the students, and instruction ... Professional teachers also understand the numerous educational issues that confront today's schools, and they can explain these to parents and other interested citizens. We believe that teachers must be such professionals'.[75] Unlike the more economically rooted report by the Carnegie forum, the National Commission for Excellence in Teacher Education is less preoccupied with concepts rooted in economistic language and like-minded measures of improvement, and less committed as a result to a view of teaching as an engineering-like activity for which it makes sense to speak of productivity, incentive, and the more efficient application of methods to procure a better product.[76]

The Commission exemplifies another conceptual orientation that is common to several of the current reform efforts in teacher education, however. In discussing programs for teacher preparation, the authors separate the various components of such programs; they argue for (i) extensive coursework in the liberal arts generally, and an academic concentration in one of them; (ii) 'systematic study and application of pedagogy — the art, history, philosophy, and science that undergird educational processes and successful teaching';[77] and (iii) field experiences of a variety of kinds within the professional component of teacher preparation programs.

A key to seeing the relevance of 'the application of pedagogy' is contained in the report's discussion of professional education activities. In introducing this area, the report contends that, 'every teacher should have a strong background in professional education, because knowledge of the subject is of little consequence if the teacher cannot convey that knowledge and help students learn at a rate and level commensurate with their age and development'.[78] As a derivative and functional area, professional education is useful in helping prospective teachers apply the knowledge, concepts, and ideas from the disciplines; such knowledge, acquired during students' liberal education experiences, can be encoded and transmitted in specific teaching and learning activities.

It is this latter process of translation that is central to professional activities in teacher education. To accomplish this, teacher preparation programs must include courses dealing with how people learn to think 'at different ages and developmental stages'; how to develop 'appropriate teaching strategies and materials'; and how to observe and analyze student performance. This entails an educational program offering 'systematic instruction in the organized research and experience-based information about teaching', and how to use this research on 'teacher and school effectiveness'.[79] An emphasis on materials and methods of instruction, the developmental stage theories now popular in educational psychology, and research on 'effective schools' thus appear central to the problems of improving teacher preparation, on the view of this commission. They form the basis for its recommendations regarding the professional aspects of teacher preparation programs.

In making recommendations for this component of teacher preparation, the authors make the usual distinction between liberal studies and professional programs for future teachers. In what amounts to an addendum to the general recommendations of the commission, nine of its members make a specific plea for at least an additional year of study beyond the baccalaureate degree. These members say that:

> we are concerned particularly about the issues of the liberal education prospective teachers should receive and about the amount of time needed to properly prepare teachers for the future.
>
> ... All prospective teachers, as part of their liberal education, should be educated in at least one academic major ...
>
> ... A minimum of four years should be devoted to the liberal arts component of the teacher education program; a minimum of five years to the total program.[80]

There are several ideas worth pondering in these recommendations. First, since an 'academic major' is stressed at the undergraduate level as a part of a student's liberal arts background, it is clear that a major in educational studies (which is pursued at the graduate level as the 'professional education' component) is not seen as a legitimate academic area of interest or specialization, and is not a part of the liberal arts tradition that comprises a course of study for the bachelor's degree. Again we see the assumption that liberal and educational studies are logically discontinuous phenomena; though the reasons for this separation are not offered or defended in this report (as is the case with other reports as well, demonstrating its common sense status), we can assume they follow from the confluence of epistemological, institutional, and historical forces discussed earlier in this chapter.

At the same time, the addendum cited suggests a four year period of study in liberal arts, with only one year devoted to professional study in education. With the importance attached to field experiences that would occupy a substantial portion of post-baccalaureate study, it is reasonable to conclude that non field-oriented courses in educational studies would occupy a small percentage of the total program of a prospective teacher.

Another perspective contained in this 'call for change' is indicative of the relationship between theory and practice it sanctions. The commission specifically recommends a one year 'induction period or internship' after work is completed for a provisional teacher's certif- cate. Central to this induction period is the view that people connected to teacher preparation should 'help the new teacher become successfully immersed in the teaching profession'.[81] While it is not clear exactly what is meant by a one year period aimed at such 'immersion', the literature on teacher socialization, the tendencies toward 'excessive realism', 'utilitarian teaching perspectives', and so on, discussed above in relation to vocationally oriented teacher preparation programs, might recur in the internships suggested by the commission.

The split between academic and professional or applied study is reinforced in the report of the National Commission for Excellence in Teacher Education. This group visualizes educational studies as primarily concerned with the dissemination of knowledge from the academic disciplines, largely through the office of educational psychology. In presenting educational studies in this way, they are pictured as functionally related to the real knowledge contained in the liberal arts disciplines, as the former adapt the ideas, issues, and concepts gleaned from academic study. The report further separates the study of education by insisting that liberal studies generally, and an academic major in particular, precede professional education activities (whether the total program requires four or five years). And in promoting a one year period of immersion that would enhance the process of teacher socialization, this report encourages the pursuit of teacher preparation primarily as an area devoted to adaptation, job survival, and pragmatic accommodation. Thus, in spite of allegations that the commission is committed to the idea of teachers as professionals rather than technicians, *A Call for Change in Teacher Education* continues the view of educational studies as an applied, secondary, derivative field, conceptually and procedurally distinct from the more liberating, knowledge-producing, non-utilitarian academic disciplines. Though perhaps accommodating educational coursework with a theoretical bent to a degree not sanctioned by more strictly vocational and technical approaches to teacher preparation, this commission provides professional studies in education a distinctive, applied rubric.

Of the commissions and groups that have been working on the reform of teacher preparation during the last few years, it is The Holmes Group that has attracted most of the attention by college and university faculty. In part this is due to the makeup of The Holmes Group itself. Starting with seventeen deans from the most prestigious of the Schools of Education in the US, this group has attempted to take the leading role in reform of teacher preparation. In attempting to increase its membership to well over 100 universities representing a substantial segment of our research community, it is fair to conclude that this group is attempting to develop a cartel of like-minded institutions that will set policy for teacher preparation, and attempt to exert its influence in state legislatures, state departments of education, national and regional accreditation agencies, and colleges and universities not members of The Holmes Group. It forms a powerful political force in the reform of teacher preparation.

The report of The Holmes Group, *Tomorrow's Teachers*, is the most comprehensive and articulate of the proposals that have been made to date, outlining policy, program, and institutional changes that would alter in fundamental ways the ideas and practices involved in the preparation of teachers. Moreover, The Holmes Group recognizes more fully than do other agencies the necessity of linking improved undergraduate education, revitalized programs in education, and the conditions and possibilities of the workplace of teachers. As a comprehensive, clearly written document, *Tomorrow's Teachers* is committed to improvement in the quality of teaching in the US public schools, and recognizes that the failure rate of past reform efforts is traceable in large part to the top down, hierarchical imposition of improvements. It is committed to the notion that teachers and other school people must be collaborators in the creation and implementation of serious changes in public school teaching and teacher preparation.

There are other perspectives and ideas contained in The Holmes Group report that are to be applauded, even if the writers are at times a bit too narrowly political and self-congratulatory in their statements. This group is clearly aiming to substantiate the importance of educational study and research within the confines of teacher preparation.

While this should not be surprising, and is in fact partially self-serving, recent attempts to erode or abolish altogether teacher preparation programs as a prerequisite for certification, and the ambiguous status of educational research within existing and contemplated programs of preparation, make this aspect of the report timely and worth reinforcing. Even though there are serious questions about the nature of the research centrally supported by The Holmes Group, and in spite of shortcomings in some of its policy recommendations, this group's insistence on the centrality of research in reconstituted programs of teacher preparation is refreshing.

The Holmes Group report contains more specific recommendations that are quite progressive in intent, and worth briefly noting here. The authors recognize that the nearly universal approval of field placements in teacher education can itself become a panacea for solving problems that are more deeply rooted. While The Holmes Group correctly recognizes that students often value such field experience more than other aspects of their program, 'rarely does the experience build upon the general principles and theories emphasized in earlier university study ... most student teachers quickly conform to the practices of their superivising teacher and rarely put into practice a novel technique or risk failure'.[82] Attentive to the dangers in a vocationally oriented approach to teacher training fostering primarily professional socialization, the authors recognize that field experiences as ordinarily structured will do little to bring about the pervasive changes in teaching that are required in order for teacher education to be effectively transformed.

As well, The Holmes Group is sensitive to the needs of what it calls 'at risk' students: those who are racially, ethnically, or culturally different, who are not afforded the privileges of the white upper and middle classes, and who often have divergent linguistic, cultural, and school-related needs. The authors recognize that such students 'receive less attention than they rightfully deserve or are assigned to inappropriate classes and denied adequate or appropriate opportunities to learn'.[83] While perhaps limited a bit in scope — in terms of both analysis and suggestions for change — The Holmes Group is to be commended for its concern in addressing the problem of students who are different. Similarly, this group takes seriously the obvious imbalance between numbers of minority teachers and students, and the need for teacher preparation advocates to offer proposals to redress this imbalance.

This speaks as well to a central assumption of *Tomorrow's Teachers*: that teaching, and teachers, are the central variables in improving the quality of public education. As the authors tell us:

> We cannot improve the quality of education in our schools without improving the quality of teachers in them. Curriculum plans, instructional materials, elegant classrooms, and even sensitive, intelligent administrators cannot overcome the negative effects of weak teaching, or match the positive effects of positive teaching ... The entire formal and informal curriculum of the school is filtered through the minds and hearts of classroom teachers, making the quality of school learning dependent on the quality of teachers.[84]

The teacher is the linch-pin of educational improvement in our schools. Thus teacher preparation is to be valued for the ways in which it can enhance the competence of the practitioner. Moreover, the quality of teaching is determined, the authors say, by the quality of student learning that results. As the primary aim of teaching, levels of learning can be utilized in assessing both practitioners and programs for preparing them.

Indeed it appears to be assumed that teaching, and education generally, is for learning. At one level the equivocation involved here can be seen in part of The Holmes Group rationale for abolishing undergraduate education majors in higher education. 'For elementary teachers, this degree has too often become a substitute for learning any academic subject deeply enough to teach it well'. The result is teachers who fail to 'know much about anything, because they are required to know a little of everything'.[85] As with other reform proposals, education is here assumed to be distinct from 'academic subjects', and an area of study less valued than such subjects — hence its unfortunate 'substitute' status for students. Further, it is assumed that an undergraduate education major can only be geared to teaching as an aim or end point, and because the preparation of teachers must be expanded, it is to be eliminated as a possible major for these undergraduates. The Holmes Group's emphasis on learning as the aim of teaching is also rather clear: 'for competent professionals, students' learning is the *sine qua non* of teaching and schooling'.[86] This orientation is also evidenced in the report's discussion of a new hierarchy in the teaching profession, with Career Professional Teacher, Professional Teacher, and Instructor classifications. Professional Teachers, who would probably constitute the bulk of the teaching force, 'would be specialists in pedagogy'. Beyond a knowledge of appropriate content acquired in general education, the Professional Teacher would be responsible for understanding 'learning problems children encounter at different ages', how to overcome these problems, and would be a 'skilled diagnostician of children's learning needs ... ' Further, these teachers would make 'judgments about when to seek outside help, and when they could remediate learning problems themselves. They would be trained in techniques of motivation and classroom management and could evaluate curricular materials'.[87]

To justify this differentiation of the teaching profession, and to provide teachers with the appropriate knowledge base they will need in order to be recognized as professionals, the Holmes Group acknowledges the importance of developing an approach to professional education that will elevate the status of teacher preparation. It is clear that for this group many of the potential contributors to the required knowledge base have been eliminated. For example, while supporting undergraduate study in the academic disciplines, they see professional education as relying on such disciplines, and not as a collaborator on a common project. This is shown in part by The Holmes Group's rejection of majors in education at the undergraduate level. 'Academic' subject matter is seen as providing the necessary 'undergirding discipline' for professional education: 'clearly, teacher education is dependent upon the arts and sciences, consistent with the primary disciplines'.[88] The role of liberal education for the work of teachers is further clarified when this group tell us that:

> the reforms of undergraduate education toward greater coherence and dedication to the historic tenets of liberal education is ... essential to improving teacher education. Teachers must lead a life of the mind. They must be reflective and thoughtful: persons who seek to understand so they may clarify for others, persons who can go to the heart of the matter.[89]

The historical roots of liberal studies as concerned with 'the expansion of the mind', reflection, contemplation, and so on, are clearly central for good teaching; they provide the content for effective instruction. Good teaching is then conceived as the process of translating that knowledge into a form appropriate for school learning. It is this process of translating academic knowledge into school activities that is instrumental in enhancing student learning. Yet the knowledge base for teaching is kept distinct from the academic disciplines themselves, as the latter provide the core knowledge on which education is dependent.

Nor is professional education to be grounded in the social,

historical, or sociological foundations of education. While *Tomorrow's Teachers* does suggest that the study of teaching and schooling could proceed in a discipline-based way (presumably through inquiry in the foundational fields of education), such study is justified because it is rooted in 'tested modes of inquiry'; and since this study would be separated (conceptually and perhaps also in terms of its placement in an overall program) from the study of pedagogy, the skills of classroom teaching, and the distinguishing dispositional requirements of teachers, the distinction between academic and professional areas remains.

Yet there is a particular focus in The Holmes Group report on an area of study that is presumed to be central for the requirements of teaching. Since curriculum as an aspect of educational studies is 'one area about which we have little compelling information and theory',[90] the attention of the Holmes Group is turned to a purportedly more reliable source of knowledge:

> Within the last twenty years ... the science of education promised by Dewey, Thorndike, and others at the turn of the century, has become more tangible. The behavioral sciences have been turned on the schools themselves, and not just in laboratory simulations. Studies of life in classrooms now make possible some convincing and counter-intuitive conclusions about schooling and pupil achievement.[91]

The behavioral sciences offer special advantages for teacher preparation: first, they are allied with a tradition of inquiry that lends credibility to education, as it can now be referred to as a 'science'. Second, this new 'science of education' can be implemented so as to achieve the primary aim of schooling: increased pupil achievement. Even though professional education is fundamentally unlike the academic disciplines that undergird it, a new teacher education effort based in the behavioral sciences will aid in improving the overall quality of education, justifying the stratification of the profession, and increasing the respectability of teachers, teacher educators, and Schools of Education.

Summary and Conclusions

We have analyzed in this chapter a rather wide array of evidence that the separation between liberal and applied studies is both long standing and deeply entrenched. It is from this basic schism that the distinction between theory and practice in education emanates. To effectively overcome this educational dichotomy, we must confront the deeper historical, conceptual, and institutional movements that propel it.

From the conceptual and institutional side of this gulf between academic and applied areas, several considerations are pertinent. Liberal education has been conceived as pertaining to the development of the mind, which liberates us from cares incompatible with wisdom — especially from such things as an obsession with physical appearance, personal gain, and social approval. In disseminating and preserving forms of knowledge, liberal education characteristically deals with general, human issues and ideas rather than the more particular or parochial concerns of future employees. Moreover, insofar as liberal education centers on the disciplines, it embodies unique methodologies, sets of problems, and modes of discourse that separate each into a proper domain. Overlying all of these features of liberal education is a view of learning and knowledge as intrinsically valuable, to be pursued disinterestedly.

The development of the modern multiversity has in some ways altered, or at least expanded, this conception of liberal studies. For institutions of higher education now admit research and development activities, and a host of professional schools, into their domain. As the university has become more integrated with the cultural, economic, and political institutions of society, it has given up some of its historic commitments and guiding principles. Yet even given this enlarged picture of the university that now accommodates professional study, Schools of Education seem more grudgingly accepted, as they do not contribute in as obvious a way to either the tenets of liberal study or this expanded conception of higher education.

Those concerned with education, on the other hand, have often exacerbated the separation between academic and professional study. Philosophers of education tend to regard theoretical inquiry as unlike practical decision making in schools, often taking the context of schooling for granted. The division between philosophical clarity and the practical dimensions of teaching thus becomes another force that cements the divorce between academic and professional study.

Teacher preparation, as the most professionally oriented wing of educational studies, has further divided these areas, as it tends to see its activities as distinct from both the academic disciplines (on which it presumably depends) and the foundational areas of education. As a vocational and technical area, those concerned with the preparation of teachers — including those now engaged in its reform — emphasize the sort of skill development, employment-related competencies, and technical rationality that are the very antipathy of the guiding principles of liberal education. Even the development of a 'science of education' in teacher preparation, as enunciated by The Holmes Group, is seen as facilitating the translation of the 'structure of the disciplines' into classroom interaction and measures of student achievement.

Thus we are left with what appears to be an intractable segregation of liberal and applied studies; within such a characterization, the most that might be hoped for is the reform of each side so that they become co-equal, conceptually distinct areas. And even this possibility seems rather remote, given the hierarchy of knowledge and domains that now exist both inside and outside higher education.

Yet the reformulation of these areas can be accomplished in a more radical way. Keeping in mind that 'radical' refers to getting at the root of things, the succeeding chapters of this book will show how the very heart of the division documented here needs to be transcended, by challenging its conceptual and institutional core. The next chapter will, in particular, challenge the epistemological and political bases of the distinction between liberal and applied studies, arguing that 'knowing' and 'acting' may not be easily separated.

Notes and References

1 This should not be seen as a critique of the people who work in these quite diverse settings. Rather, the tendencies and inclinations noted here have to do with the historical and institutional barriers that have been erected to separate these areas.

2 JOHN DEWEY, 'The relation of theory to practice in education', in *The Relation of Theory to Practice in the Education of Teachers*, the Third Yearbook of the National Society for the Scientific Study of Education, Part I (Chicago: University of Chicago Press, 1904), p. 16.

3 For instance, a brochure from a publishing house advertising a new text related to the use of drama in schools alleges that the 'article presents *useful* rather than *theoretical* premises'; see *Learning Through Dramatics: Ideas for Teachers and Librarians* (Phoenix, Arizona: Orynx Press, 1982), emphasis added.

4 I have explored this issue in a preliminary way in LANDON E. BEYER, 'Beyond elitism and technicism: Teacher education as practical philosophy', *Journal of Teacher Education*, Volume XXXVII, Number 2, March–April, 1986.

5 For example, this is discussed in JOHN HENRY NEWMAN, *The Idea of a University*, edited by I.T. KER (London: Oxford University Press, 1976), 'Editor's Introduction'.

6 BRUCE A. KIMBALL, 'Liberal versus useful education: Reconsidering the

contrast and its lineage', *Teachers College Record*, Volume 87, Number 4, Summer, 1986, p. 583.

7   CHARLES H. HASKINS, *The Rise of Universities* (New York: Henry Holt, 1923), p. 36.

8   *Ibid.*, p. 17.

9   Newman, *op. cit.*, p. 135.

10   Not all liberal arts institutions, nor all faculty and administrators within them, share this abstracted and elitist ideal. There are, in fact, institutions that embody a liberal arts tradition and whose history is infused with social activism and a commitment to the disadvantaged rather than the privileged. See, for example, HERMANN R. MUELDER, *Missionaries and Muckrakers: The First Hundred Years of Knox College* (Urbana, Illinois: University of Illinois Press, 1984).

11   WILLIAM C. DEVANE, *The American University in the Twentieth Century* (Baton Rouge, Louisiana: Louisiana State University, 1957), p. 7.

12   *Ibid.*, pp. 16–17.

13   *Ibid.*, pp. 39–40.

14   Newman, *op. cit.*, pp. 145–146.

15   *Ibid.*, p. 101.

16   ALEXANDER MEIKLEJOHN, *The Liberal College* (Boston: Marshall Jones Company, 1920), pp. 14–15.

17   *Ibid.*, p. 23.

18   *Ibid.*, p. 25.

19   *Ibid.*, p. 28.

20   A similar point was made by JOHN STUART MILL, *Inaugural address delivered at the University of St. Andrews*, 1 February, 1867 (Boston: Littel and Gray, n.d.).

21   JACQUES BARZUN, *The American University: How it Runs, Where it Is Going* (New York: Harper & Row, 1968), p. 6.

22   *Ibid.*, p. 243.

23   ALLAN NEVINS, *The State Universities and Democracy* (Urbana: University of Illinois Press, 1962), p. 16.

24   EDWARD D. EDDY, JR., *Colleges for our Land and Time: The Land-Grant Idea in American Education* (New York: Harper, 1957), p. 26.

25   See EARLE D. ROSS, *Democracy's College: The Land-Grant Movement in the Formative State* (Ames, Iowa: The Iowa State College Press, 1942), especially Chapter VIII.

26   These impulses involve categories that are ideal types, and no doubt do not fully represent any actual university or college — historically or in contemporary society. However, these categories are useful for heuristic purposes as they reflect the dominant values affecting higher education in the U.S.

27   DeVane, *op. cit.*, pp. 42–43.

28   See LANDON E. BEYER, 'Field experience, ideology, and the development of critical reflectivity', *Journal of Teacher Education*, Volume XXXV, Number 3, 1984.

29   B.O. SMITH, *A Design for a School of Pedagogy* (Washington, DC: US Government Printing Office, 1980), p. 12.

30 See MICHAEL W. APPLE and LOIS WEIS, (Eds.) *Ideology and Practice in Schooling* (Philadelphia: Temple University Press, 1983), 'Introduction.'

31 See *Plato, The Collected Dialogues*, Edited by EDITH HAMILTON and HUNTINGTON CAIRNS (Princeton: Princeton University Press, 1961), especially the *Republic*, Books VI and VII, pp. 720–772.

32 We too often, however, neglect the more human side of Plato's theory of knowledge — namely, the importance of dialogue, mutual interrogation, and discussion. As in many other instances, our appropriation of Platonic thought is often quite selective, used to bolster certain of our presuppositions.

33 This is not to say that Plato was totally unconcerned with physical training. Rather, he saw the development of physical capacities as needing to be coordinated with, and tempered by, the exercise of reason and contemplation.

34 JEROME A. POPP, 'Practice and malpractice in philosophy of education', *Educational Studies*, Volume 9, 1978, p. 282.

35 *Ibid.*, p. 283.

36 ISRAEL SCHEFFLER, *The Language of Education* (Springfield, Illinois: Charles C. Thomas, 1960), p. 75.

37 See, for example, R.S. PETERS, *The Concept of Education* (London: Routledge & Kegan Paul, 1967); P.H. HIRST and R.S. PETERS, *The Logic of Education* (New York: The Humanities Press, 1970); and R.S. PETERS, *Ethics and Education* (London: George Allen and Unwin Ltd., 1966).

38 Hirst and Peters, *op. cit.*, p. 3.

39 *Ibid.*, p. 13.

40 Peters, *Ethics and Education, op. cit.*, p. 196. Similar ideas can be found in R.S. PETERS, *Education and the Education of Teachers* (Boston: Routledge & Kegan Paul, 1977).

41 JONAS F. SOLTIS, (Ed.) *Philosophy and Education*, The Eightieth Yearbook of the National Society for the Study of Education (Chicago: University of Chicago Press, 1981), p. 2.

42 *Ibid.*, p. 9.

43 For some interesting comments on the possible contradictions between the introduction written by Soltis and a second introduction offered by Broudy, see DAVID NYBERG, 'Thank God for Babel: Analysis, articulation, autonomy', *Educational Theory*, Volume 31, Number 1, Winter 1981.

44 Soltis, *op. cit.*, p. 25.

45 *Ibid.*, p. 144.

46 *Ibid.*, p. 161.

47 Two exceptions need to be noted in this regard. First, the essay by JANE ROLAND MARTIN, 'Needed: A paradigm for liberal education'; second, the chapter by JAMES E. MCCLELLAN, 'First philosophy and education'.

48 I have explored this further in LANDON E. BEYER, 'Philosophical work, practical theorizing, and the nature of schooling', *Journal of Curriculum Theorizing*, Volume 5, Number 1, Winter, 1983.

49 This is not to deny the crucial importance of reflection, conceptual clarity, and theoretical analysis. Rather, it is to argue for an increased integration

of these things with the actual settings of schools. See LANDON E. BEYER, 'The parameters of educational inquiry', *Curriculum Inquiry*, Volume 16, Number 1, Spring 1986.

50 HARVEY SIEGEL, 'The future and purpose of philosophy of education', *Educational Theory*, Volume 31, Number 1, Winter, 1981, p. 13.

51 B.O. Smith, *op. cit.*, p. 89.

52 *Ibid.*, p. 75.

53 *Ibid.*, p. 76.

54 See KENNETH M. ZEICHNER, 'Myths and realities: Field based experiences in preservice teacher education', *Journal of Teacher Education*, Volume XXXI, Number 3, May–June, 1980.

55 See LAWRENCE IANNACCONE, 'Student teaching: A transitional stage in the making of a teacher', *Theory Into Practice*, Volume 2, Number 2, April 1963; and B. ROBERT TABACHNICK, THOMAS POPKEWITZ, and KENNETH M. ZEICHNER, 'Teacher education and the professional perspectives of student teachers', *Interchange*, Volume 10, Number 4, 1979–80.

56 LILLIAN KATZ, 'Issues and problems in teacher education', in BERNARD SPODEK, (Ed.) *Teacher Education: Of the Teacher By the Teacher, for the Child* (Washington, DC: National Association for the Education of Young Children, 1974).

57 FRANCES FULLER, 'Concerns of teachers: A developmental conceptualization', *American Educational Research Journal*, Volume 6, Number 2, 1969.

58 The view that educational foundations are in some way detached from the preparation of teachers clearly exacerbates this problem. Faculty in the foundations fields who share this view must bear some of the responsibility for the distance that often exists between teacher preparation and educational foundations, along with those who see teacher preparation in strictly technical and vocational terms.

59 B. OTHANEL SMITH, 'On the content of teacher education', in E. HALL, S. HORD, and G. BROWN, (Eds.) *Exploring Issues in Teacher Education: Questions for Future Research* (Austin: University of Texas Research and Development Center for Teacher Education, 1980), pp. 23–24.

60 See GEOFFREY M. ESLAND, 'Teaching and learning as the organization of knowledge', in MICHAEL F.D. YOUNG, (Ed.) *Knowledge and Control* (London: Collier-Macmillan, 1971).

61 There are, of course, exceptions to this general tendency. See, for example, 'Preservice teacher selection and retention', a special issue of the *Journal of Teacher Education*, Volume XXXVIII, Number 2, March–April, 1987.

62 THE NATIONAL COMMISSION ON EXCELLENCE IN EDUCATION, *A Nation At Risk* (Washington, DC: US Government Printing Office, 1983).

63 THE CARNEGIE FORUM ON EDUCATION AND THE ECONOMY, *A Nation Prepared: Teachers for the 21st Century* (Washington: Carnegie Corporation, 1986), p. 2.

64 It is worth noting that 'excellence' and 'competitiveness' have become the latest in a series of slogans that tend to obfuscate a good deal of educational discourse. For the purposes and politics of educational ideas as slogan systems, see B. PAUL KOMISAR and JAMES E. MCCLELLAN, 'The logic of slogans', in *Language and Concepts in Education*, edited by B.

OTHANEL SMITH and ROBERT H. ENNIS (Chicago: Rand McNally and Company, 1961).

65 The Carnegie Forum on Education and the Economy, *op. cit.*, p. 3.
66 *Ibid.*, p. 125.
67 *Ibid.*, p. 66.
68 *Ibid.*, p. 73.
69 *Ibid.*, p. 75.
70 *Ibid.*, p. 76.
71 See, for example, FREDERICK WINSLOW TAYLOR, *The Principles of Scientific Management* (New York: Harper, 1911); SAMUEL HABER, *Efficiency and Uplift: Scientific Management in the Progressive Era 1890–1920* (Chicago: University of Chicago Press, 1964); for the effect of scientific management ideas on schools see RAYMOND E. CALLAHAN, *Education and the Cult of Efficiency: A Study of the Social Forces That Have Shaped the Administration of the Public Schools* (Chicago: University of Chicago Press, 1962); and HERBERT M. KLIEBARD, 'Bureaucracy and curriculum theory', in WILLIAM F. PINAR, (Ed.) *Curriculum Theorizing: The Reconceptualists* (Berkeley: McCutcheon Publishing Corporation, 1975).
72 The Carnegie Forum on Education and the Economy, *op. cit.*, p. 89.
73 *Ibid.*, p. 89.
74 See LANDON E. BEYER, 'Educational reform: The political roots of national risk', *Curriculum Inquiry*, Volume 15, Number 1, Spring, 1985.
75 NATIONAL COMMISSION FOR EXCELLENCE IN TEACHER EDUCATION, *A Call for Change in Teacher Education* (Washington DC: American Association of Colleges for Teacher Education, 1985), pp. 1–2.
76 This is true in spite of the fact that the authors of *A Call for Change in Teacher Education*, in discussing the 'supply and demand for quality teachers', warn us that, 'the public must be assured that the additional funds [for teacher salaries, etc., that will be required] are purchasing quality education for children', (pp. 8–9). Such remarks, while evidencing the same economistic tendencies as the report of the Carnegie Forum, are more peripheral than is the case with the latter report.
77 National Commission for Excellence in Teacher Education, *op. cit.*, p. 11.
78 *Ibid.*, p. 12.
79 *Ibid.*, p. 12.
80 *Ibid.*, p. 15.
81 *Ibid.*, p. 16.
82 THE HOLMES GROUP, *Tomorrow's Teachers* (East Lansing: The Holmes Group, Inc., 1986), p. 55.
83 *Ibid.*, p. 31.
84 *Ibid.*, p. 23.
85 *Ibid.*, p. 14.
86 *Ibid.*, p. 29.
87 *Ibid.*, p. 39.
88 *Ibid.*, p. 46; also see in this regard PHILIP H. PHENIX, *Realms of Meaning: A Philosophy of the Curriculum for General Education* (New York: McGraw-Hill Book Company, 1964).

2
Knowledge, Ideology, and Inquiry

The demarcation of liberal and professional studies discussed in the previous chapter can be summarized by noting two general contentions. First, liberal studies are allegedly, by their very nature, preoccupied with the discovery, generation, and transmission of knowledge for its own sake, in the sort of disinterested way that is unconcerned with private gain, social circumstance, or material benefit (whether individual or social). Their sole purpose is the pursuit of knowledge and learning as its own end through discipline-based inquiries and methodologies, and the dissemination of this knowledge to students engaged in the study and appreciation of the liberal disciplines. Education on the other hand, and the professional preparation of teachers in particular, is aimed at inculcating (training for) technical competence. As a vocational domain, education fosters the development of particular skills, techniques, and dispositions that constrict or narrow inquiry. Consequently, educational studies can be regarded as the very antithesis of liberal inquiry. While the liberal disciplines expand the mind and broaden students' horizons, educational studies are aimed at more narrow technical proficiencies, job training, and the application of knowledge.

The separation of liberal from professional studies is not, of course, the inevitable result of some natural or organic process over which people have little or no control. Rather, it is the result of historical processes — both intellectual and social — that have affected the way we conceptualize and act within these domains. The view that genuine inquiry is concerned with the pursuit of dispassionate, objective, 'pure', and disinterested knowledge, can be located in the development of ideas regarding the conditions of knowledge that has a long history in

Western civilization. Liberal inquiry as discussed in the previous chapter also needs to be placed in the context of social and political movements that occurred during this period of time.

Our understanding of liberal inquiry is more critically assessed in this chapter. The epistemological assumptions that have provided liberal inquiry its special status, especially as these have been generated from the philosophy of the natural and social sciences, are of special concern in this regard. We will also consider the arguments of those who have challenged the positivistic views that undergird orientation to knowledge and inquiry, as we consider the implications of the shift from foundational epistemology to hermeneutics and praxis. This shift entails a recognition of the socially constructed nature of knowledge and the methods and criteria with which it may be ascertained. Following this, we will take up the important insights from feminist scholarship, especially the emerging perspective of a feminist epistemology, as this both undermines the older tradition of foundationalism in epistemology and points toward a revitalized conception of knowledge.

The central aim of this chapter is to demonstrate that the disinterested, objective, and context independent theory of knowledge and inquiry that lies behind liberal education is not credible, and that a reconstituted theory of knowledge must alter our view of the *artes liberales* and their separation from more useful or applied forms of inquiry. In the following chapters we will reconsider the depiction of educational studies as a pragmatic, vocationally oriented, technical domain, dominated by considerations that narrow inquiry and discourse, making it too instrumentally oriented. As we shall see, recent theoretical and practical work in educational studies has been sensitive to just the sort of revisions in epistemology and inquiry that are the subject of the present chapter.

Liberal Studies and the Domain of Knowledge

Epistemology and Certainty

To facilitate the disinterested search for knowledge and its transmission to students committed to its inherent value, the liberal arts have been divided into domains, disciplines, and departments. The aim of this division is to assist the process of inquiry by utilizing methods, questions, and perspectives that will reveal the characteristics of our objects of study. An important part of liberal education has been thought to consist in coming to understand 'the structure of the disciplines', the methods they appropriately utilize in the discovery of knowledge, and the ways in which this new knowledge can be justified. Becoming liberally educated, expanding one's mind in significant ways, is therefore importantly based on two complementary assumptions. First, it is assumed that the disciplines producing new forms of genuine knowledge can validate their claims — that the criteria they impose can be shown to be rigorous, objective, and value free. This is sometimes contrasted with artistic interpretations which are thought to be subject to, or even defined by, individual variation and subjective interpretation. Second, it has been assumed that the liberal arts are valuable because of their influence — via the knowledge objectively acquired and confirmed — on the quality of thinking of students devoted to their study. As a result of liberal learning, people will become more reflective, more tolerant or open minded, and more aware of the complexities of issues. In short, liberal study, in drawing upon the best of our cultural heritage through the incorporation of important, verifiable ideas, can deepen our intellectual awareness and curiosity, making us more discriminate, aware of complexities, respectful of ideas, and sensitive to the need for clarity and precision in our own thoughts and language.

Disciplined inquiry, in order to be seen as valuable in the way required by advocates of liberal study, must be based on processes and methods that at least hold the promise of certain, reliable knowledge. If such certainty is lacking, the very point of becoming liberally educated may be undermined. For a failure to substantiate the knowledge conveyed by the liberal disciplines will bring into question the special status which separates them from other pursuits.

Two general routes have been trodden to obtain certain and verifiable knowledge — the view we might call epistemological objectivism. The first, through philosophy, was introduced in chapter one. The other route of epistemological objectivism, through the natural and social sciences, will occupy the majority of this section.

Recall that, on Plato's view, genuine knowledge and understanding were only possible through coming to mentally perceive the realm of true Being. It is only the evanescent, other worldly Forms that provide a secure source of knowledge, and the philosopher's search must be for these embodiments of perfection as they are revealed if one follows the proper line of reasoning and inquiry.[1] For Plato, there did exist a way for the philosopher to obtain objective, disinterested truth that was pure, certain, unmediated (by misleading, fallible human and physical processes) and separated from day to day life. As such the Forms presented the possibility of obtaining the sort of secure knowledge on which philosophy, and one's own life work, might rest.

Modern, secular philosophy has not continued the search for those other-worldly phenomena with which Plato was enamored. Though there is a similarity between Plato's metaphysics and certain religious beliefs (Plato's 'theory of the psyche' is sometimes discussed as a theory of the soul, and his Forms might be thought of as existing in some Heaven-like location independent of space and time) contemporary philosophers have focused instead on the clarification and analysis of concepts, language, and more human ideas. It has not, however, abandoned the search for certainty in its formulation of knowledge claims. It is this pursuit of certainty that provides a more long lasting Platonic legacy than the theory of Forms itself.

With gradual changes away from a transcendental, metaphysical, or theocratic world view, the beginnings of the natural sciences promoted a distinctly different sort of awareness and model for knowledge. The changes brought about by scientific procedures, instrumentation, and methods of observation were to have consequences that went far beyond the domain of science per se; they served to reorient our very perceptions of self, other, and reality, as these changes ushered in a new epistemological vision and helped found new forms of social life.

In the introduction to his book entitled *Human Understanding*, sciences as well. It led, in short, to the generation of positivism in people as they reflect on the world and their own processes of reflection:

> What sort of things do we know? What kinds of certainty can our knowledge have? How do we acquire that knowledge, or the concepts in terms of which it is framed? And what part does the evidence of our senses play in this process?
> How far are our concepts — even the most basic ones — derived from sense experience? Must our claims to knowledge be backed, in every particular, by sensory evidence? ...
> ... how can we compare the merits of rival concepts? And how, in their turn, can our claims to knowledge — moral or mathematical, scientific or practical — be justified and appraised?[2]

Such questions, though quite complex and requiring in depth investigations of a sort sometimes thought needlessly theoretical and abstract, have the most profound consequences for how we understand the role of knowledge, liberal education, and the more specific question of the appropriate preparation for prospective teachers.

From the seventeenth century in Europe onward, there developed a perspective on how such questions must be answered that was to capture the spirit of the era, and that still affects contemporary thinking about knowledge and the criteria for its justification. This perspective is a part of a more comprehensive viewpoint that sees the natural world, the principles of its organization and interrelations, and human nature as equally fixed, law-like, and immutable. Scientists and philosophers during this era were instrumental in formulating the conviction that:

1 The Order of Nature is fixed and stable, and the Mind of Man acquires intellectual mastery over it by reasoning in accordance with Principles of Understanding that are equally fixed and universal.
2 Matter is essentially inert, and the active source or inner seat of rational, self-motivated activity is a completely distinct Mind, or Consciousness, within which all the highest mental functions are localized.
3 Geometrical knowledge provides a comprehensive standard of incorrigible certainty, against which all other claims to knowledge must be judged.[3]

The universe could be understood as a vast mechanism with fixed, if complicated, laws which govern the actions of physical entities. The mind operates with a set of similarly lawful principles, and by utilizing these in the process of discovering the regularities of the world, we can obtain genuine, irrefutable knowledge.

For much of this knowledge producing activity, people were interested primarily in formal relationships and formulae themselves — reinforcing the view that geometrical theorems and knowledge are a source of irrefutable knowledge. The purpose of investigating the properties of the physical world, and their relations with the objects, was thus the recording of observations and the statement of conclusions that reflected the structure of a universe governed by ordered principles, laws, and mathematical regularities. From such observations could spring real knowledge of the world, guided by the proper principles of human thought and understanding.

By attending to physical phenomena, inventing instruments and devices for more accurately recording and predicting events, increasingly sophisticated measurements could be made that would lead to the formulation of hypotheses that could be tested and verified; given a sufficient number of these observations and their verification by scientifically approved procedures, general principles could be generated that would offer mathematical precision as they reflected the immutable 'Laws of Nature'. This clearly offered the promise of genuine knowledge as certain as that posited by Plato, with the advantage of being less metaphysical and abstract, indeed less theoretical. For the key emphases were on empirical observations and empirically based generalizations that reflected the true nature of that physical reality that could be seen and recorded by all, and the analysis of such observations via the use of quantitative calculations and reasoning.

Because knowledge could be based on the regularities of nature, the principles and generalizations that resulted could be extracted from any important social or historical context. The Laws of Nature were assumed to be independent of the context in which scientists themselves might be working, so that the particular social, political, or economic exigencies of the time were epistemologically irrelevant. As a result, the findings of empiricist science had transhistorical, asocial, and extra-human qualities that further ensured their certainty and objectivity. Discounting social contexts, personal biases, and historical precedents alike, the physical sciences promised the possibility of apodictic truth and thus became the model for other domains and undertakings. The fascination with this picture of the world as ordered, mechanical, and governed by laws that were capable of being discovered, extended not only to the physical or natural sciences, but to the human and social sciences as well. It led, in short, to the generation of positivism in human inquiry.

The development and meaning of positivism has been the subject of much discussion and criticism. The term 'positivistic' is now commonly used to condemn or galvanize opposition to a position, sometimes without being very clear about to what this label refers. It is especially important that we understand the meaning of the set of ideas associated with positivism, their linkages to the mechanistic world view that preceded it, and its connection with contemporary issues. This will enable us to understand the significance of positivistic criticism and how the rejection of some of its key provisions undermines the model of inquiry associated with liberal study and the structure of the disciplines.

Like all systems of thought of any complexity, positivism is a combination of many ideas, the work of many people, and the appearance of social circumstances that cannot be precisely located in a determinate time and place. While Auguste Comte is (with good reason) usually cited as the founder of positivism, his ideas are in fact a synthesis of the ideas of earlier writers, just as Comte's thoughts were to affect those of people who followed him. Indeed it is instructive initially to see how the tenets of 'French Positivism' were shared, to varying degrees, both by Saint-Simon (who preceded Comte and had a direct bearing on his development) and Emile Durkheim.[4] It is worth citing at length the twelve tenets of positivism shared by these three thinkers, as they embody the assumptions and convictions of the age; these tenets form the core of a world view associated with positivist precepts:

1   There is but one world, and it has an objective existence.
2   The constituents of the world, and the laws which govern their movements, are discoverable through science alone, science being the only form of knowledge. Therefore that which cannot be known scientifically, cannot be known.
3   Science depends upon reason and observation duly combined.
4   Science cannot discover all the constituents of the world, and all the laws which govern them, because human powers of reason and observation are limited.
5   What man seeks to discover about the world is normally suggested by his practical interests and his situation.
6   There are laws of historical development whose discovery will enable the past to be explained, the present understood and the future predicted.
7   There are social laws which govern the interconnections between different institutional and cultural forms.
8   Society is a reality *sui generis*.
9   Social order is the natural condition of society.
10   Moral and political choice should be established exclusively on a scientific basis.
11   The subjection of man before the natural laws of history and society precludes evaluation of institutional and cultural forms in any terms other than those of conformity with these laws.
12   The positive, the constructive, supercedes the negative, the critical. The positive, the relative, also supercedes the theological and the metaphysical, the absolute.[5]

As the central principles of positivist thinking what do these ideas mean?

The first thing to notice about these twelve tenets is how much ground they cover — that is, how all encompassing are their sentiments and consequences. These ideas cover the nature of physical and social reality, the way social and personal decisions are to be made, and the very means with which one's life is to be led and measured. They form a comprehensive world view whose internal consistency and wholeness deserves consideration.

Many of the principles listed above are directed toward revealing the nature of reality and are thus ontological in character. For positivists, reality can't be understood as a constellation of separable components but is instead a whole, susceptible to objective delineation, through the use of reason and scientific observation. Moreover, social reality is governed by laws much in the same way nature is; specific social facts can be evaluated only in terms of their compliance with these laws, just as human development follows its own progressive course. Lastly, while what we seek to know is often the result of practical interests, both those interests and our ability to obtain genuine knowledge will be determined by the level of development of the historical and social period we live within. In sum, the earlier mechanistic view of the physical world that began some two centuries earlier is here given a specific content, as the ideas and world view associated with the natural scientist become the pattern for social and human existence.

Let us examine more specifically the ideas of Comte himself, the presumed founder of positivism.[6] Comte sought to defend the scientific study of society and, in providing a firm grounding for such study, to create the field of sociology. Himself a trained mathematician, Comte believed that mathematical logic was the fundamental method that lies behind all physical sciences. Using mathematical relationships in articulating and defending its principles and laws, the physical sciences found a discipline with sufficient precision and standardization. Like the physical sciences as well, social science must rely on observations and their faithful recording if it is to arrive at its own truths.

An important part of Comte's positivism was his rejection of speculative, non-empirical, abstract ideas such as those found in metaphysics. Comte also distrusted the conclusions arrived at through logical reasoning. To be truly scientific, Comte thought, we must restrict our hypotheses to events and occurrences that can be verified by the senses. Thus Comte was in important respects a 'phenomenalist', and believed that the road to truth could be travelled only by those who utilized the methods of the physical sciences, focusing on physical phenomena. As one commentator has expressed the contribution of Comte's thought:

> Comte insisted, in general, that the social sciences should be built up by inductive methods. He emphasized observation as the basis of all science. As we advance toward positive science, he tells us, imagination is more and more subordinated to observation.[7]

While imagination and creativity are not totally to be dispensed with, they will be governed by the truths that are discovered through disciplined, objective observation and mathematical reasoning. By studying the natural history of humankind (just as the biologist studies the history and development of other species), the social scientist can obtain knowledge of human society. In employing statistical measures in their observation and study of human society, social scientists may combine a reliance on empirical facts and mathematical reasoning that is at the core of all scientific certainty.

A Progressive, Comte assumed that civilization was continually advancing. Like other thinkers of his day (including the Frenchman Condorcet and those who were affected by his ideas, notably Thomas Jefferson in the United States) there existed for Comte a natural law of progress that was the foundation of human history. In a general sense, Comte thought that human civilization progressed through three states: the theological, the metaphysical, and the positive or scientific. Thus the domain of science embodies the highest form of human endeavor and provides a model for the development of human reason:

> The history of science and technology was the example *par excellence* of cumulative growth, of the progressive transformation of society by the progressive development of positive knowledge ... Thus the growth of science and the scientific attitude indicated the general direction of historical development.[8]

The natural sciences clearly served as more than an illustration of one methodology, way of knowing, or intellectual endeavor; their accumulated knowledge provided the model for knowledge of all sorts, and the methodological path by which other areas of inquiry could certify their findings.

The influence of positivism cannot be understood solely as a matter of a set of ideas discussed by a small group of academics. The real force behind Comte and his later translators and intermediaries is in their success in formulating a view of the world that had social, political, and economic affinities. In part this can be seen in the extent to which positivism was widely accepted as embodying the methods of inquiry with which to substantiate claims to genuine knowledge. As one writer has asserted with respect to Comte's vision of history and positive science:

> He did not say that history was, or was reducible to, a kind of physics; but his conception pointed in that direction — of one complete and all embracing pyramid of scientific knowledge; one method; one truth; one scale of rational, 'scientific' values. This naive craving for unity and symmetry at the expense of experience is still with us.[9]

By creating a picture of knowledge as empirical–analytic, based on objective observation, mathematical reasoning, and fulfilling a Progressive development, Comte and his descendents were able to define not only theoretical concepts like truth, validity, knowledge, and so on; they were also able to develop a set of ideas and practices that could guide research and inquiry and, perhaps most importantly, to formulate a set of convictions that affected the way people saw themselves and the larger natural and social worlds. As a world view or ideology, positivism was to influence intellectual and social life, ideas and daily interactions, in a way that went far beyond its intellectual origins:

> ... the triumph of the positive spirit as such is not to be overlooked, for out of its formalizing, generalizing, and dominating intentions it had in the meantime developed its own practice — i.e., its own technology — commonly known today as the 'software' and 'hardware' of the natural and social sciences. This is the reification proper of the positive spirit: an intellectual technology for the control and guidance or steering of human life.[10]

The proper guidance of human life was a special concern of Comte's in large part because of the political and social changes that were taking place during the 19th century. The revolutions in France and the United States had helped overturn the aristocratic, staid, and orderly societies of the past. With power being shared by larger numbers of people, the potential for instability and disruption was clearly apparent within the new, democratic state. It is within such a changing climate that Comte's social philosophy was especially provocative. 'His entire work was dedicated to the development and elaboration of a system that would resolve, once and for all, the disruptive and anarchic tendencies in the society of his time and the societies of the future.'[11] Perhaps the culminating result of Comte's ideas would be a society that is ordered, systematic, and committed to progress — and one that would short circuit the potential for revolutionary turmoil and social disarray. The prospect of social disorder is, for Comte, directly connected to the appearance of intellectual disorder and uncertainty. His theory of positive science is both academic and social in this sense. As Comte expressed this:

> It cannot be necessary to prove to anybody who reads this work that ideas govern the world, or throw it into chaos — in other words, that all social mechanisms rest upon opinions. The great political and moral crisis that societies are now undergoing is shown by a rigid analysis to arise out of intellectual anarchy.[12]

In articulating a positive philosophy, Comte's methods were designed not only to provide for a reorganization of inquiry in the human and social sciences that would result in more rigorous, irrefutable knowledge based on a natural science model, but also to help bring order and control to societies threatened with political upheaval. The proper direction of social conditions is prefigured by the state of civilization at that moment, especially which of the stages (theological, metaphysical, or scientific) is dominant at that time. Both the individual and the society as a whole must conform to the natural law of progress, and to the scientific tenets that are its culmination.

Clearly there is in these ideas a strong conservative direction. Since the laws of progress and of human development are to be modeled on the laws of the natural sciences which in fact provide their aim, existing institutions and practices are to be commended as they conform to such laws. By paying attention to (i.e., closely observing and scientifically analyzing) current social practices, the ubiquitous, extra–social laws of human development may be discovered. We can see here how, 'the very purpose and result of extending the positive scientific method to human and social phenomena are to secure in the public at large acceptance of the existing order and its predominant forces'. In a more general way, such a view:

> takes on the role of accustoming the general mind to succumb to what is, and of theoretically as well as practically fixing the

parameters of knowledge and action within the predominant configuration of the present as *reality* — while every other mode of knowledge and action falls into the realm of speculation, imagination, and the unreal.[13]

The power of a positive science of society and humanity can be seen, finally, in its ability to provide secure knowledge that will produce both intellectual and social tranquility, while preserving extant realities and moving slowly toward the perfection of humanity itself.

The legacy of the positive philosophy first systematized by Comte can be seen in many arenas. In sociology it has had a pronounced effect on social research. This is evident in the extent to which 'social theory' is to be kept separate from 'scientific social research'. While social theorists may employ suppositions, value laden perspectives, and even imaginative analyses and efforts at social reform, these are not suitable avenues for the social scientist. This is clear, for example, in the 'instrumental positivism' that dominated American sociology from the 1920s and 1930s. In his 1926 presidential address to the American Sociological Society, John L. Gillin criticized those sociologists whose major concern was not the accumulation of positive sociological knowledge but social reform. He declared, however, that such speculative pursuits would soon end:

> the application of the scientific method and the increased emphasis upon objective data have been acting as selective agents in consigning these enemies of sociology to a deserved innocuous deseutude ... Emphasis upon rigidly scientific methods will attend to them.[14]

The key to uplifting social science lay, clearly, in making it closer to the natural sciences, at least as these were viewed by the growing numbers of sociologists favoring instrumental positivism. This must include a lack of personal interest or value commitment in the observation of social phenomena, a greater reliance on statistical analysis of large scale survey data, and the renunciation of philosophical/theoretical work that lacks a scientific base. In the end the new image of the sociologist was closer to an engineer or technician than someone committed to the impassioned pursuit of truth:

> It will be necessary to crush out emotion and to discipline the mind so strongly that the fanciful pleasures of intellectuality will have to be eschewed in the verification process: it will be

desirable to taboo ethics and values (except in choosing problems); and it will be inevitable that we shall have to spend most of our time doing hard, dull, tedious, and routine tasks.[15]

Hardly productive of a glamorous or (one thinks) satisfying professional life, the social scientist's labors are justified by the important contributions they ostensibly make to the discovery of genuine knowledge.

Besides an emphasis on statistical analysis of large scale survey data, the methodological legacy of positivism can be seen in an individualistic perspective on social events, a belief in accumulationism in knowledge about social reality, and a commitment to value freedom. In conducting social research it is the beliefs, actions, and opinions of individuals that are of interest. The information thus obtained can be used inductively to accumulate knowledge that, because of its verifiability and its relationships to other verified facts, is linked to a process of progressive accumulation of knowledge. This fits well with the progressive orientation of positivism in that it assumes that the future will be brighter to the extent that it can be guided by more secure, objective, certain knowledge on which to base social policies. To realize this objective knowledge, the researcher must not allow personal or social values to intrude upon the objective determination of reality and the laws that govern it.

Positivistic tendencies have also been felt in the field of education, especially as they have become embedded in methodological and conceptual emphases. In developmental psychology for instance, there is evidence of positivism's influence in the reliance on mechanistic world views that undergird models of development.[16] These are perhaps clearest in the work of behaviorists like Watson, Skinner, Thorndike, and others, who present a world mechanically ordered around stimuli and responses, devoid of mental notions such as mind, intention, and introspection. At its most extreme, this perspective argues for the reduction of all events and actions to concrete, if complex, physical and chemical processes. While having some affinity with materialist theories of mind,[17] behaviorists have postulated an educational arena that is consistent with the drive for the dominance of the scientific method, statistical analysis, accumulation of objective facts, and value freedom; such an educational perspective extends the development of French positivism and its counterpart in this country, instrumental positivism. The result has been an effort to include only psychometric, technical analyses of educational matters as bona fide research efforts in education, while dismissing more qualitative, critical, or ethnomethodological studies. [18]

It is worth quoting one of the founders of behaviorism, Edward L. Thorndike, to capture the inheritance of positivism in educational psychology:

> We should regard nothing as outside the scope of science, and every regularity or law that science can discover in the consequence of events is a step towards the only freedom that is of use to men and an aid to the good life. If values do not reside in the orderly world of nature, but depend on chance or caprice, it would be vain to try to increase them. The world needs, not only the vision and valuation of great sages, and the practical psychology of men of affairs, but also scientific methods to test the worth of the prophets' dreams ... [19]

The primordial importance of positive science is here apparent.

Still other factors helped promote the viability of the positive science. During the era in which the force of positivism was being felt, the beginnings of a shift in economic production was being witnessed in many nations. In the United States, factory capitalism was being organized, especially in the textile mills of New England, that was to have profound social, political, and familial effects. A change in production took place that moved the economy away from a guild-oriented, often family or community-centered unit toward a system in which mass production, the division of labor, and technical advance were accompanied by wage payments and fragmented work operations for which the assembly line became the epitome; these economic shifts necessitated a change in cultural and intellectual orientation in many ways.

The influence of the industrial revolution on American social and economic life is of course multi-faceted, and well beyond the scope of this book. [20] There are, however, several ways in which this influence was supported by (and in turn supported) the emphasis on science and progress in positivism that are worth detailing. First, the success of industrialization depended on the development of procedures, organizational patterns, and physical operations that were based on technical expertise and scientific management. The development of the assembly line, for example, required specialized machinery and processes of production that would facilitate orderly, mechanical, and individualistic work routines. Sophisticated machinery and procedures that replaced the craft oriented activity of flesh and blood people were required in order that the process of manufacturing could be broken down into component parts and easily managed. Such a process was also useful because it controlled the activities of those involved in the work process. By controlling production, the newly emerging forces of capitalism also controlled labor.

A theory of knowledge and of social and human development based on science and progress is quite useful for this system of production. If the techniques and methodologies of science could be harnessed or at least incorporated into the workings of industry and manufacturing, they could aid in the expansion and sophistication of the production process. This is not to suggest that the founders and purveyors of positivism were themselves involved in the emergence of capitalistic forms of economic activity, nor that they were involved in some collusion with industrialists. Rather, some of the major tenets of positivism were in many ways inherently compatible — at the level of a cultural consciousness or ideological framework — with the demands of a new system of production and distribution.

Second, the expanding productive apparatus of U.S. society during this era required something else, beyond the provision of scientific and technological discoveries and procedures that could propel capitalist economic development. Such development also crucially depended on the formulation of broadly shared personal habits and dispositions. Such personal and social propensities can be clearly seen in a couple of major traits. One of the perspectives central to the growing industrial sector was the segmentation, compartmentalization, and individuation of people and activities. Instead of a communal or collective/social orientation, this way of seeing the social and institutional contexts of daily life emphasized the fragmentation of processes and events. To be more concrete, such fragmentation was not only inherent in the procedures of manufacture and industry, but was also implied in the separation of family from economic activity, work from leisure, occupational from avocational experience, and the like. The consciousness required for these dualisms emphasized discontinuity rather than wholeness, segmentation rather than unity. Here too positivism as a system of thought that compartmentalized activities and areas of knowledge — into scientific and non-scientific, rational and irrational, progressive and static, etc. — was useful for the world view of capitalist society. Moreover, the individualistic orientation to instrumental positivism in the United States was especially resonant to the individualized and fragmented world view of industrial capitalism. Again the affinities here are generic, indicating an overlap pertaining to the characteristic thought of the era rather than a conscious manipulation of people and events by those in positions of power.[21]

To summarize this section, the development of a mechanistic world view, commencing with the advance of secular physical science in the seventeenth century, helped propel the emergence of positivist thinking that held a new vision of knowledge, rationality, objectivity, and social and human development. Its influence went far beyond the domain of academic discussion and debate, as it captured the emerging spirit of new social, economic, and political orders. In fostering a new consciousness or world view, the ideology of positivism reciprocally reinforced the needs of a new capitalist order. Rather than thinking about the relations between capitalism and positivism on a causal model, however, it is more insightful to see these as emerging tendencies that reinforced each other in interesting ways, with each dovetailing with the other at crucial cultural points. They had a decided impact on the thoughts, values, and institutions of the day, including the conceptions of education.

Scientism, Compartmentalization, and Liberal Studies

In the previous chapter we discussed some of the changes that took place in higher education in the nineteenth century as colleges and universities emphasized research and the generation of new knowledge, especially in forms that had social and economic utility. Recall that the earlier, more scholastic orientation of liberal education had embraced the preservation of a cultural heritage, and its transmission to generations of students. It was within the older, classical conception of the university that it made sense to talk about a 'community of scholars' whose work brought them together to discuss perennial problems and issues related to the common good, including the nature of social and personal responsibility. Within such liberal arts oriented institutions, moreover, the curriculum was composed largely if not exclusively of required courses and even mandated texts, with little need for elaborate libraries, museums, or laboratories.

In an interesting history of one important liberal arts institution, Knox College, Hermann R. Muelder documents the first century in the development of that college. Beyond a specific portrait of Knox, Muelder's history presents a revealing picture of liberal arts colleges in general, providing insight into the changes that were taking place in conceptions of knowledge and in the curriculum of higher education during the latter portion of the nineteenth century. Founded in 1837, the number of academic alternatives afforded Knox College's first students was small indeed:

> [The] curriculum was so uniform for all students and so common to colleges that it could be printed on one page of the first catalogue, which was published in the summer of 1842. The courses were strong on classical languages and literature, mathematics, and philosophy or religion. There was some science but no modern literature, no modern languages, and no modern history.[22]

This uniformity in curricula and individual courses was overturned by the growing emphasis on the natural sciences and specialization in the decades following Knox's founding. Even the nature of scientific investigation changed during this era:

> The term natural philosophy was becoming [in the 1880s] archaic as scientists were less and less perceived as scholars concerned with underlying causes or with principles of reality. More and more they were regarded as experts who provided the kind of knowledge that might be of practical use in an industrial economy that was ever ready for technological innovations.[23]

The Knox College catalogue used the word 'Laboratory' for the first time in 1891; it also indicated that the natural sciences were considered, again for the first time, a 'department' of the college.[24] Such changes in the curriculum of liberal arts colleges reflected the new emphasis on science, empiricism, and practical utility that accompanied the intellectual, social, and economic grounding of positivistic thought. At larger universities the changes were even more graphic.

The advent of the research university, emphasizing especially graduate level instruction, a system of electives, and a commitment to research and scholarship (especially in the sciences) was to fundamentally reshape the mission of higher education. One of the physical changes that took place as a result of the new 'university idea' was the construction or expansion of library and laboratory facilities in which the new research ventures (and their derivative activities involving instruction to graduate students) could be carried out. Whereas libraries before this era were often thought extraneous and even treated with a certain ambivalence, in the transformed university they became central. Again, while scientific laboratories were infrequent elements of the older liberal arts curricula like those at Knox in the third quarter of the nineteenth century, by the turn of the century they became central to the changed mission of higher education institutions.

One of the leading assumptions behind this drive for increased research and inquiry was provided by the commitment to science that grew out of a positivistic inspired faith in our ability to predict and thus control natural phenomena.[25] The methods and perspectives of science were expected to show the way to the proper investigation of a range of phenomena. This is evident in the speech by Daniel Gilman (formerly president of Johns Hopkins University) to the graduates of the University of Chicago in 1903. In this speech — significantly titled 'Prospects of Science in the United States at the Beginning of the Twentieth Century' — Gilman makes the following prophetic observations:

> ... during the last century the range of science was vastly extended. *Its domain is now imperial.* When some of us were undergraduates science was restricted to the phenomena of the visible world ... Chemistry, physics and natural history ... were the chief departments ... Now all these subjects are subjected to manifold subdivisions, as branches of science; at the same time, a host of younger aspirants claim recognition as belonging to the parent system. History, archaeology, geography, meteorology, agriculture, philology, psychology, logic, sociology, and even jurisprudence and theology, are employing the scientific method, with increasing success and demand recognition in the surrogate's court, as the next of kin.[26]

Two aspects of these observations regarding the new emphasis on research are worth pondering. In the first place, Gilman is here recognizing the importance of science as the key to expanded research in areas well beyond the boundaries of natural science. Insofar as his comments reflect the growing reliance on 'the scientific method' as the potential guardian of new knowledge in a variety of domains, they fall within a positivistic world view. Nor should this be surprising, since the scientific domain held the promise of creating new technologies and products that fit well into the new role of the university as providing socially and economically useful goods. Thus the scientific study of phenomena would be justified both by its incorporation of methodologies and a world view that guaranteed objective, certain knowledge and the promise of material goods that would add significantly to the quality of our lives (and, not incidentally, help ensure that better future that was a crucial part of the Progressive credo).

Another result of the new emphasis on scientific research in higher education was the increased compartmentalization of the subjects of learning and research. The curriculum of the new university had to be divided and put into separate, even isolated departments. President Harper, of the University of Chicago, pointed to the problems associated with departmentalization in a statement published in 1986:

> The different departments are organized as departments for the convenience of administration. It is impossible in most instances to draw a sharp line of separation ... Over against the tendency to separate departments farther and farther from each other, the movement should be encouraged to bring the departments more closely together ... The need for correlation [of departments] does not receive from most of us the appreciation which it deserves.[27]

In 1898, two years after President Harper made these observations regarding the dangers of compartmentalization, his concerns were more pointed:

> An arrangement of work which is formal and which has been introduced merely for the sake of convenience must not be permitted to interfere with the best interests of students or of instructors or of the University at large. In our own University this evil seems to be greatest in the departments of science.[28]

What we are witnessing here is the beginnings of the movement to separate areas into departments, and to fragment bodies of knowledge and inquiry. As departments and sub-departments multiplied, so too did the creation of curricular choices for students. It is no accident that President Eliot of Harvard was influential in developing a system of electives during this period of time. 'The elective system', one commentator asserts, 'was a natural consequence of the division of knowledge into specialized investigations'.[29] It should not be surprising that a key argument in favor of increased specialization of subject matters and of the expansion of student electives was their ability to foster individualism for the professor (in terms of conducting research) and the student (in terms of individual 'freedom of choice' among curricula).

The growing faith in science and scientific research to ensure both certain knowledge and technological advances had the effect of separating areas of inquiry into discrete, autonomous, and multiple specialties; these educational and cultural changes reflect the ideological views that accompanied the rise of positivism. They provide evidence of the extent to which a system of social, economic, and cultural expectations accompanied the development and implementation of rather abstract, theoretical postulates and ideas; at the same time, changing social, economic, and political practices and institutions helped bolster the new trust in science and technology.

Together these intellectual and social movements fostered a world in which new divisions and distinctions would be seen as justifiable and, eventually, 'natural'. These distinctions would include such dichotomies as those between objectivity and subjectivity, theory and practice, reason and emotion, facts and values, work and leisure, and liberal and applied. More generally, the world as it came to be known during this era was increasingly compartmentalized and fragmented, with individuals and groups afforded increasingly narrow, autonomous areas of expertise. This was true of work in the academy as well as in the factory.

To the extent that this world view was founded on epistemological perspectives growing out of positivism and a new view of knowledge and certainty, we need to investigate the criticisms that have been made of these perspectives. For to the extent that the distinction between liberal and applied studies relies on the epistemology and ideology associated with positivism, criticisms of them may well alter our view of the possibilities of education within an altered view of liberal inquiry.

Epistemology, History, and Social Context

Against Foundationalism in Epistemology

In the last quarter century or so especially, there have been a number of important challenges made to the views discussed in the previous section. These challenges threaten to overturn the very core of the assumptions and points of view regarding knowledge we have inherited from the legacy of positivism, thereby altering our perceptions of inquiry and its relationship to social action.

Richard Bernstein begins his recent work, *Beyond Objectivism and Relativism*, with the observation that:

> there is an uneasiness that has spread throughout intellectual and cultural life. If affects almost every discipline and every aspect of

our lives ... as we follow the internal development in the twentieth century of both Anglo-American and continental philosophy, we can detect increasing doubts about the project of grounding philosophy, knowledge, and language. The movement from confidence to skepticism about foundations, methods and rational criteria and evaluation has not been limited to philosophy. The confusion and uncertainty in philosophy exhibits and reflects a phenomenon that is characteristic of our intellectual and cultural life ... There seems to be almost a rush to embrace various forms of relativism ...[30]

It is precisely because the parameters of the present cultural crisis are so encompassing, and its resolution so much in doubt, that the issues Bernstein and others are pointing to are so crucial — especially for the domain of education as one of our society's central cultural institutions.

While it is almost always inaccurate to pinpoint an individual or small group of people as the catalyst for subsequent ideas, the story of the current debate regarding knowledge and certainty can be encapsulated by noting the publication of three important volumes: (i) *The Idea of A Social Science and Its Relation to Philosophy* by Peter Winch;[31] (ii) *The Long Revolution* by Raymond Williams;[32] and (iii) *The Structure of Scientific Revolutions*, by Thomas S. Kuhn[33]. While the epistemological issues raised in response to the propositions embodied in positivism are complex and multi-faceted, these three volumes contain much that continues to be central in the debates that have persisted. Each has made a fundamental contribution to the critique of positivism.

In outlining the major thrust of his book, Winch sets out to realign the social sciences and philosophy, so that their interrelations can be seen and appreciated. He says that,

> to be clear about the nature of philosophy and to be clear about the nature of social studies amount to the same thing. For any worthwhile study of society must be philosophical in character and any worthwhile philosophy must be concerned with the nature of human society.[34]

The clear and distinct separation between empirical matters of fact and philosophical or normative speculation seen in Comte and later positivists, is here explicitly denied by Winch. The reasons for this denial are illuminating.

For Winch, abstract epistemological questions such as what constitutes reality are intimately connected with how different responses to such questions affect the activities of people and their conception of society. Our epistemological positions or assumptions thus directly affect how we act as social beings:

> A man's social relations with his fellows are permeated with his ideas about reality. Indeed, 'permeated' is hardly a strong enough word: social relations are expressions of ideas about reality ... a monk has certain characteristic social relations with his fellow monks and with people outside the monastery; but it would be impossible to give more than a superficial account of those relations without taking into account the religious ideas around which the monk's life revolves. [35]

Our ideas about reality, our relations with other people and institutions, and our more general cultural aims cannot be separated without reducing the authenticity of each; our social and intellectual worlds are intimately conjoined. To elucidate fully our conception of reality (and of human intelligence that helps generate it) is to illuminate the nature of our social relations.

As Winch realizes and documents in his discussion of the views of John Stuart Mill, the equivocation between the natural and social sciences central to positivistic thought explicitly rules out large areas of philosophy from having a central role in the study of social phenomena. It is this dismissal of philosophy and the touting of the natural sciences in its place that is the subject of Winch's critique. In the case of the natural scientist, Winch says, all we need to be concerned about are the accepted 'rules of the game' for doing science. Yet to arrive at an understanding of society is quite different, for *what* we study, as well as the actual study of it, are human activities. Unlike natural or mechanical phenomena that exhibit clear, determinant cause and effect relations that can lead to more or less certain predictions, human activities are not so clear and invariantly related. Human activity is unpredictable, given to revolutionary shifts, disruptions, and unprecedented activities that make them conceptually distinct from natural phenomena. What Winch concludes, thus, is that:

> the central concepts which belong to our understanding of social life are incompatible with concepts central to the activity of scientific prediction. When we speak of the possibility of scientific prediction of social developments of this sort, we literally do not understand what we are saying. We cannot understand it, because it has no sense. [36]

The heart of the positivistic program — the identification with a mechanical, predictable, objective universe susceptible to control and prediction — is thus rejected by Winch as a basis for social and human studies.

In the course of rejecting positivistic social study, Winch makes several comments about the relations between language, thought, and action that are central to the present volume. When a new, revolutionary idea is expounded and accepted by a society, it changes the way people use language. Often such ideas create new forms of language that replace or importantly modify previous linguistic forms. Yet such ideas and patterns of language use represent more than just changes in symbols and patterns of utterance; they also are embedded in, and help alter, social patterns:

> our language and our social relations are just two different sides of the same coin. To give an account of the meaning of a word is to describe how it is used, and to describe how it is used is to describe the social intercourse into which it enters.[37]

Language, ideas, and social relations thus mutually support one another, making the separation of ideas and actions implicit in positivism conceptually mistaken. In terms that reflect a growing affinity with hermeneutics as an alternative to epistemological foundationalism and positivism, Winch says that 'social interaction can more profitably be compared to the exchange of ideas than to the interaction of forces in a physical system'.[38] Human interaction and understanding, the study of social systems and relationships, cannot be subsumed under the mechanical, orderly, predictable world of the natural scientist. Positivism, finally, is misguided as it attempts to control and predict social events in the same way that scientists explain events in the physical universe.

Kuhn's analysis of empirical science takes these views a step further, and in ways that go beyond the critique of Winch in undermining the canons of positivism. While the latter author departs from the pretensions of positivistic social science, his views still support a dichotomization between natural and human events. Kuhn's central challenge to the established view of science and scientific change, however, is more radical; it involves five central points. These contributions have generated important debates in the history and philosophy of science, and are crucial for our understanding of the current situation.

First, Kuhn challenges the view of science as cumulative — the notion that scientific facts, theories, and methods are part of a linear progression by virtue of which our knowledge of the physical world is compiled. In the view challenged by Kuhn, scientific knowledge is thought to be added to the previous store of knowledge to produce an ever more sophisticated, accurate, or true picture of the natural world. Instead, Kuhn tells us, scientific change takes place through the breaking down of theories, methods, and patterns of scientific instrumentation whose viability is challenged because of their inability to resolve certain puzzles or anomalies. This perspective directly challenges the progressive view of knowledge articulated within positivism. Second, scientific work can only take place when such theories and methods unite to provide a distinctive body of ideas and practices through which problems can be identified and research programs implemented. It is the formulation of such ideas and practices into a coherent, codified set of principles that signals the establishment of a paradigm and the commencement of normal scientific work. This picture of scientific practice is contrary to the fractured, compartmentalized view of positivism that identifies a variety of dualisms. Third, a range of paradigms operate over time in the sciences, each of which forms its own body of distinctive procedures, beliefs, and commitments for a particular research community. Each of these paradigms represents a self-enclosed, internally persuasive set of images, languages, and worlds, which make an extra-paradigmatic perspective impossible. Since no paradigm is self-confirming, and since each is incommensurable with competing or possible paradigm candidates, paradigms are logically discontinuous. Fourth, Kuhn challenges the notion of science as context independent, empirically based, and ahistorical. The 'context of justification' and 'the context of discovery', to use more specific language, do not demarcate separable domains, except perhaps within an established and ongoing paradigm. Science and history are not separable. Fifth, scientific work within a paradigm rests upon a complex and interactive set of assumptions, beliefs, and observations. 'Scientific fact and theory are not categorically separable' except with a paradigm, Kuhn says, and therefore there is no such thing as theory-free, 'merely factual' data.[39]

The effect of Kuhn's work is to challenge many of the positivistic assumptions that infect our view of science, and upon which our understanding of valid, objective knowledge is based. The challenges he and others have brought to bear on our image of science have tentacles that connect a variety of areas — the social sciences, literature, mythology, religious faith, political and social theory — so as to question the very heart of the Western tradition in epistemology. A sign that Kuhn's ideas are seminal was provided by the heated and protracted debate touched off by the publication of *The Structure of Scientific Revolutions*.[40]

We can understand the collapse of assumptions surrounding science, and related views of knowledge and objectivity, as furthered by the critique of parallel or overlapping pursuits in philosophy. Propelled by what Richard Rorty calls 'Cartesian anxiety'[41] — a fear that if knowledge is not grounded at some level in Truths that are indubitable then irrationality, subjectivism, nihilism, etc., will prevail — modern philosophy took up the search for certainty in its role as guardian of claims to knowledge that are expressed by the rest of the social and cultural world.

In *Philosophy and the Mirror of Nature*, Rorty outlines the role of philosophy as a foundational study:

> philosophy as a discipline sees itself as the attempt to underwrite or debunk claims to knowledge made by science, morality, art, or religion ... Philosophy can be foundational in respect to the rest of culture because culture is the assemblage of claims to knowledge, and philosophy adjudicates such claims ... Philosophy's central concern is to be a general theory of representation, a theory which will divide culture up into the areas which represent reality well, those which represent it less well, and those which do not represent it at all (despite their pretense of doing so).[42]

Much of the history of modern philosophy is the attempt to specify the way in which it forms such a foundational and judicial grid. There are two general ways in which philosophy has attempted to provide an epistemological grounding. A key assumption, rising in part out of the mind/body dualism confirmed by Descartes, is that secure knowledge is arrived at through an accurate representation of external reality. We can, on this view, exercise our privileged access to unmediated external reality through the mind as the 'mirror of nature': that ocular device which is capable, through philosophical rigor, of accurately reflecting the objects existing in that reality. In this way epistemology as the core of philosophy was to serve as the underlying basis for all claims of knowledge — including those generated by secular, empiricist science. 'Descartes's investigation of the mind — his coalescence of beliefs and sensations into Lockean ideas — gave philosophers new ground to stand on. It provided a field of inquiry which seemed "prior" to the subject on which the ancient philosophers had had opinions. Further, it provided a field within which *certainty*, as opposed to mere *opinion*, was possible'.[43]

The other path to certainty, the nonempirical side of philosophy as foundational epistemology, was fundamentally provided by Kant. Kant's role in this evolution of philosophy was to raise 'the science of man from an empirical to an a priori level'.[44] For Kant a central philosophical question was the means by which cognition was able to organize experience through the intercession of synthetic a priori knowledge. Even though knowledge may only be brought into existence in experience, our cognitive faculty still may provide a priori elements that are necessary and universal, and hence which can serve as a ground for certain knowledge. The mind, Kant says, synthesizes the diversity of intuitions given consciousness, by the workings of concepts that have a priori claim to certainty. This theory of knowledge thus makes use of empirical intuitions that are reflected in what Rorty calls our 'glassy essence', while preserving the claims of metaphysics to be the non-empirical, rational discipline par excellence. It thus reconfirms philosophy's place as the site for adjudicating claims to Truth.

What centrally concerned the modern philosophers was the development of knowledge that was unchallengeable, non-contingent, and could enable philosophy to take its rightful place as 'queen of the disciplines'. The more recent developments of logical positivism, ordinary language analysis, and analytic philosophy share this concern. The general method by which knowledge claims are to be created and ascertained accepted the search for immediate, primordial access to empirical observations through cognitive entities that contain an a priori truth, and the development of language systems that can express the certain knowledge that results. The means of arriving at necessary truth consisted, largely, of developing systems of introspection, expression, and analysis that did not partake in the vicissitudes of social and human life. The whole point of the epistemological tradition was to rid ourselves of the merely contingent, changeable, and deceptive impressions, sensations, and social experiences in which we are normally engaged, to glimpse the Truth in respect to which all other claims of knowledge are subordinate. The cleavage between philosophical analysis and human interaction solidified the distinction between Being and Becoming that served as the central quest of philosophy as a systematic, grounding discipline.[45]

In presenting the search for foundational knowledge as essentially a chapter in the history of ideas rather than the Method to verify claims to

Truth, Rorty presents a different story of philosophy. Instead of talking about philosophy as a foundational discipline concerned with the articulation of certain knowledge, he treats knowledge claims as a behavioral, social, and pragmatic matter, based on the work of, among others, Heidegger, Wittgenstein, and Dewey. It is Rorty's celebration of the pragmatic and contextual nature of knowledge which, as we will see later, leads him to pose hermeneutics as a viable alternative to epistemology.

While there are important differences between the views of Kuhn on the nature of scientific change and the deconstruction of philosophy advocated by Rorty, it is the appearance of fundamental similarities that is crucial for us. Both writers argue for the contextualization of human thought, theorizing, and claims to the validity of ideas. Both reject the demarcation of their fields and the correlative notion of disciplinary boundaries as framing separate areas of inquiry that vouchsafe particular claims to knowledge. For Kuhn, the movement from one paradigm to another — since no theory is self-confirming and the adoption of a new paradigm always happens in the context of rejecting another, competing one — cannot be understood on the model of proof or deduction. 'The proponents of competing paradigms are always at least slightly at cross-purposes. Neither side will grant all the non-empirical assumptions that the other needs in order to make its case'.[46] Since observation is always theory-laden, objective reports of uninterpreted impressions are impossible, and the domain of values, judgments, and ideologies inevitably intrudes on the formation of 'scientific rationality'. That is why, on Kuhn's view, for proponents of alternative paradigms, though 'each may hope to *convert* the other to his way of seeing his science and its problems, neither may hope to *prove* his case. The competition between paradigms is not the sort of battle that can be resolved by proofs'.[47] Since scientific and non-scientific claims are no longer so easily divisible, the vision of science as a specialized, objective non-valuative domain is undermined, as is the view that scientific disciplines can be neatly circumscribed and disputes settled on a strictly rational basis.

Rorty makes a similar point about the evaporation of determinate disciplinary boundaries with the depletion of epistemology. As he puts this point:

> The lines between disciplines will blur and shift, and new disciplines will arise, in the ways illustrated by Galileo's successful attempt to create 'purely scientific questions' in the

> seventeenth century ... Our post-Kantian sense that epis-
> temology or some successor subject is at the center of philos-
> ophy (and that moral philosophy, aesthetics, and social
> philosophy, for example, are somehow derivative) is a reflection
> of the fact that the professional philosopher's self-image
> depends upon his professional preoccupation with the image of
> the Mirror of Nature.[48]

Since philosophy can no longer lay claim to be a foundational discipline
that evaluates claims to knowledge — any more than literary criticism,
political theory, or moral judgment, for example, can — it is largely a
matter of sociological curiosity that professional philosophers have
clung to the old pursuits and ways of life. Yet this does not mean that
established philosophical traditions must be totally abandoned or
neglected. As Rorty is quick to remind us, in terms reminiscent of
Kuhn, it may seem as though the rejection of epistemology and the
Mirror of Nature 'entail the claim that there can or should be no such
profession [of philosophy]. But this does not follow. Professions can
survive the paradigms which gave them birth. In any case, the need for
teachers who have read the great dead philosophers is quite enough to
insure that there will be philosophy departments as long as there are
universities'. The result of rejecting the imagery of epistemological
foundationalism, 'would be merely an "encapsulation" of the problems
created by this imagery within an historical period'.[49] The challenge
brought by Rorty to the dominant tradition in philosophy, and the
critique by Kuhn of positivistic views of science, contextualize these
areas, both within an historical frame and within the matrix provided
by other social, interpersonal, and political pursuits. The writings of
Winch, meanwhile, demonstrate how misguided it is to base social and
human studies on a positivistic conception of science. While Winch
partially accepted the pretensions of empiricist, positivistic science as
outlined by Comte and his followers, Kuhn, Bernstein, Rorty, and
others reject those very pretentions. Insofar as these challenges place
individual and social interaction at the center of claims to knowledge,
they may be said to be articulating a humanistic vision of knowledge.

The nature of human perception and communication are central
problems in Williams' *The Long Revolution* and add an important
dimension to the problems of knowledge. In seeing art as a kind of
creative activity that rises above more usual or 'natural' actions, artists
are conventionally elevated above other workers, Williams says. The
poet and painter are creators of works of art that — unbounded by

typical, everyday constraints and conventions — represent a different reality. The artist is pictured as suffused with 'creative imagination', and as working in a domain unlike that of the rest of us. This view of art as concerned with some alternative reality gives rise to two quite different conclusions: that the artist is an inspired creator of images that reflect a superior reality or that art is impractical, relatively useless and subordinate, since 'the real world' must be the source of our primary attention. The problem with this view of art as creative representation of some alternative reality, Williams suggests, is that it overlooks the extent to which all reality is created and not simply seen or found. At the center of almost all conceptions of 'reality', is a 'common assumption: that there is an ordinary everyday kind of perception, and that this can exceptionally be transcended by a certain kind of man or a certain kind of activity'. If we regard current experience as constituting reality, other expressions, representations, and interpretations become, de facto, examples of 'alterations of this "reality" that is shared by other men'.[50] Art becomes such an alteration since it deviates from the everyday, taken for granted reality that is assumed to be presented to us.

Yet — and here we see a direct repudiation of the tenets of positivism — all perception, all seeing, is itself an act of creation:

> There is no reality of familiar shapes, colours, and sounds, to which we merely open our eyes. The information that we receive through our senses from the material world around us has to be interpreted, according to certain human rules, before what we ordinarily call 'reality' forms. The human brain has to perform this 'creative' activity before we can, as normal beings, see at all ... [51]

Perception of even the most ordinary, common objects is the result of an active process of interpretation, learning, and acculturation. We cannot simply 'see things as they are', since all seeing, all sense-making, is unavoidably influenced by our (and our culture's) previous seeing, interpretation, and sense-making. We do not have access to a world independently constituted and disconnectedly observed. We cannot construct a platform from which we can accurately, objectively, and independently see reality simpliciter. The view of art as the product of creative imagination that is qualitatively different from ordinary sense perception is, accordingly, mistaken. 'Reality *as we experience it* is ... a human creation; all our experience is a human version of the world we inhabit'.[52] All perception, all reality, has a peculiarly human face that can not be rejected or avoided, despite the attempts by positivists to discount those human and social contexts. Art, as a kind of material and ideational activity, may create worlds unlike those we are used to; but the creation of art is not different in kind from the creation of what we typically label 'reality'.

What follows from this is a rejection of some profound dualisms: perception and interpretation, subject and object, art and reality, and culture and politics. No longer is it possible to isolate either side of these supposed opposites since our life experiences are constituted by events, people, and actions that can be separated only analytically. More concretely, art and life are no longer separable in the way that we have thought. For art is concerned with communication, and expresses experiences that can become incorporated into the viewer's own perceptions, understandings, and experiences. Further, this process of communication is essentially a shared or social phenomenon. The artist communicates to his/her audience via the employment of particular symbols, images, and ideas. As such art is 'an extension of our capacity for organization: a vital faculty which allows particular areas of reality to be described and communicated'.[53] Because all perception, all living, necessarily involves an important creative component, art is a crucial, human, and communicative experience.

Communication involves people in a multitude of overlapping contexts and domains. As individuals and members of social groups, we develop perceptions, assumptions, and values that are central to our identity and way of life. The process of forming a community is one of sharing common perceptions, meanings, and purposes. It is important to recognize the seamless nature of such a process of communication and community building:

> It is of the utmost importance to realize this sense of communi-
> cation as a whole social process ... The fatally wrong approach,
> to any such study, is from the assumption of separate orders, as
> when we ordinarily assume that political institutions and con-
> ventions are of a different and separate order from artistic
> institutions and conventions. Politics and art, together with
> science, religion, family life and the other categories we speak of
> as absolutes, belong in a whole world of active and interacting
> relationships, which is our common associative life.[54]

The separation of art from life — as well as the demarcation of object and subject, thought and action, reason and feeling — is rejected in favor of a complex, interactive, and human/social world that is dynamic, created, and learned. It presents an alternative to the static, discovered, found world of the positivists. As such it articulates not only an alternative set of issues and ideas but quite literally a different reality and way of being in the world.

From Confrontation to Conversation

If writings in epistemology, the philosophy of the social and natural sciences, and cultural studies have undercut many of our cherished beliefs about knowledge and certainty that have grown out of positivism, they have also suggested alternative ways of understanding claims to knowledge, understanding, and meaning. These amount to proposals to replace the search for certainty with one aimed at justified belief, productive disagreement, conversational vitality, and communal and social possibility.

Kuhn does not discuss hermeneutics in his book on scientific revolutions (he does elsewhere, however[55]) yet he does anticipate such a discussion in his thesis on incommensurability and paradigm conflict. Kuhn, you will recall, says that the movement from one paradigm to another is not understandable on the model of deductive proof, but is closer to a gestalt switch, for which 'conversion' is a more apt description. It is only through persuasion, in which continued and prolonged probing, discussion, and dialogue take place, that scientific change can ensue — even when such change originates as part of normal scientific work.

It is the repudiation of an obsession with 'the scientific method', and the forms of control sanctioned by a technological consciousness that crystalizes in the adoration of 'the expert', that is one of the central notions of Gadamer's articulation of hermeneutics. Philosophical hemeneutics, he says,

> corrects the peculiar falsehood of modern consciousness: the idolatry of scientific method and of the autonomous authority of the sciences and it vindicates again the noblest task of the citizen — decision-making according to one's own responsibility — instead of conceding that task to the expert. In this respect hermeneutic philosophy is the heir to the older tradition of practical philosophy.[56]

One of the features of hermeneutics, then, is its fundamentally democratic, humanist, and practical impulse.[57] It aims at supplanting the search for truth with the conversation of people whose ideas are propelled by the practical necessity of engaging in actions that are morally just and politically efficacious. It is the legitimation of this conversational context, and its open continuation, that is central for Rorty:

> Hermeneutics sees the relations between various discourses as those of strands in a possible conversation, a conversation which presupposes no disciplinary matrix which unites the speakers, but where the hope of agreement is never lost so long as the conversation lasts. This hope is not a hope for the discovery of antecedently existing common ground, but simply hope for agreement or, at least, exciting and fruitful disagreement.[58]

Since paradigms (and those loosely held together theories, perceptions, and assumptions that make possible social life and personal identity) create and reinforce worlds that are incommensurable, the search for a 'disciplinary matrix' is futile, as is the view of truth as correspondence. The only avenue left open is that of conversation — the making of judgments, points of contact and disagreement with others, and the continuation of dialogue within some social context. Instead of 'accurate representation', of a found reality, the search is for interesting exchange, mutual understanding (even where disagreement is expressed and continues), protracted dialogue, and social action. Participants in the search for knowledge no longer work toward a fixed, consensual end point; rather, hermeneutics views conversational participants as 'persons whose paths through life have fallen together, united by civility rather than by a common goal, much less by a common ground'.[59]

This lack of a common goal and a common ground is furthered by Rorty's pursuit of 'edifying philosophy', which the author sees as essentially a continual questioning of received wisdom through hermeneutic dialogue. Philosophers concerned with edification, 'are reactive and offer satires, parodies, aphorisms. They know their work loses its point when the period they were reacting against is over. They are **intentionally** peripheral ... [They] want to keep space open for the sense of wonder which poets can sometimes cause — wonder that there is something ... which (at least for the moment) cannot be explained and can barely be described'.[60] The ability to capture uncertainty, mystery, and the barely knowable perhaps signifies the chief virtue of open ended, hermeneutic conversation.

This quality of hermeneutics prevents it from becoming a systematic, essence-seeking philosophy in the style of positivistic epistemology. In this sense hermeneutics is not a 'discipline' at all, nor is it a program of research aimed at realizing what epistemology failed to accomplish (in short, it is radically discontinuous with the tradition it abolishes). Edifying philosophy, while not exactly replacing the older epistemological tradition, makes an allegiance to the latter seem like an error of judgment or a case of bad taste. As Rorty expresses this, 'hermeneutics is an expression of hope that the cultural space left by the demise of epistemology will not be filled — that our culture should become one in which the demand for constraint and confrontation is no longer felt'. Instead of such a demand, hermeneutics is seen as a struggle against the assumption that 'there is a permanent neutral framework whose " structure" philosophy can display' — the assumption, that is, that 'all contributions to a given discourse are commensurable'.[61] Though hermeneutics may give rise to new forms of language, altered projects, and new ways of proceeding, these are only 'accidental byproducts. The point [of edifying philosophy, or hermeneutic conversation] is always the same — to perform the social function which Dewey called "breaking the crust of convention", preventing man from deluding himself with the notion that he knows himself, or anything else, *except under optional descriptions*'.[62] Because edifying philosophy is always reactive, convention-breaking, and rebellious in this way, it sanctions new forms of discourse without seeking to encapsulate any into a philosophic 'system'. It is not the replacement for positivism that is sought, but rather its contextualization as an historical, social, and political phenomenon that produced a particular type of world and person.

The sanctioning of the rebellious, the novel, and the unconventional is embodied in the person whom we might regard as one of the clearest contemporary exemplars of an edifying philosopher, Paul K. Feyerabend. In the introduction to his seminal work, *Against Method*, Feyerabend writes that, 'science is an essentially anarchistic enterprise,' and follows this with the admonition that, 'while perhaps not the most attractive political philosophy, [anarchy] is certainly excellent medicine for **epistemology**, and for the **philosophy of science**'.[63] In order for science to progress it must not only legitimate, but actively construct and sponsor, alternative theories, points of view, and beliefs — even those that have previously been rejected. As a Dadaist — the label he prefers[64] — Feyerabend

> is utterly unimpressed by any serious enterprise and ... smells a
> rat whenever people stop smiling and assume that attitude and
> those facial expressions which indicate that something impor-
> tant is about to be said ... a worthwhile life will arise only when
> we start taking things **lightly** and when we remove from our
> speech the profound but already putrid meanings it has accumu-
> lated over the centuries ('search for truth'; 'defense of justice';
> 'passionate concern'; etc., etc.)[65]

As if to confirm his edifying role, Feyerabend instructs the reader to
'remember me as a flippant Dadaist and not as a serious anarchist'.[66]
Such sentiments propel Feyerabend to insist that '**the only principle
that does not inhibit progress is**: anything goes'; there is no universal
method, set of procedures, or table of rules that can be relied on.[67] In
short, the notion of a scientific method is a myth that only inhibits
knowledge and leads to dogmatic assertions in science, and to
totalitarianism in political and social affairs.

Both science and philosophy are forced to give up their claims to
providing epistemological foundations and certainty. The view of
Truth as ahistorical, universal, non-contingent, and evaluative of
cultural claims to knowledge must, as a result, be abandoned. Truth
becomes supplanted by 'warranted assertability', knowledge by judgment, and a historicism by social and cultural context/valuation. The
death of positivism is accompanied by the celebration of more contextualized forms of human discourse and interaction. The positivistic
reliance on objective, socially neutral observations and corresponding
quantitative analyses as guarantors of transcendent truths has been
misguided. Equally misplaced has been our faith in conceptual analysis
in philosophy — as it makes available the findings secured through an
alleged 'mirror of nature' — as the foundation for certain knowledge.
The critiques discussed above show how knowledge, validity, and
understanding are necessarily embedded in social situations, human
contexts, and ideological presuppositions, and are socially constructed
rather than found. Not only is this the case in the study of social
situations and human interactions (as Winch, for example, demonstrated), but these same considerations also apply to the natural sciences,
the domain that positivists since Comte believed to be the proper basis
for knowledge in all spheres.

To summarize, the view of secure knowledge as socially and
historically removed, ascertained though objective, neutral observa-

tions of a discovered physical and social universe, whose truths could be extended by articulating the laws of experience and derivative algorithmic calculations, must give way to alternative explanations and criteria for knowledge. These new criteria focus on a contextualized, communal picture of knowledge in which understanding is intimately related to the actions of people, where knowledge matters because of the way it fosters social interaction, mutual understanding (if not agreement), democratic, communal participation, and more preferable worlds. Such a humanized, contextualized view of knowledge alters fundamentally what we can reasonably require or expect from education and social situations.

A contextualized view of knowledge is also central to recent writing in feminist studies. Several writers have indicated how foundational knowledge, empiricist science, and objectivity — the hallmarks of positivism — are fundamentally masculine enterprises, and how a feminist epistemology might alter our view of knowledge and the domain of science. These writings provide important insights into the dynamics of gender and knowledge.

Gender, Science and Knowledge

Positivist science has relied on objective perception and clear, especially mathematical and logical, analysis. In utilizing objective perception and abstract analysis, scientists could more accurately control and predict phenomena. Such prediction and control were at the center of the positivist's search for knowledge. Evelyn Fox Keller outlines the development of this reliance on objectivity:

> With the modern era ... a new form of perception came into being: a self-detachment that enabled men to conceive of an autonomous universe, 'operating without intention or purpose or destiny in a purely mechanical or causal way'. Indeed, it is often argued that the very success of modern science and technology rests on a new methodology that protects its inquiries from the idiosyncratic sway of human motivation.[68]

While Keller is quick to point out the advances of modern science that took place as a result of adopting such a detached, non-human perspective, it is a mistake to regard this description of science as itself neutral or objective:

The objectivist illusion reflects back an image of self as autonomous and objectified: an image of individuals unto themselves
severed from the outside world of other subjects (animate as
well as inanimate) and simultaneously from their own subjectivity. It is the investment in impersonality, the claim to have
escaped the influence of desires, wishes, and beliefs — perhaps
even more than the sense of actual accomplishment — that
constitutes the special arrogance, even bravura, of modern man,
and at the same time reveals his peculiar subjectivity. [69]

In spite of assumptions to the contrary, the image of science (and, by
implication, the scientific self) as separate, autonomous, and isolated
from people and events documents the very thing positivists have
denied: the inclusion of subjectivity in their own presuppositions and
scientific actions. This subjectivity is based on a static, removed,
masculine model of behavior and propriety. The very heart of the
positivist's program, thus, is founded on an ideological presupposition
involving gender: the equivocation between 'objective' and 'masculine'
(and of course the corollary: 'subjective' and 'feminine').

These equivocations go beyond the alarming fact that most scientists are men. They have to do with the ways in which scientific activity
itself has been masculinized. It is contained, for example, in the forms of
language we have developed to describe scientific activity:

When we dub the objective sciences 'hard' as opposed to the
softer (that is, more subjective) branches of knowledge, we
implicitly invoke a sexual metaphor, in which 'hard' is of course
masculine and 'soft' feminine. Quite generally, facts are 'hard',
feelings 'soft'. 'Feminization' has become synonymous with
sentimentalization. A woman thinking scientifically or objectively is thinking 'like a man'; conversely, a man pursuing a
non-rational, non-scientific argument is arguing 'like a
woman'. [70]

The very categories and terms we use to describe scientific activity are
gender based; thus the imbalance between men and women in science is
an effect, rather than a cause, of the way we have thought about
scientific knowledge.

This way of conceptualizing science and scientific methodology
has, Keller says, important psychological origins. Following to some
extent the ideas of Freud and Piaget, she says that the child's recognition that there is a reality separate from her/his own ego is facilitated

when the child begins to gain independence from his/her mother. Children gradually realize that their own situations are separate from those of others. They learn to recognize and, eventually, to tolerate their separateness. Yet the clear separation of self from other that may be the result of this process of individuation carries with it its own hazards. It is the very boundaries between 'self' and 'other' that must become relaxed, fluid, and dynamic if the capacity for mature, adult love is to be realized. Both an exaggerated sense of self as identical with 'the other' and a sense of self as completely individuated create problems for adults. The peculiar problem of modern science, within this scheme, lies in its embrace of the second, individuated position. The clear, fixed separation of self from other is both an emotional and cognitive obstacle that must be overcome.

The celebration of objectivity and its role in science is bolstered by at least three complementary social facts. First, in a culture characterized by gender inequalities, it becomes 'natural' to assume that what is masculine should be more highly regarded. Given the existence of patriarchal social relations, activities that can be labeled 'masculine' will be automatically, as it were, seen as desirable. Second, the rise of modern science, as we have seen, promised the methodology to guarantee certain, objective, non-contingent knowledge. This promise led to the view that the sciences were the 'new gatekeepers' for knowledge. Thus the view of science as both certain and masculine in operation was doubly influential in our culture's embrace of 'the positive science' of nature and society. Third, the fact that science and technology contributed directly to the growing industrial and corporate economy further added to our culture's approbation of a masculinist science. We are witness here to the intersection of gender inequities, epistemological presuppositions, and social and economic preoccupations — a very strong mixture indeed. Little wonder that the vision of knowledge that has been generated by these forces has been so resistant to challenge and critique. It is not hyperbole to say that such challenges threaten the very bases of some of our most deep seated cultural and ideological convictions. The gender-based tentacles of these convictions run deep and wide, as Ruth Bleier has recently documented:

A patriarchal mode of thought dichotomizes the world into systems of control and domination. From the patriarchal division of the 'civilized' world into public and private spheres that institutionalized the division into the political world of men and the domestic world of women, there has developed a coherent scheme of dualities: men are to women as culture is to nature, as mind is to body, as subject is to object, as domination is to subordination.[71]

Patriarchy as world view, science as objectified masculinity, and technological advance as socioeconomic utility combine and recombine in various ways — ones that frequently serve to strengthen each element in this equivocation.

In addition to clarifying and critiquing the dominant, masculine and objectivist view of science, several writers have explored the parameters of a new feminist science and epistemology. While an alternative tradition that might supplant the masculinist forerunner may still be some distance off,[72] the outlines of an altered view of knowledge are instructive. As outlined in her recent book *The Science Question in Feminism*,[73] Sandra Harding discusses five aspects of feminist inquiry that can contribute to our understanding in ways that masculine science does not:

1   The unity of Hand, Brain, and Heart in Craft Labor.
2   Women's Subjugated Activity: Sensuous, Concrete, Relational.
3   The 'Return of the Repressed' in Feminist Theory.
4   The Bifurcated Consciousness of Alienated Women Enquirers.
5   New Persons and the Hidden Hand of History.[74]

Unlike the separation of mental and manual labor characteristic of masculine work in capitalist society, women scientists have practiced 'craft labor' in which both mental and manual labor — as well as emotional involvement — are fused. Going beyond the separation of mental and manual labor that has been rejected by Marxists, feminists have critiqued the tacit devaluation of caring as an important aspect of craft work.[75] The fact that such elements are characteristically a part of women's unpaid labor in the home (as well as a part of 'women's work' when it is paid) reflects the social nature of such distinctions, of course (the assertion of some socio-biologists aside[76]), and the gender divisions embedded in our culture. A feminist epistemology would:

> ... hold that appeals to the subjective are legitimate, that intellectual and emotional domains must be united, that the domination of reductionism and linearity must be replaced by the harmony of holism and complexity ...[77]

The subjects of scientific inquiry would no longer be seen as distant, passive, and non-binding. Rather, the 'craft of science' would centrally include relationships between organisms, including the scientist herself.[78] In this way feminist science would integrate the aspects of experience that reflect women's social life and that have been disintegrated by masculine experience.

As opposed to masculine/positivist science, a feminist epistemology 'is an interested social location ("interested" in the sense of "engaged", not "biased") the conditions for which bestow upon its occupants scientific and epistemic advantage'.[79] As opposed to masculine activity that is based on abstractions, autonomous presumptions, and the ethereal, women's experience is characteristically based on more tangible, physical or material ways of being in the world.

Another central focus of a feminist epistemology involves the reunification of philosophical and empirical knowledge. Philosophers have assumed that their experience — for example, in becoming separate, discrete individuals — can be generalized as *the* human experience. Given this assumption, the problem of emotional and psychological separation is a human problem. The experience of women is implicitly denied in this conception. While males typically experience separation anxiety that is overcome only by successful domination and control, feminist epistemology requires a more interactive model in which reciprocity becomes central to human interaction. Understanding this model of development as relational requires that we 'recover and write the histories of women and our activities into the accounts and self-understanding of the whole social relations.'[80] If the concrete historical experiences of women can correct the excesses of abstract masculine science and philosophy, they can formulate experience (ideas and practices) that move toward a revised epistemology and corresponding reality.

In researching the experience of women, the very distinction between inquirer and subject of inquiry becomes blurred as the subject-object dichotomy reflective of masculine domination is replaced. In the end the experience of women's understandings becomes definitive; there will be several forms of feminist 'reality' — reflecting the variousness of women's actual, concrete experience — 'but they should all be regarded as producing more complete, less distorting, and less perverse understandings than can a science in alliance with ruling-class masculine activity'.[81]

Unlike the reputed advances brought about by masculine, objectivist forms of understanding, feminist epistemology highlights the historico-social embeddedness of its contributions to understanding. 'Feminist science and epistemology projects', Harding writes, 'are not the products of observation, will power, and intellectual brilliance alone — the faculties that Enlightenment science and epistemology hold responsible for advances in knowledge. They are expressions of ways in which nature and social life can be understood by the new kinds of historical persons created by these social changes'.[82] The trans-historical, presumably socially boundless domain of masculine knowledge will give away to the contextual, historical relations of real people.

It would be difficult to imagine an alternative view of science and knowledge that so openly contradicts the tenets of positivism. What a feminist epistemology outlines, in fact, are not only alternative conceptions of, and ideas about, social experience, but the centrality of integrated, relational, concrete, physical and material, historically defined consciousness that makes the subjugation of women a central part of its inquiry.

Keller ends her volume on the relations between gender, ideology, and science with an important reminder:

> To know the history of science is to recognize the mortality of any claim of universal truth. Every past vision of scientific truth, every model of natural phenomena, has proved in time to be more limited than its adherents claimed. The survival of productive difference in science requires that we put all claims for intellectual hegemony in their proper place — that we understand that such claims are, by their very nature, political rather than scientific.[83]

What, then, are we to make of the hegemonic claims of positivist science, and how might we counter the political program it embodies?

Knowledge and Ideology: Toward Participatory Communities

The critiques of positivism provided by historians and philosophers of science, social scientists and cultural analysts, and feminists, persuasively expose the shortcomings of the positive science first articulated as a system of thought by Auguste Comte. In place of the principles of positivism, we might pose the following summary of a contextualized, human gender, and community-centered search for knowledge:

> The 'nature' of 'reality' will never be finally and unquestionably revealed, since what we call reality is part of an active, dynamic

process in which what we see and name, and the sense we make of it, are social and communal constructs. There are multiple realities to be created, each of which may claim to disclose aspects of experience heretofore hidden, none of which may be objectively 'proven' beyond question and debate. While observation and reason are important tools in helping make sense of experience, their masculinist-inspired separation from 'emotion' and sensuality calls into question their usefulness for human understanding. The only 'laws' that govern physical or social interactions are those constructed by people with specific interests and values, and can only be authenticated within communities that encourage open discussion, the breaking of convention, and the widest possible participation. Moreover, this participation must acknowledge the need to reconsider the bases of participation, as we break down social, communal, and gender-specific presuggestions.

As with positivism, there is in this conception of knowledge a barely concealed political and social theory. This theory advocates genuine participatory practice in areas now obstructed for many of us; in particular, economic, cultural, familial — as well as 'political' — areas must be transformed. Further, the alternative view of knowledge outlined here would mandate the removal of material and ideological barriers to such democratic possibilities.[84] This would necessitate the rather widespread redistribution of wealth and power in society, the creation of educational practices that would help abolish ideological and material obstacles to participatory inclinations, and a commitment to altering forms of injustice that block these things.[85]

This view of knowledge and understanding would alter fundamentally the world created under the influence of positivism, gender discrimination, and the capitalistic drive for technological advance and domination. Instead of a fragmented, compartmentalized world dominated by various dualisms that are propelled by a masculine drive for control and domination and fueled by commitments to abstract certainty, competitive struggles, and precise, colourless reasoning, the new world would be quite different. A contextualized world emphasizes connection, interdependence, and commitment; fragmentation gives way to more holistic, dynamic, and interactive communities; and control and competition for positions of dominance take a back seat to nurturance, communication, and cooperation. The world associated with such ideas would be one in which a multitude of perspectives and practices would be not only tolerated but encouraged. These ideas can only obtain meaning, though, in practical actions within particular, concrete settings — the spirit of this world view is destroyed if they languish as merely 'interesting ideas'.

This altered reality would effectively undermine some of our most cherished ideas (and ideologies) regarding liberal education. An 'expansion of the mind', though of course an important part of all education, expresses at best a half-developed understanding; there is no longer much sense to be made of pursuing 'knowledge for its own sake' (unless this is a coded way of saying we are pursuing knowledge for the sake of something sanctioned by those who control cultural, economic, and political resources); to be disinterested is to be, in a fundamental way, anesthetized to the power and value of knowledge; and to be committed to the pursuit of 'pure knowledge' and Truth is to pursue a dangerous and ideologically impregnated illusion.

Knowing and Acting are experienced as a unitary whole in such a world. Like the other dualisms discussed and rejected in this chapter, we can see how the propagation of these phenomena as binary opposites has arisen because of the cultural dislocations that arose out of the necessity to control the access to decisions and actions (especially, in our culture, by gender, social class, race, ethnicity, and age). Their dismantling will, likewise, entail the prolonged and multi-faceted reorganization of our central institutions: the family, the media, the arts, our political practices and economic institutions, and our schools.

The remainder of this book will explore the ways in which the study of education is implicated in the alterations in knowledge discussed in this chapter. For an abandonment of some of our most central convictions regarding liberal inquiry, and a revised view of hermeneutic practice and inquiry, leaves us with more than the vision of technical or vocational competence that is sometimes associated with educational studies. Education, and the specific matter of how to prepare teachers, may embody some of the central practices that articulate and embody alternative realities. These possibilities will concern us in detail in the proceeding chapters.

Notes and References

1 See Plato's *Symposium* for the steps necessary to glimpse the Forms; this can be found in EDITH HAMILTON and HUNTINGTON CAIRNS, (Eds.) *The Collected Dialogues of Plato* (Princeton: Princeton University Press, 1961), pp. 526–574; see especially the speech of Diotima, pp. 553–563.

2   STEPHEN TOULMIN, *Human Understanding* (Princeton: Princeton University Press, 1972), p. 7.

3   *Ibid.*, pp. 13–14.

4   I am indebted in the following to the discussion in CHRISTOPHER G.A. BRYANT, *Positivism in Social Theory and Research* (London: Macmillan, 1985).

5   *Ibid.*, pp. 12–22.

6   JOHN C. GREENE, *Science, Ideology, and World View* (Berkeley: University of California Press, 1981), Chapter 4, 'Biology and social theory in the nineteenth century: Auguste Comte and Herbert Spencer'.

7   CHARLES A. ELLWOOD, *A History of Social Philosophy* (New York: Prentice-Hall, Inc., 1938), p. 372.

8   Greene, *op cit.*, p. 64.

9   ISAIAH BERLIN, 'Historical inevitability', in *Four Essays on Liberty* (New York: Oxford University press, 1969), p. 43.

10 GERTRUD LENZER, *Auguste Comte and Positivism: The Essential Writings* (New York: Harper and Row, 1975), p. xxii.

11 *Ibid.*, pp. xxxii.

12 J.H. BRIDGES *et. al.*, (Translator) *System of Positive Polity* (London: 1875–1877), Volume IV, p. 83.

13 Lenzer, *op. cit.*, p. xiii.

14 JOHN L. GILLIN, 'The development of sociology in the United States', *Publications of the American Sociological Society*, Volume 21, pp. 24–25.

15 Cited in Christopher G.A. Bryant, *op. cit.*, p. 138.

16 See, for example, RICHARD M. LERNER, *Concepts and Theories of Human Development*, second edition (New York: Random House, 1986), Chapter two, 'Philosophical models of development'.

17 For example, see D.M. ARMSTRONG, *A Materialist Theory of the Mind* (London: Routledge and Kegan Paul, 1968); for an extended discussion of the philosophical issues involved, see C.F. PRESLEY, (Ed.), *The Identity Theory of Mind* (St. Lucia, Queensland: University of Queensland Press, 1967).

18 Increased credibility of alternative approaches to research in education has recently been witnessed. Yet the most acceptable research projects in many institutions and academic journals are still thought to consist of statistical, positivistic, psychometric studies. See the reductionist tendencies in DANIEL TANNER and LAUREL TANNER, 'Emancipation from research: The reconceptualist prescription', *Educational Researcher*, Volume 8, Number 6, June, 1979.

19 Cited in F.S. MARVIN, *Compte, The Founder of Sociology* (New York: John Wiley and Sons, Inc., 1937), pp. 196–197.

20 See, for example, RICHARD EDWARDS, *Contested Terrain* (New York: Basic Books, 1979); HARRY BRAVERMAN, *Labor and Monopoly Capital* (New York: Monthly Review Press, 1974); DAVID NOBLE, *America By Design* (New York: Alfred A. Knopf, 1977); and JAMES O'CONNOR, *The Fiscal Crisis of the State* (New York: St. Martin's Press, 1973).

21 This idea will be dealt with in more detail in chapter 3, as we discuss the

extent to which ideological hegemony has been influential in the development of educational theory and practice.

22 HERMANN R. MUELDER, *Missionaries and Muckrakers: The First Hundred Years of Knox College* (Urbana: University of Illinois Press, 1984), p. 7.

23 *Ibid.*, p. 219.

24 *Ibid.*, p. 204.

25 This is not to say that the advocates of increased emphasis on research in the graduate-oriented university were themselves positivists or even scientists (as we use that term today). Yet the increased faith in science and technological advances (furthered by their utility in economic and social terms, as discussed above), aided by the promises of a positive science, were part of the educational establishment's fascination with scientific research. Here again we see a multiplicity of forces aligned so as to serve as a catalyst for institutional and cultural commitments.

26 DANIEL C. GILMAN, *The Launching of a University and Other Papers* (New York: Dodd Mead and Company, 1906), pp. 238–243, emphasis added.

27 'Sixteenth quarterly statement of the President', *University of Chicago Record* 1, number 28, 1896, p. 384.

28 'Twenty-fifth quarterly statement of the President', *University of Chicago Record* 3, number 32, 1898, pp. 199–200.

29 CHARLES WEGENER, *Liberal Education and the Modern University* (Chicago: University of Chicago Press, 1978), p. 24.

30 RICHARD J. BERNSTEIN, *Beyond Objectivism and Relativism: Science, Hermeneutics, and Praxis* (Philadelphia: University of Pennsylvania Press, 1983), pp. 1–3.

31 PETER WINCH, *The Idea of a Social Science and its Relation to Philosophy* (London: Routledge and Kegan Paul, 1958).

32 RAYMOND WILLIAMS, *The Long Revolution* (Harmondsworth, Middlesex, England: Penguin Books Ltd., 1961).

33 THOMAS S. KUHN, *The Structure of Scientific Revolutions*, second edition, enlarged (Chicago, University of Chicago Press, 1970).

34 Winch, *op. cit.*, p. 3.

35 *Ibid.*, p. 23.

36 *Ibid.*, p. 94.

37 *Ibid.*, p. 123.

38 *Ibid.*, p. 128.

39 Kuhn, *op. cit.*, p. 7.

40 See Bernstein, *op. cit.*, 'Postempiricist philosophy and history of science', pp. 20–25.

41 RICHARD RORTY, *Philosophy and the Mirror of Nature* (Princeton: Princeton University Press, 1979), p. 3.

42 *Ibid.*, pp. 136–137.

43 *Ibid.*, p. 138.

44 *Ibid.*, p. 138.

45 This is analogous to the separation of 'art' and 'life' mandated in a good deal of modern aesthetic theory. See LANDON E. BEYER, 'Aesthetic theory and the ideology of educational institutions', *Curriculum Inquiry*, Volume 9, Number 1, Spring, 1979; and LANDON E. BEYER, 'What role for the

arts in the curriculum?' in CARL GRANT, (Ed.) *Preparation for Reflective Teaching* (Boston: Allyn and Bacon, 1983).

46 Kuhn, *The Structure of Scientific Revolutions*, *op cit.*, p. 148.

47 *Ibid.*, p. 148, emphasis added.

48 Rorty, *Philosophy and the Mirror of Nature*, *op cit.*, p. 392.

49 *Ibid.*, p. 393.

50 Raymond Williams, *The Long Revolution*, *op. cit.*, p. 16.

51 *Ibid.*, p. 18.

52 *Ibid.*, p. 18.

53 *Ibid.*, p. 34.

54 *Ibid.*, p. 39.

55 See THOMAS S. KUHN, *The Essential Tension: Selected Studies in Scientific Tradition and Change* (Chicago: University of Chicago Press, 1977).

56 HANS-GEORG GADAMER, 'Hermeneutics and social science', *Cultural Hermeneutics*, Vol. 2, p. 316.

57 Jurgen Habermas is one of the most important figures in this tradition. For example, see *Knowledge and Human Interests*, Translated by JEREMY J. SHAPIRO (Boston: Beacon Press, 1971).

58 Rorty, *Philosophy and the Mirror of Nature*, *op. cit.*, p. 318.

59 *Ibid.*, p. 318.

60 *Ibid.*, p. 370.

61 *Ibid.*, pp. 315–316.

62 *Ibid.*, p. 379, emphasis added.

63 PAUL FEYERABEND, *Against Method: Outline of an Anarchistic Theory of Knowledge* (London: Verso Edition, 1978), p. 17.

64 *Ibid.*, p. 21.

65 *Ibid.*, p. 21.

66 *Ibid.*, p. 21.

67 *Ibid.*, p. 23.

68 EVELYN FOX KELLER, *Reflections on Gender and Science* (New Haven: Yale University Press, 1985), p. 69. The quotation within Professor Keller's comments is from NORBERT ELIAS, *The History of Manners* (New York: Pantheon, 1978), p. 256. The use of the word 'men' in this quotation is intentional.

69 Keller, *op. cit.*, p. 70.

70 *Ibid.*, p. 77.

71 RUTH BLEIER, *Science and Gender: A Critique of Biology and Its Theories on Women* (New York: Pergamon Press, 1984), pp. 164–165.

72 For discussion of some of the central questions that must be addressed in such a theory, see DONNA HARAWAY, 'In the beginning was the word: The genesis of biological theory', in *Signs: Journal of Women in Culture and Society*, Volume 6, Number 3, 1981.

73 SANDRA HARDING, *The Science Question in Feminism* (Ithaca, NY: Cornell University Press, 1986).

74 *Ibid.*, pp. 142–161; the discussion which follows is indebted to this section of Professor Harding's work.

75 Also see NEL NODDINGS, *Caring: A Feminine Approach to Ethics and Moral Education* (Berkeley: University of California Press, 1984).

76 For example, see E.O. WILSON, *On Human Nature* (Cambridge: Harvard University Press, 1978).
77 Harding, *op. cit.*, p. 144.
78 For an example of the kind of scientific work that might result, see EVELYN FOX KELLER, *A Feeling for the Organism: The Life and Work of Barbara McClintock* (New York: Freeman, 1983).
79 Harding, *op. cit.*, p. 148.
80 *Ibid.*, p. 154.
81 *Ibid.*, p. 158.
82 *Ibid.*, pp. 160–161.
83 Keller, *op. cit.*, pp. 178–179.
84 I have discussed these ideas more fully in LANDON E. BEYER, 'Schooling for moral and democratic communities', *Issues in Education*, Volume IV, Number 1, Summer, 1986; also see chapter 4.
85 See Habermas, *op. cit.*; and LANDON E. BEYER and GEORGE H. WOOD, 'Critical inquiry and moral action in education', *Educational Theory*, Volume 36, Number 1, Winter, 1986.

3
Educational Studies and Ideology

The contextualization of knowledge and inquiry, the pursuit of realities that diverge from the elitist, separatist, and masculinist conceptions of knowledge growing out of a positivistic epistemology, gender stratification, and capitalist demands for increased technization, have implications for numerous aspects of Western culture and society. Chief among these is the study and practice of education.

This chapter is concerned with a view of education that responds to the contextualized view of knowledge detailed above, as we consider various theories of education as social reproduction. The following chapter considers in more detail some of the inadequacies of this body of literature, and lays the conceptual groundwork for a view of teacher preparation as praxis.

After looking briefly at the central tenets of structural functionalism in education, this chapter will outline the view that schools are important agents of economic reproduction. This will be followed by the more elaborated view of schooling as an agent of cultural reproduction. Such theories tell us much about the social role of schooling in advanced industrial societies. Yet they also tend toward their own sort of functionalism, as school policies, practices, and outcomes are seen as fitting into and reinforcing existing social and economic structures. This tendency has been exposed as inadequate by several writers who have examined the specific ways in which students, teachers, and others often resist the socially useful messages of the school's curriculum and pedagogy. These resistance theories will also be discussed in this chapter. This literature has exposed the myth of educational neutrality, as it has uncovered the linkages between education and larger social political, and economic institutions and practices. The last section will examine in some detail a recent attempt to not only critically assess the social/structural effects of schools, but to reassess the nature of inquiry in education. This produces a view of education responsive to the contextualization of inquiry and also points to some of the inadequacies in the critical literature with which we are here concerned.

Education and Social Context

Technicism and Schooling

In an exceptionally important essay dealing with recurring issues in the study of curriculum, Herbert M. Kliebard has argued that the field itself is 'characterized by an overwhelmingly ameliorative orientation'.[1] Such an ameliorative stance, Kliebard continues, may in part be created by 'the huge constituency of teachers, school administrators, and supervisors who exert continual pressure on those who conduct research for answers to such practical questions as, how can I improve my teaching, which are the best programs, and how can I recognize and reward a good teacher'.[2] As everyone is aware, teachers in classroom situations are continually confronted with such practical questions which, given the density and pace of classroom life, require immediate, practical response. Frequently the requirement for some kind of action or intervention on the part of the teacher eclipses the opportunity for a more sustained, reflective analysis of related educational ideas.[3] Yet in a larger sense, as Kliebard again cogently argues, one problematic consequence associated with such an immediate, pragmatic model of teaching 'revolves around the effort to develop a kind of technology of teaching leading to the performance of certain presumably effective behaviors in the absence of any fundamental understanding or conception of what kind of activity teaching is'.[4] It is very easy to conceive of and confront teaching, within such a pragmatic orientation, as a technical enterprise, with success and failure measured in rather technical and quantifiable terms (e.g., as exhibited by scores on achievement tests or instruments used to identify 'exceptional children', ratings on supervisory evaluation forms, and so on). Another consequence of this pragmatic, technological orientation to teaching is an overemphasis on teaching technique and method, abstracted from any principled, sophisticated understanding of the educational ideas and ideals which stand behind and give such methods meanings.[5]

In his very insightful book entitled *The Reflective Practitioner*, Donald

A. Schon nicely captures a way of thinking that has dominated our conception of professionalism. This view of the professions coincides with and furthers many of the assumptions of positivism, as it identifies our commonsense view of the ways in which education, research, and practice are related. 'Technical Rationality' asserts that:

> professional activity consists in instrumental problem solving made rigorous by the application of scientific theory and technique. Although all occupations are concerned, on this view, with the instrumental adjustment of means to ends, only the professions practice rigorously technical problem solving based on specialized scientific knowledge.[6]

On this view, the professions are characterized by the application of specialized, scientific knowledge to problems and practice. This knowledge base provides the foundation for dealing with concrete, specific situations. The professional applies the proper knowledge to the precise situation, much as we might apply the principles of construction in building a house. The professional is seen as the mediator of knowledge and practice via the technical application of scientifically proven principles.[7]

Within educational studies, we have often been guided and informed, if not actually dominated, by such technical rationality. A substantial number of educators seem to limit their investigations into the nature and effects of schooling — into what counts as effective school practice — to two broad, technical areas: those dealing with measures of (usually individual) academic achievement, on the one hand, and socialization effectiveness on the other. Though in many instances these two areas have been collapsed into a single pedagogical perspective, the traditions of academic achievement and socialization still form a good deal of the conceptual apparatus that underlies our collective sense of what schools are about.[8] Each of these traditions, in addition to being directed and dominated by technical concerns — e.g., as evidenced recently in the move toward Competency Based Teacher Education[9] — views the function or purpose of educational institutions in technical terms, and as socially and politically neutral. In effect, such technical concerns have served to defuse and displace more fundamental political and ethical debate within education, as we have embraced the myth of social neutrality.

Perhaps the most well known analysis of the allegedly neutral socialization effects of schools may be found in Robert Dreeben's essay, *On What Is Learned in School*.[10] Much of Dreeben's explication of what has come to be called the 'hidden curriculum' of school[11] is concerned with how family life and school life each make a contribution to larger social experience. The structural/functional view of socialization embraced by Dreeben moves the author to acknowledge what he labels an 'ideological caveat': he explains to the reader that, 'the main purpose of this analysis is to present a formulation, hypothetical in nature, of how schooling contributes to the emergence of certain psychological outcomes, and not to provide an apology or justification for those outcomes on ideological grounds'.[12] In addition to not providing the reader with any such ideological justification, Dreeben also fails to examine the possible ideological functions of the 'psychological outcomes' he considers. It is this tendency to construct a non-ideological, apolitical, technical analysis of the socialization effects of schooling that has been influential in thinking about educational issues. Socialization thus becomes a technical search for the 'best way' or 'most effective method' to promote the adoption of the appropriate social norms in students; under such a technical rubric, these norms are, correlatively, conceived of as 'given' rather than socially constructed and to that extent problematic, open to critique, and changeable.[13] This approach relies on the objectivist view of knowledge dismissed in the previous chapter, as it presupposes discovered worlds that can be found but not replaced, and a neutral platform from which to view the reality of schooling.

In the achievement model, likewise, knowledge has been typically thought of as unproblematic. Such epistemological and ideological questions as, what is the nature of educational knowledge, how is the selection process that produces 'school knowledge' itself governed, whose knowledge gets into schools, what is to count as an instance of having learned something, and the like, are often not considered; in their place, concerns about how best to structure, implement, package, and evaluate those forms of knowledge that find their way into classrooms become the central issues for educational investigation. Thus the achievement tradition becomes more and more given over to bureaucratic concerns for control, efficiency, and certainty, leaving the content and form of school knowledge unexamined.

Both the achievement and socialization traditions may be viewed as important aspects of the technicist and functionalist perspectives in education, and as responding to the ameliorative concerns of school people outlined earlier; the content and organizational form of schools are treated as authoritatively pregiven, usually from 'outside' or 'above'. The possible latent functions of the selection process itself, and of

schooling in general, go unrecognized and unnoticed, thereby confirm-
ing and legitimating the perception of schools as neutral sites for
knowledge acquisition and socialization. Since only immediate, predominantly technical concerns are manifest in the thought of these
educators, the less than immediately obvious effects of schooling
become at best secondary, and the school's perceived status as
politically neutral confirmed. Floud and Halsey point out the social
consequences of such a position:

> The structural functionalist is preoccupied with social inte-
> gration based on shared values — that is with consensus — and
> he conducts his analysis solely in terms of the motivational
> actions of individuals. For him, therefore, education is a means
> motivating individuals to behave in ways appropriate to main-
> tain society in a state of equilibrium. [14]

The assumption of neutrality on the part of educational theorists
and practitioners has come under increasing scrutiny and been called
into question from several quarters. Among others, this assumption has
been seriously questioned by what has been called the 'new sociology of
education', by educational philosophers and historians, and by theorists
of economic and cultural reproduction. This has led to extensive debate
and discussion regarding the precise nature of the relationship between
classroom activities and the larger social order. It is the assumption of
social, political, and economic neutrality implicit in the traditions
outlined already that theories of economic and cultural reproduction are
challenging. By examining the outlines of the discussions surrounding
these complex issues, we will be in a better position to see how
educational studies must be expanded to investigate such ideological
concerns and perspectives. We will, subsequently, also be able to extend
and enlarge upon the parameters of the 'reproduction debate', while
increasing the cogency of this critical educational perspective and
formulating an alternative perspective that respects the critiques offered
and yet goes beyond them.

While the bulk of this chapter will be concerned with recent
critically oriented investigations of the ideological role of schooling, it
is important to understand that the linkages between education and the
larger array of institutional matrices has a long and important history.
Numerous scholars and practitioners have been concerned with the
relations between educational and other institutions, and the more
recent literature on social reproduction is only now possible given the
legacy of this earlier writing.

For example, James B. Macdonald clearly saw that all educational curricula have important political components and consequences:

> I suspect that in many ways all curriculum design and development is political in nature; that is, it is an attempt to facilitate someone else's idea of the good life by creating social processes and structuring an environment for learning ...
>
> Curriculum design is thus a form of 'utopianism', a form of political and social philosophizing and theorizing. If we recognize this, it may help us sort out our own thinking and perhaps increase our ability to communicate with one another. [15]

Education, specifically here the design and implementation of school curricula, is an essentially political phenomenon. It cannot be adequately understood by using only the technical perspective that we sometimes assume defines educational studies.

Another important legacy of the critical inquiry in education that has bolstered current scholarship in the field is a focus on the forms of discourse that dominate our communications. Several writers have argued that an exclusively technical language system does a disservice to the complexities of educational theory and practice. Some of the most impassioned and poetic commentary in this area has been provided by Dwayne Huebner; our educational vision is dangerously narrowed when we utilize an exclusively technical discourse:

> ... there standing before the educator is a being partially hidden in the cloud of unknowing. For centuries the poet has sung of his near infinitudes, the theologian has preached of his depravity and hinted of his participation of the divine; the philosopher has struggled to encompass him in his systems, only to have him repeatedly escape; the novelist and dramatist have captured his fleeting moments of pain and purity in never-to-be-forgotten esthetic forms; and the man engaged in curriculum has the temerity to reduce this being to a simple term — 'learner'. [16]

The technical rationality and language of educational discourse serves to define our work in ways that hide, rather than disclose, multiple realities.

Writers like Macdonald and Huebner — in addition to other educational scholars like Dewey, Counts, Rugg, and others [17] — have developed the platform on which more contemporary critical scholars can stand.

Schooling as Economic Reproduction

It was with the publication of *Schooling in Capitalist America*, by Samuel Bowles and Herbet Gintis,[18] that attempts to situate schooling as one of a number of important institutions that together help perpetuate the current social order gained recent respectability. These authors view the social function of schooling as a fundamentally economic one, responding to the needs of a particular form of economic organization. This position is forcefully advanced, in fact, in the authors' view of socialization:

> Our critique of education and other aspects of human development in the United States fully recognizes the necessity of some form of socialization. The critical question is: What for? In the United States the human development experience is dominated by an undemocratic, irrational, and exploitative economic structure. Young people have no recourse from the requirements of the system but a life of poverty, dependence, and economic insecurity.[19]

Schools serve to produce a 'finished product' that will have sufficiently acquired the requisite skills and dispositions to ensure the maintenance of American corporate capitalism; educational institutions function in a way that guarantees the reproduction of this economic form. There are, on the authors' view, four main components to this relationship between educational and economic structure. These include: (i) an adequate and appropriately trained labor supply provided by the educational establishment; (ii) social relationships within schools that can be used to 'facilitate the translation of labor power into profits'[20]; (iii) a system of acknowledging, rewarding, and reinforcing personality traits that is shared by the school and the economy; and (iv) a stratified and hierarchical way of thinking about one's relationship with others, developed in schools through a differential system of status and distinctions, which has utility in the market place. Some specific examples from Bowles and Gintis's own research may help in clarifying how, for the authors, a principle of correspondence exists that reproduces social class structures and perpetuates capitalist modes of production. Looking at such examples will also allow us to see why theorists of economic reproduction see the posture of social and political neutrality with respect to educational institutions fostered by technical rationality and structural functionalism as an ideologically useful myth.

Bowles and Gintis argue that the social relationships within schools correspond to the division of labor, along hierarchical lines, within the economic order. Within educational institutions, vertical lines of authority exist and become part of everyday classroom experience, with students at the low end of the power continuum, followed by teachers and administrators. This pattern of domination is duplicated in many work places: individual workers stand on the bottom rung of the authority ladder, while the supervisor stands above them, with the manager/owner at the top. Just as this pattern of social relations in the sphere of economic production creates alienated labor, and an alienated work force, so too is the student alienated from his or her own educational experience. By training students in the public schools to regard these kinds of social relations and patterns of dominance as 'normal' or necessary, students learn to habituate themselves to patterns of thought and ways of acting that assure the continuance of analogous relations of production in capitalist industry. As with many day to day decisions in the factory, the corporation, or the state bureaucracy, educational decisions are made by those 'above', with little or no input from students whose daily lives are informed if not defined by such decisions. As well, students are typically evaluated in terms of criteria over which they have little control. This way of making educational decisions, i.e., via people who in some way stand above and independent of students themselves, serves to produce in each student, 'the types of personal demeanor, modes of self-presentation, self-image, and social-class identifications which are the crucial ingredients of job adequacy'.[21] In this way schools 'process' people who come to the marketplace with the skills and attitudes necessary for the smooth, efficient operation of the economic machinery. 'By attuning young people to a set of social relationships in schools similar to those of the work place, schooling attempts to gear the development of personal needs to its requirements'.[22]

Bowles and Gintis further argue that schools function to prepare particular social groups for determinate occupational slots, while reserving different occupations for other groups. Different behavioral norms are enacted and enforced depending on which track or stream a student is enrolled in. As differently oriented classrooms develop their own sets of dispositional rules, social relations of widely varying sorts are facilitated. It is in the correspondence between the social relations within each curricular track and the norms mandated by particular occupational slots that the potency of our economic system for school settings may be seen. 'Thus in high school, vocational and general tracks emphasize rule-following and close supervision, while the college track tends toward a more open atmosphere emphasizing the internalization of norms'.[23] Just as supervised rule following—in contrast to internalization of norms—is a mark of stratification within schools, so these same differences may be seen in the subsequent job prospects of each group. Since the working class ethos of supervised rule following tends to recur in working class schools and classrooms, social class distinctions and their perpetuation are fostered by differing social relations within the educational establishment.

In contrast to technical rationality and the achievement and socialization traditions, theorists of economic reproduction view the activities of schools as intimately tied to the demands of a hierarchical, alienating economic system. School experience furthers the interests of certain groups and classes while effectively curtailing those of others. In arguing for a correspondence between schooling and economic form, Bowles and Gintis expose the perniciousness of the former by virtue of its complicity with the latter.

While the analysis provided by such theorists of economic reproduction is illuminative in its characterization of how school life may be tied to economic form, we need also to recognize the very real shortcomings of the 'correspondence theory' that undergirds it.[24] There are several ways in which such an analysis is misleading. In the first place, it does little in the way of clarifying how the exigencies of classroom life — the daily ebb and flow of educational practices — actually contribute to the continuance of an unequal distribution of goods and services within capitalist society. What Bowles and Gintis have provided, though in many ways insightful, is little more than a functional view of schooling, with particular inputs and outputs; what happens inside schools, the actual classroom exchanges and forms of knowledge that may in some way solidify social and economic forms, is for the most part neglected.[28] For example, the question of school knowledge itself — how it gets selected, organized, and evaluated, who benefits from these processes as they exist in schools, and the like — is not explored by the authors. Though Bowles and Gintis do make some insightful remarks about the economic ramifications of the hidden curriculum, even this phenomenon is isolated and abstracted from classroom activities in a way that makes it difficult to situate the latent functions of schooling within a larger, more coherent contextual theory. This is more than just an academic or tangential deficiency, especially for those interested in how the activities of teachers, administrators, and others may concretely serve ideological interests, and in understanding how educational activities might be redirected so as to serve different interests. In short, for those involved in trying to decipher the relationship between education and ideology, especially in terms of identifying and developing strategies for intervention, the abstracted nature of the critique by Bowles and Gintis is less than helpful.

Secondly, the relationship between schooling and economic form is itself too unproblematic in at least two ways. Though the points of contact between schools and a capitalist economy make any notion of neutrality seem naive, to suggest a simple one-to-one correspondence, as the authors of *Schooling in Capitalist America* do, may obscure more than it reveals. As we will see more clearly in a later section of this chapter, many students 'caught' in the alienating classroom situations Bowles and Gintis describe are by no means passive; they are frequently quite adept and creative in exposing, and struggling against, the realities of school life that the authors describe. In short there are many 'cracks' or 'crevices' in the foundation wall provided by corporate capitalism that affects schools, some of which are created by students themselves, which make any simple correspondence theory less than tenable. A much more concrete, detailed examination of schools is necessary in order to perceive these crevices. Indeed, we might say that the abstracted, macroscopic analysis of Bowles and Gintis must be corrected by a more feminist vision of classroom life that explores its concrete, palpable experiences and forms of expression.

Just as the school-based side of the correspondence coin is overly mechanistic (and perhaps pessimistic), so too is the work or occupation-based side. While we need to be aware of how the control of workers under capitalism is linked to the way personality traits, dispositions, and skills are promoted so as to increase profit potentials, we must also realize the real and often dramatic contestations that have taken place over just such issues by workers.[25] Just as students are not the passive recipients of norms and dispositions which they are powerless to resist or modify, workers have historically been influential in fighting against the forms of domination and control which Bowles and Gintis argue characterize the workplace. Indeed, the reproductive metaphor may itself serve an ideological function in persuading us to take a management orientation to those whose work and educational lives we seek to understand.[26]

Thirdly, and perhaps most important for our purposes, theorists of economic reproduction such as Bowles and Gintis, by the very nature of their analysis, focus too narrowly on the economic sphere in understanding the ideological role of contemporary schooling. They see schools as responding to the demands of a relatively isolated, mono-lithic form of economic production, and fail to take adequate notice of how other social institutions may be related to school practice and a particular ideological perspective. The social and ideological functions of educational institutions are not fully revealed by addressing only their rather narrow economic purposes and affects. This, of course, is not to deny the connections between schools and economic production. Rather, to expose the ideological functions of schooling and make them a subject for analysis, we need to go beyond 'merely' their relation to economic form, without losing sight of this vital aspect of social reproduction. This is precisely where theories of cultural reproduction have been helpful.

Schooling as Cultural Reproduction

As noted above, a basic flaw in the view that schools function as agents of economic reproduction is a decided lack of concern with the domain of knowledge itself. The formal, organized body of school knowledge, and its possible ideological, social, and political purposes, are not systematically addressed. It is just this relationship between the selec-tion and organization of curricula and the power relations extant in society that Michael F.D. Young has explored in interesting and incisive ways.[27]

In discussing the state of the art of American sociology of education, Young suggests that a predominantly functionalist view-point 'presupposes at a very general level an agreed upon set of societal values or goals which define both the selection and organization of knowledge in curricula'.[28] Such a consensual perspective has had a clear impact on the kinds of educational research and analysis that we saw, for example, in the writings of Dreeben on socialization. Yet Young's remarks here can be viewed as moving beyond the critique offered in the work of Bowles and Gintis to suggest that, at least until recently, 'even the best American work in the sociology of education has been concerned with the "organization" or "processing" of people (whether pupils or students), and takes the organization of knowledge for granted'.[29] This criticism is as applicable and illuminating for the work of correspondence theorists as it is for more structural/functionalist analyses of American schooling. Indeed it is the attempt to locate curriculum content in a broader cultural perspective that forms the basis for the 'new sociology of education' proposed by Young.

Young begins his analysis with the assumption that 'those in positions of power will attempt to define what is to be taken as knowledge, how accessible to different groups any knowledge is, and what are the accepted relationships between different knowledge areas and between those who have access to them and make them available'. [30] Those groups who have influence upon and access to what is considered appropriate or valid knowledge will also influence which groups wield political and economic power in the larger social order. With all the discussion of what has been termed the 'knowledge explosion' during this century, it is dangerously easy to forget that knowledge forms are not uniformly available to all social groups or classes, and that whether particular groups have access to validated forms of knowledge or not may have real economic and political consequences both individually and collectively.

Since not all forms of knowledge can become part of the curriculum of formal schooling, some process of selection becomes unavoidable. Curricula become differentiated in this process of selection, so that certain kinds of knowledge become separated and distinguished from other categories. But something in addition to differentiation takes place in the process of selecting curricular forms for incorporation within the educational system — they become stratified and specialized as well. Now the processes of differentiation and stratification are so enmeshed in our way of thinking about educational issues — are so much a part of the functional ideology of educational debate — that it is difficult to think of school knowledge being differentiated without it being of greater or lesser worth. Indeed this is just the point. As Young argues, such a separation between curriculum being simply different as opposed to of greater or lesser worth 'suggests that assumptions about the stratification of knowledge are implicit in our ideas of what education "is" and what teachers "are"'. [31]

An intriguing question here is how to account for this conflation between the logically distinct activities of stratification and differentation in curriculum selection, how to account for this commonsense assumption. Here is where understanding the interaction between school knowledge and power relations in society becomes crucial. For the stratification that takes place within our schools and universities is intimately connected with economic rewards and political power. Placing more value on certain forms of knowledge within schools, and restricting the access to such knowledge, has the effect of adjudicating between those who will enjoy political and economic power and those who will not.

What Young and others are suggesting is that schools 'process' knowledge, in addition to 'processing' people in the way that Bowles and Gintis suggest. Both processes in turn need to be linked with the unequal distribution of resources in advanced capitalist economies. How knowledge is selected and organized, in addition to how dispositional elements of classroom practice affect students' consciousness of themselves and others, therefore become important for understanding the ideological role of schools in maintaining and legitimating the current set of institutional patterns and arrangements. Perhaps an example will clarify the relationship between knowledge in schools and economic and political power.

In considering why technical expertise has come to be considered what he calls 'high status knowledge', Michael W. Apple argues that,

> A corporate economy requires the production of high levels of technical knowledge to keep the economic apparatus running effectively and to become more sophisticated in the maximization of opportunities for economic expansion ... production of a particular 'commodity' ... is of more concern that the distribution of that particular commodity. To the extent that it does not interfere with the production of technical knowledge, then concerns about distributing it more equitably can be tolerated as well.[38]

The reason for this emphasis on the production of technical knowledge in, for example, the fields of medicine or engineering, is that industry within a capitalist economy requires not an equitable distribution of such knowledge, but rather its increased production, to ensure its economic solvency; this in turn necessitates, as we previously noted in the development of the modern university, the increasingly specialized training of a relative few technological experts who can further expand the requisite forms of high status knowledge. Thus the needs of an economic system for increased technical and administrative knowledge of a specific and (importantly) specifiable kind help define the way in which our universities and colleges confer legitmacy on particular kinds of curriculum content. Significantly, as a result, 'cultural institutions "naturally" generate levels of poor achievement'.[33] Only a limited amount of knowledge distribution is a prerequisite to the maintenance of economic security for corporate capitalist industry; thus the process of selecting and organizing curriculum content can become stratified, indeed *must* become stratified, and at the same time comfortably produce both low levels of proficiency and substantial amounts of institutionally-defined deviance for specific students and social classes.

To return to our example of medical expertise, the fact that this high status knowledge is perceived in particular ways, with a definite aura of taken-for-granted respectability, and its access simultaneously limited by rather restrictive admissions policies on the part of medical schools, has definite social consequences. Only students with a particular social history and class standing will be eligible to receive such knowledge. And inasmuch as different economic and social rewards accompany the successful mastery of high status knowledge such as this, social class distinctions and divisions will be maintained by stratifying this knowledge. We can see here how technical concerns and a posture of amelioration surrounding the achievement rubric of educators may in fact hide and at the same time assist the economic and political functioning of schools in US society.

A reiteration of the general point Young emphasizes is instructive for the purposes of this chapter. The control of a society's mechanisms governing knowledge production and allocation is directly related to the relative power of individuals and groups in society. Since discrete knowledge forms are accorded quite different levels of status and reward, who controls their production and distribution, and in whose interests these things function, becomes crucial. Put another way, the question of whose knowledge gets into schools, who it benefits, how alternative production schemes would effect questions of social control and organization, and the like, are seen by Young as fundamental questions for sociologists of education. It is not an accident, for example, that most history taught in schools is essentially military history, and that a serious program of labor, women's, and Black history does not, by and large, find legitimacy within the confines of US public schools.[34]

Like Young, Basil Bernstein views school knowledge as crucial in informing the quality of school experience and its relationship to social control within the wider society. Bernstein's analysis centers on those social and historical changes, especially those associated with the demands of an increasingly specialized division of labor, which have helped change the format for curricular offerings and pedagogical relationships.[35] He attempts to combine a macro theory of cultural reproduction with at least the outline of an analysis of classroom life at a more detailed, micro level. Bernstein seeks to relate changes in educational and curricular organization with specific shifts in the division of labor. To do this the author devises sociolinguistic categories with which he attempts theoretically to explain and characterize changes in curriculum, pedagogy, and evaluation within education.

The author of *Class, Codes and Control* suggests that we think about educational institutions generally as consisting of certain periods of time or 'units'; each subject area can then be understood as being allotted a specific number of such units. These units can be further differentiated on the basis of what goes on during them, their 'content', and by whether they are compulsory or voluntary for a given group of students. Hence we can, Bernstein suggests, 'take a very crude measure of the relative status of a content in terms of the number of units given over to it, and whether it is compulsory or optional'.[36] This will provide some indication of the status of particular knowledge in school settings.

Yet Bernstein suggests there may be a more important perspective from which to view the contents of the school's curriculum. He develops this perspective by articulating the categories of classification and framing, as they can be applied to the curricular and pedagogical relationships within schools. By 'classification', Bernstein means not the content of curricular areas, but the relative insulation or isolation of subject matter within the school's curriculum. Strong classification schemes, where subject matter is increasingly authoritative, produce a sharply divided, compartmentalized curriculum; an example would be the typical US high school, with specific time blocks accorded each subject area and little if any interdisciplinary activity or cooperation. Weak classification schemes denote a blurring or weakening of curricular boundaries, as for example in many preschools and 'open classrooms', and in some colleges and universities emphasizing inter-disciplinary courses. In such classrooms subject matter will be more interdependent, perhaps even to the extent of being unrecognizable. Thus, on Bernstein's view, 'classification focuses our attention upon boundary strength as the critical distinguishing feature of the division of labor of educational knowledge. It gives us ... the basic structure of the message system, curriculum'.[37]

Framing, on the other hand, refers to: (i) the pedagogical rel-ationships in the classroom, and the relative amount of control, by teacher and student, over what is studied. Again, framing does not refer explicitly to the content of the curriculum, but to the relative freedom of school people to organize, select, and pace the subjects of instruction. Bernstein also mentions framing in the context of (ii) the boundaries between 'non-school everyday community knowledge'[38] and school knowledge, though this distinction is secondary to the first one mentioned above. Educational frames, like classification schemes, can be either weak or strong, 'weak' framing indicating a substantial amount of control over the selection, pacing, the timing of the curriculum, 'strong' framing indicating little control over such curricular decisions. Essentially, framing refers to the extent to which curriculum decisions are made within the classroom rather than handed down by some person, committee, or agency outside the context in which they are to be implemented.

Bernstein recognizes that there is no necessary or logical connection between the strength of classification and the strength of framing schemes. Weak classification may be combined with strong framing, for example, in computer-assisted instruction that is multi-disciplinary; just as a classroom wherein students and teachers decide the order and timing of traditional subject area study would be an example of strong classification teamed with weak framing. Bernstein devises these categories not in an attempt to describe the logic of classroom organization, but to explain theoretically the changes in curricular form that have taken place via a four part typology of educational transmissions. This typology allows us to view historical changes in curriculum along the two dimensions of classification and framing, and to correlate these changes with transformations in the wider society.

At another level of analysis, Bernstein uses the notions of classification and framing to generate two types of educational 'codes'. He identifies integrated codes as those wherein subject matter boundaries are blurred and insulation reduced; whereas collection codes are typified by strong boundaries between identifiable subject areas. The adoption of either educational code will have effects that go beyond the realm of school knowledge. Differing pedagogical and evaluation forms will affect the personal identities of teachers and students, the power relations within the classrooms, and the concept of personal property. Moreover, 'principles of power and social control are realized through educational knowledge codes and, through the codes, enter into and shape consciousness'.[45]

Under collection codes the subject matter is the source of personal identification for both students and teachers. Subject matter, or a particular person's mastery of it, becomes authoritative; the acquisition of such subject matter knowledge defines competence or ability in individuals. Within such classrooms, both teacher and student will tend to identify with their particular subject matter specialization. This will have an impact upon not only their sense of academic affiliation, but also upon the social relations within any given classroom. As Bernstein puts this point, 'it is the subject which becomes the linch-pin of the identity. Any attempt to weaken or *change* classification strength (or even frame strength) may be felt as a threat to one's identity and may be experienced as a pollution endangering the sacred'.[40]

Power relations within classrooms also become altered or modified due to the kind of educational code embodied by a particular group of students and teachers. When collection codes are dominant, the teacher is seen as authoritative, insofar as he or she 'possesses' that knowledge which the group desires. Since identities are constructed according to the possession of particular kinds of knowledge, and teachers viewed as people who embody such knowledge, a special status is conferred upon them which has a decided effect on the dynamics of power within the classroom. Students are seen, and see themselves, as relatively power-less just because they do not possess what the teacher dispenses, namely, knowledge of that subject matter. Under integrated codes, however, the authority of the subject matter, and of the teacher in his/her embodiment of it, is replaced by some more general organizing principle under which subject matter is subsumed. Various principles governing the relations of teachers to subject matter taught may be selected and codified under a system utilizing integrated codes, affecting both pedagogical practices and their evaluation. An example of one such organizing principle is the view that growth and self-development ought to dominate pedagogy and evaluation in schools, as may be found in many informal classrooms.

The concept of property is similarily modified by the adoption of either educational code. Within integrated codes, it is not the possession of some particular kind of knowledge that is sought, but rather some more general, typically dispositional, quality; examples of such qualities include interactions denoting cooperativeness or therapeutic adjustment to a large group of peers. Students' conceptions of what it means to possess something, what property consists of, gets mediated by the kind of educational code implicit within the group. On the other hand, 'knowledge under collection [codes] is private property with its own power structure and market situation. Children and pupils are early socialized into this concept of knowledge as private property. They are encouraged to work as isolated individuals with their arms around their work'.[41]

Bernstein argues that there has been, within the educational establishment, a shift from collected to integrated codes. There is decreasing emphasis, especially at the elementary school level, on the acquisition of subject matter, with a corresponding increase in the integration of curricular forms under some more general principle of organization. It is this shift which Bernstein suggests is reflective of changes in the division of labor in the wider society.

Social integration and control are understood by Bernstein chiefly in terms of the concepts of mechanical and organic solidarity. 'Organic solidarity is emphasized wherever individuals relate to each other through a complex interdependence of specialized social functions'.[42] Such a sense of solidarity will recognize and attempt to integrate differences among individuals. On the other hand, 'mechanical solidarity is emphasized whenever individuals share a common system of beliefs and common sentiments which produce a detailed regulation of conduct'.[43] It is the shift from mechanical to organic solidarity that Bernstein sees as intimately tied to changes in educational transmissions from collected to integrated codes.

There are four specific reasons why, on Bernstein's account, the shift from mechanical to organic solidarity, and from collected to integrated codes in education, has taken place. These are that: (i) knowledge has been increasingly differentiated and diverse; (ii) changes in our conception of the division of labor,

> are creating a different concept of skill. The in-built obsolescence of whole varieties of skills reduces the significance of context-tied operations and increases the significance of general principles from which a range of diverse operations may be derived. In crude terms, it could be said that the nineteenth century required submissive and inflexible man, whereas the late twentieth century requires conforming but flexible man;[44]

(iii) the integrated code contains a greater potential for 'egalitarian education'; and (iv) in advanced industrial societies social control becomes increasingly a cause for concern. Such societies need to somehow make sense of and control a multiplicity of symbolic systems while regulating personal choices. The interpersonal control found in integrated codes may, Bernstein concludes, 'set up a penetrating, intrusive form of socialization under conditions of ambiguity in the system of beliefs and the moral order'.[45]

For Bernstein, changes in curriculum form, from collected to integrated codes, reflect and help support broader changes in society, from mechanical to organic solidarity, as the demands of an industrialized economy necessitate divergent forms of socialization. As the conception of private property and relations of power which attend it accompany an evolving sense of labor specialization, it is important that the 'messages' communicated through the organized symbolic system of the school — its curriculum — coincide with these broader social and economic transformations. By making subject matter less authoritative, and hence curriculum less insulated, those perceptions of property and power that were being solidified within the larger society were reinforced by the pedagogical practices and evaluation forms within the school.

The analyses of Young and Bernstein extend our understanding of the relationships between the curriculum and the wider social structure in several important ways. They present in rather broad outline the ways in which both curriculum form and content need to be seen relationally — i.e., as intimately tied to wider questions about the distribution of power in society. These writers go beyond a monolithic conception of the imperatives of capitalism, as they document the complicated cultural processes involved in educational change and continuity.

Yet such critiques also share some of the failings noted earlier with respect to the work of economic theorists such as Bowles and Gintis. Though Young and Bernstein both deal with the domain of educational knowledge, their analyses are offered at a level which seems at times excessively theoretical and abstracted from the actual functioning of schools, and the work of teachers and students. Neither Young nor Bernstein is concerned, in short, with how the phenomenon of cultural reproduction actually pervades the lives of school people on a day-to-day basis. Hence, as we saw in the writings of Bowles and Gintis, little help is given in terms of understanding how the dynamics of school life fit into such a theoretical perspective. In addition, little analysis is offered of 'culture' itself. While clearly not operating with an economistic model, the concept of culture and how it is involved in the process of ideological domination and reproduction is underdeveloped. Lastly, the work of Young and Bernstein, perhaps because of its macrolevel perspective and lack of concern for the day-to-day experiences which comprise life within schools, to a large extent leaves out of consideration how the activities of people both fit within their framework and, importantly, how and when such activity may be less than completely functional in this regard. By analyzing curriculum form and content at such an abstracted level, apart from the operation of schools and classrooms, it is easy to forget that quite diverse groups and individuals, with various desires, wants, and purposes, occupy those social and educational roles discussed by theorists of economic and cultural reproduction. What we need, then, is a more fine-grained analysis of how people operating within specific educational and social contexts facilitate the ideological role of education.

Schooling and the Dynamics of Reproduction

Theories of social reproduction and ideological domination have been furthered of late by a number of attempts to integrate a critical perspective in education with a sensitivity to the day to day curricular, pedagogical, and evaluative activities of classrooms. This group of writers has attempted to integrate the intricacies of theoretical argumentation over issues of domination, social control, and cultural reproduction with the particularities of classroom life. Part of the reason for this integration has to do with a particular sensitivity to the predicaments of students and teachers whose activities in classrooms are the source of an abiding ethical concern.

One of the best current collections of writing in this vein is to be found in the collection of essays entitled, *Ideology and Practice in Schooling*.[46] By looking at two representative samples of this work, we can obtain insight into the dynamics of this body of literature, and how it extends previous work in the critical analysis of education.

The dynamics of culture and its reproduction as discussed in this book are divided into two parts. The first deals with culture as a commodity and its relationship to ideology, as writers examine the ways in which curriculum form and content are related to the dynamics of cultural reproduction and contradiction. The latter portion of this work is concerned with ideology as part of the lived experience of cultural groups.

In connection with ideology and the commodification of culture, Joel Taxel provides an analysis of children's fiction that has been written about the US Revolution. Looking at this literature in historical perspective, Taxel divides these books into four periods: (1) 1899 to 1930, (2) 1937 to 1953, (3) 1959 to 1961, and (4) 1967 to 1976. The works included in periods 1 and 2, Taxel says, are 'dominated by a selective, simplistic, and conservative view of the Revolution that ignores the complexities and ambiguities evident in most historians' explanations of that event ... such fiction should not reduce a historical event to a caricature, as many of the novels do'.[47] An important part of this 'Whig' interpretation of the Revolution is that its protagonists were committed purely to principled reasons for participation — e.g., the value of representative government and individual liberty — and not to material or economic interests. Some historians, on the contrary, have suggested that participants in the Revolution were as much concerned with questions of who would rule after the revolution was accomplished as they were with the reasons for its occurrence. Such participants, these historians claim, were concerned with economic factors such as the 'conflict between social classes, and issues relating to racial and sexual justice and equality as motivation of the Revolution'.[48]

While most of the works written in periods 3 and 4 continue the same conservative thrust, there are significant differences in emphasis and tone. One book, Sally Edwards' *When the World's on Fire*, explicitly adopts a progressive/revisionist perspective, highlighting the duplicity of fights for freedom (for white settlers) while continuing the enslavement of Blacks. The fact that this work is already out of print only serves to highlight the difference in interpretation it embodies.

In summarizing his analysis of thirty-two children's novels, Taxel underscores an important contention:

> ... the authors have drawn selectively from the range of interpretations of the Revolution. Despite changes in tone and emphasis, and several exceptions, the sample *as a whole* is dominated by a vision of the Revolution as a struggle to secure political rights and independence from Britain. Missing from the overwhelming majority of books is any discussion of the internal conflict over who should rule at home.[49]

The issue of selectivity is clearly central here. From the universe of possibilities (of interpretation, character development, narrative form, and so on) a rather narrow, politically expedient depiction of events emerges. This depiction furthers a view of the Revolution that is based on consensus, motivated by pure, extra-individual and social concerns, and independent of ideological and material interests. Such a perspective is not only partial and perhaps inaccurate but is functional as it develops in students and children forms of consciousness regarding conflict, participation, and consensus that diminish our expectations of current realities and possible alternatives. The form and content of culture as a commodity — as this develops in books and school curricula — needs to be seen as containing perspectives and messages that are hardly neutral politically and ideologically.

Similarly, the elements of ideology as a part of the dynamics of lived culture need to be critically assessed. In her chapter, 'Becoming clerical workers: Business education and the culture of femininity',

Linda Valli illustrates how gender stereotyping, domination in the workplace, and cultural reproduction infect the day to day activities of students in a high school class. Her study nicely illustrates the intersection of gender and social class determinants of the reproduction of American society through schooling.

The division of labor assumed by the school programs and students revolves around and reinforces sexual divisions in the home and the workplace. The connections among sexism, personal relationships, and job possibilities were highlighted in a presentation made to these students by a job placement spokesperson: 'Look professional. Your best source for that is *Glamour* magazine. It regularly runs sections for the professional woman: her image, what to wear, how to get a job. Dress like you already have the job, like you would to find a boyfriend. That's a good parallel. You have to attract someone'.[50] The idea of 'attraction' is important in this context. Just as women must present themselves in particular ways to sexually attract a prospective male friend and spouse, so they must use a style of dress, appearance, and seductiveness to find and retain a job. The teacher of this business education class emphasized such elements in private conversations: 'You might do her [student in the class] a favor. She's a pretty girl. She could do a lot with herself and I don't think she's doing it. A lot of women in businesses are making appearance an important part of their day. She could capitalize on that. She puts herself together very nicely. She was wearing some very sexy shoes the other day'.[51]

Yet the gender stereotyping and social class inequities that pervaded this program were due to more than the imposition of norms by adults. The development of inequalities was already part of the student's own consciousness and expectations. For example, when a student was asked why the nameplates for women employees read, 'Beth', 'Jo', 'Susie', etc., while nameplates for men read, 'Mr. Gleeson', and 'Mr. J.C. Stone', she responded with, 'I don't think there is anything behind the difference. I think it's just a matter of preference'.[52] On other occasions these young women made similar remarks:

> office work is mostly for women because it's typing and a lot of guys don't like to type ... girls are secretaries, you know.
> Women shouldn't do construction work. Men are stronger and that's just the way it should be. Secretary jobs are probably for women mostly. That's just the way things are.
> Boys don't take the class because boys aren't secretaries.
> They're more into manual labor. That's just today's society.[53]

What these sentiments indicate is the extent to which categories of gender, work, personal relationships, domination, and class are deeply embedded in the consciousness of students. Valli's study details how ideological hegemony is reinforced through commonsense assumptions and the experiences of schooling. Yet this study also raises the possibility of critically assessing these assumptions, and in the process helping generate alternative practices.

The research of Taxel and Valli, like that of others, unpacks a number of the complexities and contradictions of schooling as cultural reproduction. It clarifies as well the complexities of schooling in forming students' dispositions, attitudes, and beliefs. While the authors indicate how the dynamics of cultural reproduction take place in schools, they show how a simple, reductionist theory of ideological domination is inadequate.

Other studies have looked at how students frequently resist the messages of schools. One of the most often discussed of these is Paul Willis, *Learning to Labour: How Working Class Kids Get Working Class Jobs*.[54] Divided into ethnographic and analytic segments, Willis details the interplay between the school and work lives of working class boys attending secondary school in an industrial town in England. The relationship between this group's organic culture and the formal experience and culture of the school is used by Willis as an example of how working class ideology and cultural forms help reproduce class distinctions. In the process social control is maintained not by the overt intervention of some repressive state apparatus, or any other 'outside' coercion, but by the development and solidification of cultural hegemony, or that 'range of structures as well as values, attitudes, beliefs and morality that in various ways support the established order and the class interests which dominate it'.[55] The development of hegemonic control of a citizenry is to be understood not as being imposed by the overt, conscious manipulation of one group by another, but by the dominance of certain ideas, values, and perspectives that differentially affect members of particular social and ethnic groups.

The group of working class boys of which Willis writes, collectively referred to as 'the lads' by the author, forms their own counterculture while being immersed within the 'official' or dominant culture of the school. They consciously exploit whatever openings they can either discover or create within the existing culture of the school in ways that allow some measure of control over their own lives. Indeed the lads define themselves in part at least on the basis of their opposition to the established routines, activities, and general cultural life sanctioned by the school. Here we get some insight into the complex nature of culture itself. The lads' oppositional activity, Willis writes, 'is expressed mainly as a style. It is lived out in countless small ways which are special to the school institution, instantly recognized by the teachers, and an almost ritualistic part of the daily fabric of life for the kids'.[56] Specific instances of such student opposition are numerous: e.g., engaging in imaginary dialogue by silently mouthing words during instruction, derisive laughter as a teacher or another student passes in the hallway, and a chorus of cracking knuckles during class. Now all of these actions can be seen as mere instances of deviant behavior from troublesome or delinquent students. Yet for the lads such gestures have another meaning; they become symbolic occasions which solidify their rejection of the formal organization of the school, and their correlative status as members of a select and, at least in their own minds, superior cultural and social group.[57]

Another group of students within this secondary school, the 'ear'oles' (so termed because of their tendency to just sit and listen), accept and comply with the authority structure and culture of the school; these are the students who at least superficially comply with the rules and regulations of the school, who identify with the cultural activities and patterns embedded in the institution. Such students, as one might expect, help provide the day-to-day, concrete cultural symbols that the lads reject. The ear'oles acceptance of school rules, their dress, hair style, and mannerisms, are equated with the established culture of the school, just as such cultural patterns and the formal curriculum become part of a broader perspective felt as distant and alien by the lads. The formal organization of the school, including both overt and hidden curriculum forms and the mode of culture which is engendered and embodied in the ear'oles, is rejected by the lads. Rejection of school rules and authority, and the social relations they produce, is thus seen by the lads as symbolizing their rejection of the dominant, middle class culture of the school. Considering dress, for example, Willis says, 'it is no accident that much of the conflict between staff and students at the moment should take place over dress. It is one of the current forms of a fight between cultures. It can be resolved, finally, into a question about the legitimacy of school as an institution'.[58] Dress and personal attractiveness, as well as smoking and drinking, are used by the lads as cultural symbols, ways to substantiate their repudiation of the ear'oles and school culture generally. The following excerpt from a poem written by one of the lads in an English class, illustrates the social uses of such cultural symbols:

> On a night we go out on
> the street
> Troubling other people,
> I suppose we're anti-social,
> But we enjoy it.
>
> The older generation
> They don't like our hair,
> Or the clothes we wear
> They seem to love running
> us down,
> I don't know what I would
> do if I didn't have the gang.[59]

Yet the culture of the school is not rejected only because the lads find it alienating and foreign. An essential ingredient of this refusal to participate in the official culture is that in a significant sense it is not real for the lads, it has no relationship to the working class world which surrounds them, their families, and their friends. The lads respond to school by embracing the more familiar and meaningful cultural forms of the working class, while rejecting any notion of intellectual work which the school embodies. One crucial ideological distinction is thereby formulated in the lads' rejection of schooling and school culture. Mental and manual labor — 'book learning' versus work on the shop floor — become separate categories for the lads, and one of the central divisions which sustains their class identity. The reproductive function of schools is furthered by such distinctions and by the very rejection of official culture by the lads. In rejecting mental labor, and the ear'oles as the personification of such labor, the lads maintain their own class standing and help cement social class distinctions.

In this way what Willis terms 'penetrations' made by the lads — this group's rejection of school culture as in some way ingenuine and its simultaneous utility in providing opportunities for contestation — contain inherent social contradictions. In asserting the superiority of masculine working class jobs and culture, in preferring manual to mental labor, the lads are also complying with the division of labor along sexual lines. Thus in penetrating the dominant school culture, in exposing it as foreign and alienating to their own experience, the lads implicitly further such sexual and economic divisions. Social reproduction is actually enhanced in the very process of resistance by the lads.

Willis's study is important for several reasons, and has clear implications for correspondence theories such as those offered in the writings of Bowles and Gintis and for reproduction theories like those of Young and Bernstein. Willis illustrates, in convincing detail, how and why such theories fail in their analysis of reproduction. It is simply not the case that the needs of capitalist production result in the imposition of certain dispositions, personality traits, and ways of thinking on students who acquiesce to and act on such economic needs. The studies of Taxel and Valli similarly show the inadequacies of an impositional model. At least some important elements of the capitalist work force and culture are produced in the process of rejecting the skills, propensities, and cultural symbols necessitated by capitalist production and perpetuated by schools; the contradictions built into the lad's penetrations of the official culture serve to solidify social class standing and working class ideology. The response of the lads within school gives them strength as members of a valued group while equipping them for employment that will ensure the continuation of their class history and social status.

Secondly, Willis shows how a particular set of economic realities is accompanied by various social and cultural forms that the lads find persuasive. A good deal of the lads' rejection of mental labor and book learning, for example, has to do with the discontinuity between the cultural symbols upheld by the school (voluntary rule following, specific styles of dress and personal appearance, a certain sense of sobriety, and the like) and the working class culture in which the lads themselves live. The world of the lads contains its own network of cultural symbols and values, far removed from the dominant culture of the school. These cultural forms are not perceived as something other than, or in addition to, their economic and social standing. For the lads these cultural patterns are felt to be an essential ingredient of daily life, a part of their existential reality.

What this implies, in a more general way, is that we must see cultural and economic forms — ideology and the relations of production — as intimately linked and conjoined. These areas are not separable. While it may be politically useful for people to think of culture, especially those forms which potentially serve emancipatory interests, as abstracted from daily life and social exchange, we must begin to see economic and cultural phenomena as equally productive forces. *Learning to Labor* provides an excellent example of how ideological forces persist in the day-to-day lived experiences we all share in. As ideological influences, the cultural images which tie the lads to their social and economic positions contribute to the reproduction of social class divisions and the development of hegemony. No intervention by a 'repressive' or 'dictatorial' state is necessary to perpetuate the social order in its present form. Thus to understand the ideological role of education requires a sensitivity to how cultural forms reinforce and interpenetrate ideological influences and economic 'needs', and how these are sometimes self-contradictory.

Beyond Reproduction: Reconstructing Educational Inquiry

Writings that expose the latent ideological function of schooling have contributed a great deal to our understanding of the contextualization that is necessary within educational study. They have exposed the meritocratic, liberal and functionalist view of education as not only false but politically misleading. If we are to adequately comprehend educational studies, we must enlarge our perception so as to take into account this more contextual view.

As broadening as these analyses have been, however, they have not always taken into account the larger revisions in inquiry and action in education that are implicated. Chapter four will deal with ways in which the critical perspective outlined here can become part of the larger project of creating new possibilities. Leading up to this project, and enlarging on the critical view of schooling so as to broaden the base of educational inquiry, we need to explore how social reproduction points the way toward reconstituted inquiry in education.

In *Understanding Education*, Walter Feinberg begins to undertake just this revision in educational inquiry.[60] For the thesis of Feinberg's book is that, 'education is best understood by recognizing that one of the functions of any society is that of maintaining intergenerational continuity — that is, of maintaining its identity as a society across generations and even in the context of many possible and significant changes, and that it is the activity and institution of education, both formal and informal, that carries on this function'.[61] It is the school's role in maintaining intergenerational continuity — or in serving as an instrument of social reproduction — that provides the basis for Feinberg's understanding of schools and their possible transformation.

Understanding Education is divided into two major parts. Part I provides a review of (i) the empirical research tradition, by looking at the IQ controversy and related issues, and behavioral theory in education; (ii) the sort of conceptual analysis embodied in the philosophy of education; and (iii) the more critically oriented research of revisionist historians.

In conceptualizing achievement and socialization in functional terms, researchers share an important characteristic — one that Feinberg says typifies empirical research generally. Proponents tend to take an uncritical, nonproblematic view of the inculcation of particular forms of knowledge and dispositional traits, rather than seeing these as normative propositions requiring justification. Neither tradition self-consciously addresses questions such as why particular forms of knowledge and personality attributes are stressed rather than others, nor the grounds over which such matters might be adjudicated. The result is an isolation of such research from larger social issues and debates, with the appearance of value neutrality, amoral posturing, and 'scientific' objectivity. Educational understanding based upon this emphasis from empirical research is decontextualized, detached from social life generally.

The important point here is that the empirical tradition characteristically regards values as extraneous to educational analysis:

> whether a value is seen as an attribute of the researcher (such as expressed in a decision made about the importance of a project) or as an attribute of the subject of the research, it is perceived first and foremost as something that attaches itself to an individual. Values, according to the empirical tradition, are to be understood as the preferences of individuals.[62]

It is this tendency to individualize questions of value, disconnecting them from any important institutional and social context, that is most misleading about the empirical research tradition. For, the author continues,

> when we think about research within an institutional setting ... such as a school, values must be understood in quite a different way. An institution is a systematized set of practices, expectations, and procedures, coordinated toward some special social purpose ... in which values have already been crystallized. When we understand values in this way, then we can begin to see that they cannot be turned on and off at will because they do not belong simply to a single will of an individual or an aggregate of individuals ...
> Thus the values that are at work in an institutional setting

do not belong simply to the subjective preferences of the researcher or to the researcher's subjects. Rather they are embedded in the very practices that constitute the institution that the researcher is investigating ... Insofar as values are seen as but attributes of individuals, the basic assumptions of the institution will remain at the taken-for-granted level and will not become objects for rational deliberation.[63]

In a curious way, conceptual research tends toward the same sense of decontextualization. As we have seen, such research, largely rooted in the traditions of analytic philosophy, deals with the analysis of linguistic forms as these embody educational concepts. Within analytic philosophy of education, it is not surprising that much research deals with issues that seem to be of contemporary interest to the research community and/or the public at large.

In abstracting concepts from the practices and contexts from which they arise, conceptual analysis within educational research has fragmented and trivialized its findings. This tradition of educational research, like the empirical tradition, dismisses or ignores the context of its own research efforts. Both approaches to understanding education seek to separate educational from social theory.

Much the same can be said for traditional historical research in education. Accepting the rhetoric and avowed intentions of reformers from Horace Mann to James B. Conant to Ernest L. Boyer, historical inquiry to a large extent fails to critique the underlying structure and assumptions of education as a social system. Too often it is assumed that the establishment of the common school, for instance, was brought about by the personal, humanitarian efforts of individuals committed to emphasizing individual opportunity, without examining the social and economic patterns that dominated and which, therefore, influenced how claims to justice, fairness, and equality were understood. Such research accepts a surface reality and fails to connect historical events with underlying social commitments.

One area which has begun to look more closely and critically at such structural features of society, and which Feinberg says has challenged our belief in the universal benefits brought about by schooling, is what has come to be called revisionist history. Based on the work of such scholars as Katz, Greer, Karier, Violas, and others, this group of historians has urged us to see beneath the rhetoric of educational reform, and to analyze education in relation to other social realities.[64] These writers have attempted to make problematic what is usually taken for granted in historical analysis, and to see the educational system from the point of view of those 'on the bottom' rather than from the reformer's own statements and intentions.[65] As such, revisionist historians have partially reconnected the ties between educational and social theory severed by empirical and conceptual research, and overlooked by more traditional forms of historical analysis.

When traditional historians accept as given the perspective provided by school reformers, 'the historian encounters the danger of coming to think that *because* a certain agent *thought* his acts were morally commedable, in fact they were. This traditional stance can go a long way in explaining how it is that some traditional historians have often overlooked the racism and class bias in early school reform'.[66] Once the perspective of the reformer is assumed, and his/her intentions and rhetoric accepted as the basis for historical judgment, the realm of ethical debate becomes obscured and debased. Indeed what seems to be happening in such cases is that psychological information — people's states of mind, avowed purposes, and intentions — displaces ethical judgment. What Horace Mann 'had in mind', for instance, may be of some psychological interest, and may be relevant to understanding the character of this educational reformer, but has little bearing on the value judgments that one can make regarding Mann's actions. In a sense, then, traditional historians either fail to make what we normally think of as moral claims, or else articulate such claims based on propositions that are, in a strict sense, irrelevant.

Yet if traditional historians' accounts are overly connected with the expressed intentions and commitments of reformers, the critique offered by revisionists also fails to take seriously enough the need for an extended discussion of values and normative frameworks. An example of this occurs in Katz's discussion of social control and imposition. Katz sees two aspects to the term 'imposition': first, 'there is the imposition that is set upon the child when ... his education is designed for external, societal ends'; second, 'there is the imposition set upon the parents when their culture and aspirations are overlooked'.[67] These are logically distinct forms of activity, one dealing with a certain type of education and the other with superimposing practices on people in spite of their differing cultural affinities. The problem with Katz's discussion of imposition is that he conflates these two forms of activity, discounting the possibility that in any given situation they may be contradictory. Recognizing this difficulty in his later work, Katz attempts to resolve it by siding with those at whom reforms were directed — that is, by taking the opposite side to that defended by traditional historians in understanding educational reform.[68] Yet the consequences of this shift in focus are themselves problematic, as can be seen in the attempt by parents to impose practices that seem to violate their own cultural position.

Consider the case where a candidate for the school committee, who was herself a member of the subordinate social group, reportedly advocated a return to such presumably 'impositional' (given Katz's first criterion) ideas as issuing report cards, inflicting corporal punishment, and withdrawing sex education from the curriculum. Katz himself refers to such practices as impositional and as conforming to 'bourgeois values'.[69] Labeling such actions as impositional and bourgeois, however, violates one of Katz's characterizations of such activity — namely imposing values contrary to that group's aspirations. This is not merely an oversight on the part of this historian, but reflects a confusion brought about by the failure of revisionists to develop a fully articulated normative framework on the basis of which ethical decisions can be made. To that extent they share a failing with more traditionally oriented historical investigations.

In placing their research orientation within the parameters of those who were recipients of reform proposals, revisionists like Katz curtail the array of ethical judgments that are possible. Since Katz's conceptual scheme is grounded 'in the values of the minority culture ... his framework allows little room for judgments of false consciousness to be made by the historian, [and] thus ... denies the use of an important critical tool'.[70] To a large extent Katz sees the interests of the reformers and those at whom reform was aimed as oppositional. Because of this he assumes that the guiding ideas and commitments of these groups were similarly at odds. Yet in picturing educational reform as involving disputes between groups that are fundamentally dichotomous, what Katz fails to recognize 'is that workers and owners sometimes shared a large part of the ideological superstructure of American society. The political platform of the local school board candidate that Katz tells us about ... is but a recent manifestation of this shared ideology'.[71] In a sense, revisionist historians may have implicitly accepted the framework of traditional historians in seeing disputes over reform efforts in excessively personalized, dualistic terms. While such scholarship is valuable in undermining our reliance on the expressed intentions of reformers, it has failed as yet to provide a larger framework with which the ideological nature of both reform and particular responses to it may be understood.

The perspective offered by the revisionists, thus, is itself ethically inadequate, in an interesting way. For as Feinberg insightfully points out:

> it is precisely because people can be mistaken about their own interests and because their expressed desires can be molded inappropriately from the outside that a full understanding of education needs to be able to maintain its critical force without just appealing to what people want or desire. In some cases we need to understand why people want or desire in the particular way they do.[72]

'To be mistaken' about one's interests and for desires to be 'molded inappropriately' are, of course complex and contentious matters. Disallowing such possibilities, denying the occurrence of false consciousness and, correlatively, to side with individuals or a social group in struggles where their own sentiments may be ideologically laden, reflects the lack of an encompassing, critically oriented value framework with which education can be understood.

To understand and evaluate the expressed concerns of people and groups, we need a theoretical framework that is open to critical commentary and responsive to material circumstances. The failure of revisionist historians to be open and responsive in this way has led to their work being less helpful than its critical edge might lead us to believe. Feinberg's critique of this revisionist literature is extended in his discussion of social reproduction and access to knowledge. His discussion details how educational inquiry generally is in need of reconstruction.

Since schools as socially reproductive institutions are involved in the process of helping students understand, interpret, and act on the world, they are concerned with the distribution of knowledge. The way in which knowledge is distributed will be affected by extant forms of consciousness, skill requirements, and social interaction. A basic issue is what people take to be 'real' or important knowledge, and how this is obtained within a given social structure. In other words, the starting point for this analysis is the *perception* of what is known by the participant — i.e., what sorts of knowledge allow her/him to function within that social system. The question which thus arises is how institutions function so as to distribute knowledge which is tied to and supports these perceptions — knowledge that enhances, in the process, social reproduction.

Feinberg guides the discussion of how knowledge distribution takes place by positing two analytic categories: scope and level.[73]

'Scope' refers to the structure of knowledge that people acquire and the 'range of activities and ideas over which various individuals are presumed to be aware'.[74] 'Level', by contrast, is used to signify the depth of awareness of an individual or group with respect to a knowledge base. Different levels of knowledge acquisition effect variations in the status which accompanies specific social roles.

A social role embodies certain skills and excludes others. To be a doctor in contemporary United States society, for example, is to be certified as a legitimate member of a group whose role embodies specifiable skills or 'skill clusters'. If we take the scope of the medical profession as a whole to include the dispensing of medicine, the level of knowledge involved will differ for a doctor as compared with a pharmacist or nurse, since the latter roles are understood to possess a relatively lower knowledge level. Educational institutions reproduce skill clusters and thereby maintain hierarchical relationships between workers.

Feinberg extends this analysis by using the concept of a 'knowledge code' to represent the learning of specific skills and consciousness. Formal education is to be understood 'as a consciously designed and institutionalized system of instruction that functions to maintain a given knowledge code and to further the pattern of intellectual development that is associated with it'.[75] Moreover, different individuals will perceive a particular knowledge code in different ways, depending upon the point of view attached to the cluster of skills under which they fall; this differential perception of knowledge codes is designated by Feinberg by the term 'frame'. Stability is maintained as long as there is a tight bond between a knowledge code and its relevant frames; such a bond indicates general acceptance that the clustering of skills and the definition and distribution of high status knowledge comprise 'a natural process or are of fundamental benefit to all'.[76] Yet the potential for instability, and thus for social change, exists when the bond between code and frame is challenged and made problematic, and when this is communicated to others.

Understanding Education details how social structures are necessarily involved in maintaining intergenerational continuity, and how it is that the educational system of contemporary United States society is involved in this process. It distributes knowledge codes (skill clusters and forms of consciousness) and correlative patterns of development in such a way that students' acquisition of discrete skill clusters and forms of consciousness maintain the existing knowledge code. The knowledge distributed in this manner is acquired at a certain level and is of a particular scope, thus furthering the division of labor based on such a hierarchical rendering. Changes in social structure require a recognition that current patterns of knowledge level and scope are not 'given' or natural, but the product of historically identifiable forces. This is why historical investigations, especially those which incorporate a normative framework compatible with a full analysis of 'the facts' of education, are important for movements aimed at social change: understanding the historical nature of existing patterns is to understand their constructed nature, and hence the possibilities of deconstruction and reconstruction.

Educational and social change may be brought about more specifically, by making the relationships between knowledge codes and frames more problematic. Here Feinberg's treatment of medical knowledge is especially suggestive. The dominant code within the medical system of the United States centers around maximizing technologically-oriented medical knowledge. This results in 'the need to increase the corpus of medical knowledge and technique at an ever increasing pace', a need that is facilitated by specialization within the medical profession.[77] Emphasis becomes placed on the diagnosis and treatment of various illnesses and diseases through an increased use of technically sophisticated medical equipment and procedures. Yet maximizing the growth of medical knowledge is seen as discontinuous with the distribution of medical services — the application of such knowledge. Indeed, the aim of maximizing growth is consistent with the inequitable distribution of medical care. Moreover, this emphasis on the maximal growth of knowledge does not give credence to 'the need to also understand particular situations. Many of the problems of health are the result of situationally generated factors and do not require a highly sophisticated understanding of the sciences of the human organism to comprehend'.[78]

While Feinberg's book details how the concepts of scope and level might be used to understand the distribution of medical knowledge, it is important to see how the author's analysis might be applied to more specific school settings as well. This may help us see the usefulness of the theory Feinberg provides for the more concrete situations and problems faced by school people. Let us look in some detail at a recent ethnographic study of the relationship between the culture, language and work patterns of two communities in the mid-south, as undertaken by Shirley Brice Heath in her book, *Ways With Words*.[79]

Heath's ethnography deals with the different linguistic and cultural practices of a predominately white neighborhood, Roadville, and a Black community, Trackton. Her investigation of these two communities uncovers some of the important social differences between them — from their divergent child rearing and interactional patterns to the various cultural values and traits that infuse each. In addition, Heath documents how forms of language in childhood and early school settings carry over into work patterns, mostly in the local textile mill. Of special interest is how the patterns of language use correspond to the different occupational roles of mill workers, in large part based on their vocational and social position within the mill itself. As opposed to the lower paid mill workers, the 'townspeople' have a more cosmopolitan attitude. The latter group's status and power helps generate a cultural distinctiveness that is obvious to all. 'Townspeople not known by name can be identified immediately by Roadville and Trackton residents: clothes, bearing, speech, and habits and talking from or with pieces of paper mark them. They see themselves as being "in the main stream of things"'.[80]

A part of being in 'the main stream of things' is operating with the appropriate linguistic and cultural emphases. Consider the following description of a mill executive's use of language within his everyday routine:

> the mill executive talks with and from written materials, following habitual ways of taking meaning from written sources and extending it to shared background experiences with conversationalists ... As both mill executive and father, he repeatedly moves from labels to discussion of the features of the items labeled, to questions about the reasons for and uses of these. Through preschool, school and work, these seem natural, 'logical' ways of proceeding ... Well-meaning and conscientious executives despair that neither white nor Black mill workers seem to find these ways of organizing and talking about transferring knowledge into action 'natural'.[81]

The ability to use written and oral expression in relatively standardized, systematic, orderly ways, is representative of mill executives' usage of and training in linguistic patterns. Such linguistic usage might reasonably be said to help constitute a particular level of knowledge regarding work in the textile mill, as well as a different scope of knowledge, which results in a specific knowledge code.

Contrast the patterns of language use of the mill executive sketched above with the residents of Trackton. Heath describes in detail the early experiences that Trackton children have with language, and how these contribute to the development and continuation of a particular cultural formation. In summarizing these experiences, the author comments that 'flexibility and adaptability are the most important characteristics of learning to be and to talk in Trackton. Children learn to shift roles, to adapt their language, and to interpret different meanings of language according to varying situations'.[82] In discussing the use of oral story-telling in Trackton, Heath points out still other dimensions of language use that delineate important differences from the culture of 'towns-people'. For the residents of Trackton:

> the best stories are 'junk', and anyone who can 'talk junk' is a good story-teller. Talkin' junk includes laying on highly exag-gerated compliments and making wildly exaggerated com-parison as well as telling narratives. Straightforward factual accounts are relatively rare in Trackton and are usually told only on serious occasions ... Trackton's stories [include] wide-ranging language play and imagination which embellish the narrative.[83]

This pattern of language use emphasizes creative divergence, spon-taneity, and improvisation, qualities that diverge significantly from the standardized patterns of language employed by mill executives. Moreover, the linguistic experiences of children in Trackton run contrary to the operation of the school: 'it is as though the school is not expected to link with or reinforce the norms of story-telling in the home, church, and community'.[84]

Both children of executives and workers learn to use language and to understand the social, cultural, and vocational patterns in which they live on a day to day basis. The particular forms of language, though, differ for each. The mill executive regards his use of language and communication skills as natural and expresses a level of knowledge that is related to his status and control. As a 'townsperson' who enjoys certain wealth and privilege, his knowledge code consists in the requisite skills, aspects of consciousness, and forms of communication through which these are expressed. The residents of Trackton, in emphasizing the expressive, divergent possibilities of language, especi-ally in oral forms, operate with a different level of knowledge and a distinctly different knowledge code. Not only are the skills they use in their vocations different, the cultural and linguistic tendencies they acquire help maintain their subordinate economic and social position. Moreover, because schools embody linguistic and cultural forms that are alien to them, residents of Trackton acquire a specific frame through which the knowledge of the townspeople is foreign, 'unnatural', and even somewhat mysterious. Through the development of these divergent knowledge codes and frames, then, the social setting Heath describes — with its system of stratified social relations, economic prospects, and cultural forms — is reproduced. Here we see in more concrete terms how intergenerational continuity is maintained through the perpetuation of linguistic and cultural practices that generate knowledge codes and frames that promote social stability. The school plays a key role in the promotion of such stability in its incorporation of particular forms of language and culture.

Our usual way of interpreting such diverse linguistic patterns and knowledge codes is to see the language of Trackton residents as inferior, and a reflection of the 'culturally deprived' nature of such groups. Suppose, however, that we attempted to loosen the bond between the dominant knowledge code and the frames represented by the mill executive and workers. Such a loosening might well alter the usual assumptions that attend cultural deprivation theory, and result in a more genuinely pluralistic and democratic vision of culture and language, as well as a demystification of those forms currently in use by the socially advantaged. An initial step in this direction might be the articulation of a value system which sees the more aesthetically pleasing linguistic forms of Trackton (emphasizing creative reinterpretation, spontaneity, improvisation, embellishment, and so on) as alternative, but no less valuable, forms of communication. Indeed, at least in certain respects, the more linear, stylized, systematic forms of expression embraced by the townspeople might be seen as artistically impoverished and uninspired. If such a system of values could be incorporated into the schools, both knowledge codes and frames might be altered. The residents of Trackton might in that event see the 'legitimate' linguistic patterns of the townspeople as less mysterious, unnatural, and foreign. The development of skills and forms of consciousness might likewise be altered, thereby making social reproduction in its present form more problematic. Thus changing knowledge codes and frames, skills clusters and forms of consciousness, might promote progressive social, cultural, and economic shifts.

To engage in such activity requires that ethical debate be made the center of educational dialogue. Arguing for a commitment to general education, Feinberg stresses that social function of education 'primarily intended to further social participation as a member of the public through the development of interpretive understanding and normative skills'. The kind of education needed, hence, is 'that form of instruction that involves the development of free persons, persons who are, at least in principle, capable of making unmanipulated judgments on the basis of reason and theoretical understanding, but who also find solidarity with their fellow human beings'.[85] The values of freedom, non-manipulation, the ability to understand and utilize practical and theoretical understanding, and social commitment, comprise the basis of a normative framework.

Feinberg's analysis goes beyond other theories of social reproduction in several ways. First, the normative framework provided is critically oriented, in the sense that it allows us to see how certain values and ideas, even those of a minority culture, may arise because of manipulated judgment and false consciousness. It is not necessarily the case that the sentiments of those oppressed by current social forces are themselves ideologically progressive. By insisting upon a critically oriented normative framework through which actions and sentiments can be evaluated, Feinberg goes beyond other writers who tend to identify, perhaps too quickly, with a particular class-based expression. Second, this framework places the role of ideas in promoting social stability within a theory of hegemony. Since dominant, ideologically embedded ideas, images, and values generally serve to limit the consciousness of a social collectivity, they are not the special province of a single group or class. Third, Feinberg shows how intergenerational continuity is concerned with the distribution of knowledge into particular skill clusters and forms of consciousness. By further subdividing such knowledge into dimensions of scope and level, we can see how educational mechanisms reinforce social structures and promote stability across generations. Fourth, the author describes the linkages between current skill clusters and forms of consciousness. This description not only illuminates current patterns of social reproduction, but also suggests how these may be altered. Fifth, the possibility of reworking the nature of schools as sites for social reproduction is enhanced by an understanding of how knowledge codes are perceived by those with particular frameworks. If the bond between codes and frames can be made problematic, we may be able to alter existing patterns of reproduction. Sixth, Feinberg documents the importance of interpretive and normative understanding of the sort provided by general education, in effectuating such altered patterns of reproduction.

The critical tradition has not been as responsive as we might have hoped to the demand for alternative directions that can reverse the patterns of exploitation and inequality brought about by the social dimensions of school practice. This can be seen in at least two arenas. On the one hand, there has been a growing awareness of this dearth of more progressive possibilities on the part of theorists who have been active in constructing socially relevant analyses.[86] The tendency toward cynicism — a feeling that, if schools are tightly controlled or determined by dominant social patterns, our efforts to promote change might be politically impotent — has been recognized by these and other writers as an outgrowth of some critical analyses of education. Unchecked, such cynicism can easily lead to social paralysis and a wholesale rejection of critically oriented literature. At the same time, the lack of practical alternatives has been a particularly difficult issue for those working within programs of teacher preparation, and who want to alter current forms of educational practice in concert with our students. Frequently the response by students to critical analysis takes the form of, 'now that I understand something of the processes by which schools reproduce social, political, and economic patterns, and that such reproduction is not desirable, what can I do to reverse these things in schools?' Answers to such questions have been necessarily tentative, piecemeal, and even at times overly defensive. We have not developed at all fully, even at a theoretical level, strategies that encourage the development of alternative realities. Uncovering the hidden realities of educational practice needs to be connected with the articulation of an alternative perspective with which to construct alternatives. The research of reproduction, resistance, and contradiction theorists is very helpful in this regard. The normative and interpretive analyses contained in *Understanding Education* further this commitment to reconstruction. The following chapter takes up the more specific question of appropriate values for the concrete transformation of school activities.

Notes and References

1   HERBERT M. KLIEBARD, 'Persistent curriculum issues in historical perspective', in WILLIAM PINAR, (Ed.), *Curriculum Theorizing: The Reconceptualists* (Berkeley: McCutcheon Publishing Corporation, 1975), p. 41.
2   *Ibid.*, p. 42.
3   LANDON E. BEYER and KEN ZEICHNER, 'Teacher education in cultural context: Beyond reproduction', in THOMAS S. POPKEWITZ, (Ed.), *Critical Studies in Teacher Education: Its Folklore, Theory and Practice* (Lewes: Falmer Press, 1987).
4   Kliebard, *op. cit.*, p. 43.
5   See JOHN DEWEY, 'The relationship of theory to practice in education', in *The Relation of Theory to Practice in the Education of Teachers*, the Third Yearbook of the National Society for the Scientific Study of Education, Part I (Chicago: University of Chicago Press, 1904).

6   DONALD A. SCHON, *The Reflective Practitioner: How Professionals Think in Action* (New York: Basic Books, Inc., 1983).

7   *Ibid.*, p. 24.

8   See, for instance, WILLARD WALLER, *The Sociology of Teaching* (New York: John Wiley and Sons, 1932); and HOWARD EBMEIER and THOMAS L. GOOD, 'The effects of instructing teachers about good teaching on the mathematics achievement of fourth grade students', *American Educational Research Journal*, Volume 16, No. 1, Winter, 1979.

9   For critiques of these traditions, see Beyer and Zeichner, *op. cit.*

10 ROBERT DREEBEN, *On What Is Learned in School* (Reading, Massachusetts: Addison-Wesley Publishing Company, 1968).

11 See PHILIP W. JACKSON, *Life in Classrooms*, (New York: Holt, Rinehart, and Winston, 1968), chapter one, 'The daily grind'.

12 Dreeben, *op. cit.* pp. 85–86.

13 MAXINE GREENE, 'The matter of mystification: Teacher education in unquiet times', in *Landscapes of Learning* (New York: Teachers College Press, 1978).

14 J. FLOUD and A.H. HALSEY, 'The sociology of education: A trend report and bibliography', *Current Sociology* (1958), p. 171.

15 JAMES B. MACDONALD, 'Curriculum and human interests', in William Pinar, *op. cit.*, p. 293.

16 DWAYNE HUEBNER, 'Curricular language and classroom meanings', in Pinar, *op. cit.*, p. 219.

17 For example, see JOHN DEWEY, *Democracy and Education* (New York: Macmillan, 1916); HAROLD RUGG, (Ed.), *Democracy and the Curriculum: The Life and Program of the American School* (New York: D. Appleton-Century Company, 1939); THEODORE BRAMELD, *Cultural Foundations of Education: An Interdisciplinary Exploration* (New York: Harper and Brothers, 1957); and GEORGE S. COUNTS, *Dare the Schools Build a New Social Order?* (New York: Day, 1932).

18 SAMUEL BOWLES and HERBERT GINTIS, *Schooling in Capitalist American* (New York: Basic Books, 1976).

19 *Ibid.*, p. 130.

20 *Ibid.*, p. 129.

21 *Ibid.*, p. 131.

22 *Ibid.*, p. 131.

23 *Ibid.*, p. 132.

24 See MICHAEL W. APPLE, *Ideology and Curriculum* (Boston: Routledge & Kegan Paul, 1979).

25 MICHAEL W. APPLE, 'The other side of the hidden curriculum: Correspondence theories and the labor process', *Interchange*, Volume 11, Number 3, 1980/81.

26 See *Ibid.*, and RICHARD EDWARDS, *Contested Terrain: The Transformation of the Workplace in the Twentieth Century* (New York: Basic Books, Inc., 1979).

27 MICHAEL F.D. YOUNG, 'An approach to the study of curriculum as socially organized knowledge', in *Knowledge and Control* (London: Collier-Macmillan Publishers, 1971).

28   *Ibid.*, p. 26.
29   *Ibid.*, p. 26.
30   *Ibid.*, p. 32.
31   *Ibid.*, p. 36.
32   Apple, *Ideology and Curriculum*, *op. cit.*, pp. 36–37.
33   *Ibid.*, p. 37.
34   JEAN ANYON, 'Ideology and US history textbooks', *Harvard Educational Review*, 1979, 40.
35   BASIL BERNSTEIN, *Class, Codes, and Control, Volume 3: Towards a Theory of Educational Transmissions* (London: Routledge and Kegan Paul, 1975).
36   *Ibid.*, p. 87.
37   *Ibid.*, p. 88.
38   *Ibid.*, p. 89.
39   *Ibid.*, p. 94.
40   *Ibid.*, p. 96.
41   *Ibid.*, p. 97.
42   *Ibid.*, p. 67.
43   *Ibid.*, p. 67.
44   *Ibid.*, p. 110.
45   *Ibid.*, p. 111.
46   MICHAEL W. APPLE and LOIS WEIS, (Eds.), *Ideology and Practice in Schooling* (Philadelphia: Temple University Press, 1983).
47   JOEL TAXEL, 'The American Revolution in children's fiction: An analysis of literary content, form and ideology', in Apple and Weis, *op. cit.*, p. 64.
48   *Ibid.*, p. 65.
49   *Ibid.*, p. 74.
50   LINDA VALLI, 'Becoming clerical workers: Business education and the culture of femininity', in Apple and Weis, *op. cit.*, p. 220.
51   *Ibid.*, pp. 220–221.
52   *Ibid.*, p. 225.
53   *Ibid.*, p. 228.
54   PAUL WILLIS, *Learning to Labour: How Working Class Kids Get Working Class Jobs* (Westmead, Farnborough, Hampshire, England: Gower Publishing Company Limited, 1980).
55   MADELINE MACDONALD, *Curriculum and Cultural Reproduction* (Milton Keynes, England: Open University Press, 1977), pp. 68–69.
56   Willis, *op. cit.*, p. 12.
57   *Ibid.*, p. 12.
58   *Ibid.*, p. 18.
59   *Ibid.*, p. 22.
60   WALTER FEINBERG, *Understanding Education: Toward a Reconstruction of Educational Inquiry* (New York: Cambridge University Press, 1983).
61   *Ibid.*, p. 6.
62   *Ibid.*, p. 44.
63   *Ibid.*, pp. 44–45.
64   See, for example, MICHAEL B. KATZ, *The Irony of Early School Reform: Educational Innovation in Mid-Nineteenth Century Massachusetts* (Cambridge, Massachusetts: Harvard University Press, 1968); COLIN GREER, *The*

Great School Legend: *A Revisionist Interpretation of American Public Education* (New York: Basic Books, 1972); CLARENCE J. KARIER, *Shaping the American Educational State*: *1900 to the Present* (New York: The Free Press, 1975); and PAUL VIOLAS, *The Training of the Urban Working Class*: *A History of 20th Century American Education* (Chicago: Rand-McNally College Publishing Company, 1978).

65 DAVID TYACK, *The One Best System*: *A History of American Urban Education* (Cambridge, Massachusetts: Harvard University Press, 1974).

66 Feinberg, *op. cit.*, p. 124.

67 *Ibid.*, p. 126.

68 MICHAEL B. KATZ, *Class, Bureaucracy, and Schools*: *The Illusion of Educational Change in America* (New York: Praeger, 1971).

69 Feinberg, *op. cit.*, p. 127.

70 *Ibid.*, p. 127.

71 *Ibid.*, p. 138.

72 *Ibid.*, p. 145.

73 In his treatment of knowledge, forms of consciousness, and skill clusters, Feinberg develops analytic categories and a terminology that sometimes overlap with the terminology used by Basil Bernstein, *op. cit.* This is only coincidental and does not reflect a similarity of meanings in these two writers. Feinberg's discussion is substantially different from Bernstein's.

74 Feinberg, *op. cit.*, p. 161.

75 *Ibid.*, p. 164.

76 *Ibid.*, p. 165.

77 *Ibid.*, p. 186.

78 *Ibid.*, p. 195.

79 SHIRLEY BRICE HEATH, *Ways with Words*: *Language, Life, and Work in Communities and Classrooms* (New York: Cambridge University Press, 1983).

80 *Ibid.*, p. 236.

81 *Ibid.*, pp. 261–262.

82 *Ibid.*, p. 111.

83 *Ibid.*, p. 166.

84 *Ibid.*, p. 166.

85 Feinberg, *op. cit.*, p. 229.

86 See GEORGE H. WOOD, 'Beyond radical educational cynicism', *Educational Theory*, Volume 32, Number 2, Spring, 1982; MICHAEL W. APPLE, *Education and Power* (Boston: Routledge & Kegan Paul, 1982); LANDON E. BEYER and GEORGE H. WOOD, 'Critical inquiry and moral action in education', *Educational Theory*, Volume 36, Number 1, Winter, 1986; and LANDON E. BEYER and MICHAEL W. APPLE, (Eds), *The Curriculum*: *Problems, Politics and Possibilities* (Albany, New York: State University of New York Press, in press).

4
Education, Moral Action and the Practice of Possibility

Since public schools must be situated within a broader social context that gives meaning to their pedagogical, curricular, and evaluative practices, a technical framework for educational studies is simply inadequate. Such a framework isolates educational experiences and ideas, dislocating them from social, political, and ideological matrices from which a substantial part of their significance is derived. At the same time, the pitfalls of such an isolated perspective on education point to problems in the way we have thought about liberal inquiry in institutions of higher education as well. The epistemological critiques of positivism presented earlier, together with the development of more contextual, human, and social approaches to inquiry fostered by hermeneutics, expose the shortcomings of liberal inquiry as this has taken place historically. The division between reconstituted forms of inquiry and allegedly applied areas like education becomes harder to sustain.

As important as theories of social reproduction have been in teasing out the linkages between educational theory and practice and larger social realities and ideological presuppositions, they also share some important drawbacks that need to be critically discussed. Studies of the social roles of schooling have tended to disclose the existence of realities that are often hidden and unnoticed. Indeed, the ideological purposes of schooling may be most readily served by keeping such connections hidden. While theories of social reproduction have served a significant disclosure function, though, they have not generally been accompanied by alternative ideas and practices around which schooling may be reformulated. This is not to deny the value of the critical literature we have examined or its importance for researchers, teachers, and students. Rather, we need to inquire into the meaning of this literature for the concrete redirection of educational possibilities. Not only will this result in improved educational activities, it will also be in keeping with the unification of thought and action, and the generation of alternative worlds, that are the central themes of this volume.

As we have seen, important differences exist among critical theorists regarding the constitutive questions and assumptions surrounding the nature of educational theory and school practice, and the social, cultural, and political theories from which they draw. Such differences aside, there is a sense in which this tradition generally is overly separated and immunized from other educational and social theorists and practitioners. There is always the danger, especially given the contemporary educational and political climate, that 'social reproduction' as a school of thought will become simply another in a series of slogan systems that has infiltrated educational discourse.[1] Moreover, the tendency for authors of this literature to speak only to one another, and in occasionally too unreflective and jargonesque a way, makes the danger of insulation that much more real.

In connection with this tendency toward isolation, there is a central epistemological and ethical problem with at least some views of social reproduction. As Feinberg notes, we have not taken seriously enough the need for a set of moral principles and convictions that can be used to critique current educational theory and practice, and alternatives to these phenomena as well. This has resulted in a premature applause for alleged resistances to ideological domination in schools. If we seek what Raymond Williams has called 'the practice of possibility',[2] we cannot assume that all reactions to current forms of domination are justifiable. The rejection of the former fundament of positivism for the construction of ways of thinking and acting outlined in chapter two should not be replaced by a new, equally problematic fundament, represented by appeals to one particular group, social class, or class fragment. Adopting such a fundament and restricting our moral discourse to those who share it, has resulted in too closed a system of debate, and too few proposals for alternative educational practices.[3]

The critical body of literature concerning the ideological role of schools discussed in chapter three also suffers from an alarming lack of productive debate among proponents, and between adherents to that orientation and others. To a disturbingly large extent, reactions to this literature have been of two basic kinds: a generalized and unreflective rejection of any sort of critical perspective in education by those 'outside' the field, on the one hand; or acrimonious, frequently per-sonalized, polemical reprisals by those 'inside' the field, on the other.[4] Both reactions are unhelpful.

A concern for how this body of scholarship may be extended and modified so as to reorient educational theory and school practice in ways that can be transformative lies at the center of this chapter. This is not 'merely' a problem of applicability. Nor does this concern reflect the view that all theory must be translatable into particular classroom realities in some immediate, obsessively pragmatic way.[5] Yet if this literature is to be more than a scholarly endeavor in the way liberal inquiry often is — if it is to help effect a genuine praxis, uniting knowledge and action — we must pay attention to the forms of discourse, styles of thinking and feeling, and ways of interacting with others that will assist in its efficacy.

In remaining mindful of the real contributions that theories of social reproduction have made, as well as the tendencies toward insulation and division that have too often typified both adherents and antagonists, the question of how revisions in some of the tenets of this tradition may lead to progressive, practical transformation is taken seriously. To accomplish this, we must be more self-conscious about the moral principles, normative frameworks, and political convictions that guide our interchange with others.[6] Insofar as our vision is founded on a set of moral, political, and cultural ideals, we must both clarify these commitments and be able to create opportunities for dialogue with those who may not be inclined toward that vision, in the process of creating new possibilities. A first step in building the kind of normative framework emphasized earlier lies in seeing the shortcom-ings in the ethical stance of social reproduction and resistance perspec-tives.

Moral Principles and Normative Judgments

Educational Inquiry and Normative Discourse

To be more specific about the kinds of issues that animate the current discussion, let us look at two specific cases where more careful attention to the nature of normative judgments might serve as a corrective to theories of social reproduction. These examples are representative of at least one strand of that body of literature in general, and are employed for their illustration of the issues to be addressed.

Consider again the study that has arguably received more attention and scrutiny than any other in recent critical educational dialogue, Paul Willis' *Learning to Labour*.[7] Recall that in his discussion of 'the lads', Willis notes the ways in which this group expressed an opposition to the culture of the school, whose rules, regulations, and modes of interaction were oppressive and demeaning to them. They thus created and maintained their own system of oppositional symbols and tendencies, helping establish the legitimacy of their own cultural identity. Such creative acts are fully understandable, given the social, historical, and economic context within which the lads lived and worked. Moreover, the author was concerned to capture the spirit and contradictory nature of these acts, showing how ideological forms that attend the culture of dominant groups are often mediated or rejected in actual practice. As Willis puts this, 'the logic of a living must be traced to the heart of its conceptual relationships if we are to understand the social creativity of a culture. This always concerns, at some level, a recognition of, and action upon, the particularity of its place within a determinate social structure'.[8] The dynamics of lived cultural experiences, their sociohistorical and contradictory natures, makes any simple 'rational' understanding of them misleading and at best partial.

Yet Willis says the actions of the lads occur not only *within* a 'determinate social structure', but that they 'penetrate' the ideology that blends with the culture it supports. How to understand the meaning of this claim is made clearer by the author's view of consciousness. In his analysis of penetrations, Willis writes that consciousness:

> is a privileged source of information and meaning if properly contextualized and ultimately the only stake in the struggle for meanings. It is part of the cultural level and relates most basically to it as the immediate expression of its law. It binds in with it, and has a consistency, validity, and directly developmental role with respect to its complexity. Consciousness is in any conceivable sense 'false' only when it is detached from its variable cultural context and asked to answer questions.[9]

As a part of culture, the development of discrete forms of consciousness can only be understood in the context of those social and historical forces through which the 'law' of culture is manifested. Thus understanding the lads' opposition to school, and their efforts to empower their own cultural images, can only be undertaken, and evaluated, in the context out of which they arose. 'False consciousness,' then, only exists if we take the cultural meanings of the lads out of their experienced context, and interpret them using other criteria.

Again, consider Michael W. Apple's essay, 'Old humanists and new curricula: Politics and culture in *The Paideia Proposal*'.[10] In applauding Mortimer Adler's proposals that schools be non-tracked, general and liberal, and especially that they should be non-specialized and non-vocational, Apple also points to contradictory effects of such school practices. Basically, he thinks that downplaying the vocational goals of schooling 'flies in the face of what a large portion of high school students choose as the ideal function of schooling'.[11] For many students — Apple relies on Sirotnik's findings of 30 per cent here[12] — schools are not seen as so much serving the purposes of 'intellectual development' as to 'prepare for employment, to develop saleable skills, and to develop an "awareness of career choices and alternatives"'.[13] As Apple puts his objection to Adler's proposal:

> to deal only with 'academic knowledge', with the high status culture of the old humanists ... is to forget that for many working class and minority students such knowledge represents little that is directly relevant to either their actual lives or their future economic trajectories. In fact ... working class students will quite often partly reject the world of the school. These students rightly sense ... that the knowledge and social relations considered legitimate by the educational system will have less objective pay-off in the end for these students ... than school people and others promise.[14]

Since the humanistic knowledge Adler is promoting for schools is not seen as relevant by a large segment of the student population (for good economic and social reasons), Apple rejects the separation of academic from vocational instruction. 'Not to take vocational issues seriously also risks cutting oneself off from the sentiments of large numbers of students ... We need to find ways of integrating work and education together ... in a way that does not give over the schools to the needs of the powerful'.[15] While this issue is a complex and interesting one, as is the issue raised by Willis' treatment of culture and consciousness, it is how they are addressed — the *kind* of dilemma they are taken to represent — that needs to be highlighted.

The central difficulty with these analyses is a conflation of empathic understanding with a normative judgment of what must be considered competing conceptions of empowerment, knowledge, and action. While we may understand the actions of the lads much more completely and contextually with the aid of Willis' analysis, to see their cultural symbols and actions as ideologically penetrating is to make a radically different claim. Furthermore, to say that the consciousness and derivative activities of the lads can only be understood by reference to the 'law' of the cultural level, is to lock our judgment within the perspective of that social group; judgments of false consciousness are therefore denied legitimacy. In addition to making us more sensitive to the cultural meanings of the lads, Willis is ultimately making an epistemological and moral point about how we are to regard the activities of this group of secondary students. Similarly, when Apple suggests that Adler's prescriptions regarding academic knowledge are incorrect because they disavow an affiliation with those who see the function of schooling in radically different, vocationally oriented terms, he is at least tacitly siding with 'the working class' on a similar question.

Both Willis and Apple, in affiliating with a version of the Marxist tradition, and with a theory of social reproduction that is allied with it, have articulated an identification with the working class. Even though their own writing is aimed at going beyond the mechanistic correspondence theories like that outlined in Bowles and Gintis in *Schooling in Capitalist America,*[16] their analyses are still written within those presuppositions that provide a new epistemological fundament within a particular social group. The values, symbols, and forms of identification that this group avows become the basis for interpretation and judgment. For Willis, applauding the 'penetrations' of the lads — indeed, seeing their actions *as* ideologically penetrating — is mandatory precisely because they occupy a subordinate, exploited class position. In the same way, Apple's approval of some form of 'vocational education' is mandated by that group's class-based conviction regarding academic knowledge.[17]

What this discussion reflects is the tendency for attention to be focused on a particular class segment in deciding normative disputes; the arbiter of such conflict is to be the sentiments, perspectives, or proclivities of that class. An identification with the working class as the vanguard of social change as detailed in at least certain forms of Marxism, has generated the sort of perspective illustrated above.

The problem with this tendency is that it reduces moral issues to questions of social acceptability, where 'acceptability' is defined by reference to the working class. Questions of moral judgment are settled by reference to the sentiments and actions of a particular social group. This generates a theory of moral decision making known as 'social moral relativism'.[18] This theory is normatively indefensible, and has partially contributed to the incestuous nature of discussions regarding the ideological role of schools. For debate is curtailed when possible participants do not share this presupposition. How, on the contrary, are we to understand the nature of moral judgments?

When we say, 'Bill has a moral obligation to keep his promise' we do not mean that he should keep his promise insofar as he is an historian, scientist, father, or any other particular kind of person. Instead, we normally mean that Bill is obliged to keep his promise just insofar as he is a *human being*, capable of deliberation and action on the basis of principle rather than whim, self-interest, or caprice. We mean that, absent special circumstances or undisclosed and extraordinary features about the situation, Bill is obliged to keep his promise. 'Principles of morality' oblige people to do certain things under specific and articulated conditions, and to avoid contrary actions. More generally, 'keeping our promises' is what is required when we take the moral point of view.[19] As Frankena puts this:

> when one says 'history tells us' or 'science tells us' something, let us say P, then one is subscribing to P, but one is also taking, or purporting to take, the historical or scientific point of view, and claiming that P is true or rationally justified by the evidence from that point of view ... When one says 'P is a principle of morality' one is taking or purporting to take the moral point of view, subscribing to P from that point of view, and claiming that P is rationally justified by the facts as seen from that point of view or that everyone who views the facts carefully from that point of view will eventually also subscribe to P.[20]

Now such moral understanding need not be reflected in the actions we take in any given situation. Insofar as fallibility is a part of the human condition, we may know what our moral obligations are and yet not fulfill them. Again, we may be puzzled about whether a particular principle, or a contemplated action, is morally permissible or not. Thus, we need not assume that all moral principles arise unequivocally in an a priori, analytic way that only requires careful introspection. Rather, insofar as moral principles hold, and moral judgments and actions are possible, certain actions are permissible or impermissible from the moral point of view, and those who experience the same conditions and who take the moral point of view will act in a similar manner.

Moral principles may be most easily understood, perhaps, by contrasting them with other principles of conduct, say the principles of self-interest or social advantage. When we say one follows the principle of self interest, we mean that person does whatever he/she thinks will bring the most gain — however that person chooses to define 'gain'. To go back to our previous example, if Bill decides that not keeping his promise will result in financial gain, then insofar as he is acting on the basis of self-interest alone (as opposed to moral principle), he may not keep his promise. Adding the possibility of *enlightened* self-interest complicates the picture a bit, but does not alter the basic pattern of decision making. Whether Bill considers only short-term interest, or includes longer term considerations as well, the basic question he asks is, 'what will provide me with the greatest happiness/comfort/satisfaction?' Or take the case of acting on the basis of what is socially acceptable. If Bill asks, in deliberating on whether or not to keep the promise made, 'will my social group approve?' or 'what are the currently fashionable positions on promise-keeping or promise-breaking?' he is acting on the basis of social convention. In both the cases of self-interest and social convention, 'the moral point of view' has been abridged. It is this point of view that allows us to critique both egoism and social convention as the basis for action.

We can think of moral principles, then, as providing a means of overriding actions based on self-interest or social approval convenience. What moral guidelines provide us are ways of deciding between competing (self or social) interests. 'By "the moral point of view" we mean a point of view which formulates a court of arbitration for conflicts of interest. Hence it cannot (logically) be identical with the point of view of any particular person or group of persons'.[21]

Moral judgments, as normally understood, are convictions about what is right or proper, based upon the available facts at our disposal, and upon those *moral principles* that can withstand challenge and defense.[22] When we are confronted with some moral issue or dilemma, that is to say, we have an obligation to acquire all the relevant information possible, and to consider this in light of moral principles that have withstood scrutiny within the universe of moral discourse. Accordingly, there is a sense in which moral judgments — like scientific observations, statistical analyses, and historical interpretations — can never be certain, if we mean by that infallible and beyond dispute. Yet this should not unduly concern us, since as we have seen no area of human understanding — even that represented by 'the hard sciences' — can attain that status. As a hermeneutical activity, moral reasoning replaces the framework of positivism with the necessity of interpretation, reflection, and discussion.

What we mean when we say that 'morally, Bill has to keep his promise' is that given all the facts of the situation, the relevant moral principle(s), and reflective inquiry, Bill must keep his promise, looked at *from the moral point of view* as that is understood within the current conversational context. Within these confines, the activity of keeping his promise is not open to disputation. On the other hand, it is possible that particular facts may later come to light, or that our understanding of proper reflection, moral principles, and the 'real world,' may undergo hermeneutical transformation, in ways that would have just-ified Bill's breaking his promise. In this sense it is never the case that moral judgments are absolutely settled. But, to reiterate, this is not as terrible as it might sound, since none of scientific principles, logical truths, or empirical facts provide such absolute certainty either. Indeed moral judgments are not fundamentally different, in an epistemological or ontological sense, from other kinds of phenomena. Yet this does not mean, at any particular moment, that our moral judgments are 'relative' in some simplistic sense, nor dispensable; nor does this imply that moral judgments can be grounded in a particular social group. Insofar as moral practice is required, it is not possible for us to be tentative. In the end, we have no choice but to take those actions that are morally required, based on the best available factual information and the most defensible principles, as these are understood within the community of moral discussants.

Several points need to be emphasized about the normative judg-ments that have become embedded in theories regarding the linkages between education and ideology, and their consequences. First, in relying on a particular interpretation of Marxist theory which sees an identification with the working class as paving the way toward social transformation, moral judgments become narrowly circumscribed. While cultural ethnocentrism is always a possibility for which we need to be on our guard, we also need to be mindful of how the sentiments and actions of people can be inappropriately shaped. Certainly identif-ication with oppressed groups and individuals is important for under-standing the nature of culture and social dynamics, and as a catalyst for social change; yet this cannot be the sole basis for normative judgments of the sort that are ubiquitous in social and educational life. Second, the cause of this identification is a replacement of the foundations of positivism with a new foundation — namely, the ideas and actions of the working class. In an ironic way, this reliance on a new fundament may have come about because of the entrenched nature of the older epistemological tradition — with its search for certainty. Third, as a foundation for making moral judgments, a reliance on the sentiments of the working class has resulted in a short circuiting of discussion and of the redirection of social and educational practice. Since this new paradigm gives a privileged status to the ideas of one particular class, discussion becomes limited to those who share that position. New terminologies, patterns of discourse, and functional myths thus become established and encoded.[23] This explains, in part, why dialogue between social reproduction theorists and others tends to be so non-substantive. Fourth, if we understand the development of moral judgments on a model of hermeneutics, what we must be about is the encouragement of conversations about what the appropriate moral principles are, and the creation of communities within which exchanges and actions can take place. As Williams has said, such discussion is only hindered by the 'polemical habit of measuring everything against a pure (and therefore often undefined) essence called Marxism'.[24] An allegiance to a new fundament for moral decision making will, in the end, be less practically helpful than we would like. Fifth, the creation of such conversations is crucial if we are to develop theories of schooling and education that have the possibility of transforming lived experience and if they are to work toward the creation of an informed praxis.

Throughout this discussion, our previous critiques of positivism, and the importance of normative frameworks for educational studies, frequent mention has been made of the central place of democratic participation. Some conception of democracy is crucial for participatory dialogue, the creation of knowledge and attendant realities, widespread social conversation, and collective action. Reforming educational studies along democratic lines that can serve as a moral, social, and communal grounding is in need of extended discussion.

Educational Visions of Democracy

Discussions regarding the possible role of US schools in promoting a democratic social order are as old as attempts to establish a system of publicly supported education. Educational institutions have been both applauded and chastised for efforts to establish programs that will further particular democratic ideals and practices. From Thomas Jefferson's proposals for a system of schools in Virginia, to Horace Mann's call for school reform in the second quarter of the nineteenth century, to the recent report of the National Commission on Excellence in Education, America's schools have been called upon to advance a variety of purportedly democratic purposes.[25]

One problem that has repeatedly plagued such discussion is that the nature of democracy has itself undergone substantial, periodic revisions over the course of our history. This has resulted in schools aiming to fulfill a number of functions, related to one or another of the visions of democracy currently favored by other social institutions and practices.[26] Moreover, there are important conceptual and ideological differences among the various interpretations of democracy that are presented. Each serves to support or subvert the interests of specific social groups. A fundamental problem facing schools in this regard is that these interests are themselves often contradictory, so that by supporting certain versions of democracy, other views may be neglected, even explicitly opposed.[27] We cannot expect educational institutions uniformly to support a vision of democracy if there are in fact numerous visions comprising a constellation of competing interests and claims to action that do not allow for any straightforward synthesis.

The problems associated with schools as sites for democratic ideas go even deeper than these conceptual and ideological differences. Our very conception of democracy has become withered at its roots, making problematic the possibility that schools can assist in promoting any substantial vision of democracy. Not only are there multiple realities surrounding conceptions of democracy, but the very conditions under which these realities might be debated, clarified, and acted on are increasingly difficult to locate. The reasons for this are complex, but basically reflect fragmentary, chaotic and confused attempts to embed moral dialogue in a society that regards democratic participation with some ambivalence. As long as moral discourse remains in this state, possible moral principles will remain obscure, with refuge increasingly sought in various forms of emotivism.[28] The inability to provide a suitable context for the discussion of democratic ideas is also the result of a loss of communities within which such discourse can become meaningful and prompt the requisite social action.[29] Surrounded by larger institutional structures favoring technization, commodification, and the therapeutic privatization of social relations, we have all but lost a sense of the collective social good so necessary for discussion of democratic ideas.[30] Documenting the demise of moral discourse and genuine community participation, and their consequences for discussions concerning democracy, is an important part of revitalizing and clarifying democratic actions.

We also need to document the relevance of education for rebuilding moral discourse and genuine communities. The outlines of an alternative approach to schooling that responds to the social trends identified will follow our analysis.[31] The basic argument is that we need to reconstitute democracy as a cultural form — one that helps further those moral and collective pursuits that are a central part of the social transformation that is now required. As a part of this transformation, schools can play an important role in helping realize fully participatory democracy.

Given the confusion and contentiousness surrounding the concept of democracy, some preliminary remarks are in order. First, democracy is intimately tied to a set of values regarding the nature of social justice, equality, freedom, responsibility, respect for persons, and social engagement. To undertake democratic action is to act in ways that are consistent with such values, principles, and commitments (begging the question, for now, of what these principles and commitments should be). Second, this view of democracy has an affinity with some of the recent literature concerning a reconstructed civic education.[32] Recently, several critical analyses of the concept of civic education have appeared that suggest a new role for 'public philosophy'. These writers 'look upon political philosophy as a form of civic educational *agency*, exploring its value as a moral and cognitive message system, judging it by its capacity to *inspire* just action in daily life'.[33] Insofar as democracy is more than an intellectual or cognitive matter, it affects the actions, positions, and commitments that form the heart of our common, day-to-day interactions. Connecting this view with the previous point regarding the centrality of values within democracy, I would agree that, 'a value commitment involves a disposition to relevant action ... and not simply the acceptance of various abstract propositions about democracy or the passive endorsement of a set of ideals.'[34] Third, and building on this last point, rejuvenating the concept of democracy includes overcoming a number of dualisms: thought and feeling, theory and practice, idea and action, objective and subjective, rational and emotional, and leaders and followers. If the concept of democracy is to be a force for enlightened social action and reconstruction, the duplicity involved in such ideologically based antagonisms must be rejected. Fourth, democracy must refer to a way of life, a cultural form, that goes beyond political and civic affairs. It involves fundamentally a commitment to the broadest possible participation in decision making by those whose interests are involved in the everyday workings of economic, familial, cultural, aesthetic, and educational arenas. In short, democracy is here conceived as a way of life that empowers people to act in those situations and institutions comprising the bulk of human existence, guided by a set of values and principles consistent with that vision of participation, and grounded in actions that overcome ideologically based dichotomies in the pursuit of socially just action.[35]

Moral Discourse and the Importance of Community

Alasdair MacIntyre, in *After Virtue*, claims not only that moral theory has undergone a fundamental debasement in modern society, but that we have even lost the ability to use moral language sensibly. As MacIntyre expresses this:

> what we possess ... are the fragments of a conceptual scheme, parts which now lack those contexts from which their significance derived. We possess indeed simulacra of morality, we continue to use many of the key expressions. But we have — very largely, if not entirely — lost our comprehension, both theoretical and practical, of morality.[36]

The collapse of genuine moral discourse and the demise of authentic communities have occurred for several reasons. In looking at some of the more theoretical or academic reasons for the former, as well as some of the more general social causes associated with the latter, I do not mean to imply a strict separation between these domains. Some of the most interesting questions surrounding the discourses on morality and community concern the interconnections between academic inquiry and patterns of social evolution.

There are several elements within the traditions of academic inquiry that have served to weaken the authenticity and potency of moral discourse. First, within the domain of philosophy (of which ethics is an important component), the widespread acceptance of investigations centering on ordinary language and conceptual analysis has supported the view that moral debate can be separated from social context. As we saw earlier, in chapter two, the usual way linguistic analysis proceeds is to identify 'ideal types' that embody the essential elements of the concept under discussion: for example, that indicate what 'autonomy', 'justice', or 'freedom', properly mean. Commonly an appeal is made, at least initially, to the way such concepts are used in typical situations, in clarifying the meaning of these terms. Subsequently, these concepts may be analyzed for their possible internal contradictions, relations with other concepts and terms, implications for further analysis, and the like. The intent is to arrive at a more precise characterization of what a given concept entails, so that ambiguous or incorrect usages of language may be pinpointed and corrected.[37]

As a result of this sort of abstracted and decontextualized treatment of concepts, philosophical clarity and the resolution of concrete dilemmas and problems may be perceived as separate, even antagonistic, endeavors. The proper relationship between concrete problems and conceptual clarity is a contentious matter for many philosophers. Yet in regarding conceptual sophistication as disconnected from any important material context, we tend to overlook the important political and ideological struggles that take place around these concepts and related ideas that provide them with human significance. We forget the political struggles involved in linguistic disputes when we focus on a dislocated clarity.

Another factor that has promoted the dissolution of moral discourse relates more specifically to the scholarly traditions embodied in institutions of higher education in the US, as discussed in chapter 2. Recall that beginning in the late nineteenth century, the image of the university as an association of scholars committed to the conservation and dissemination of our cultural heritage was modified by an allegiance to research that had the potential to develop new products and commodities. The modern university became more closely allied with social, economic, and governmental institutions, and responsive to the demands of the growing corporate sector. University faculty became geared to the production of new knowledge. Such knowledge could be most productively pursued within increasingly narrow, specialized disciplinary and sub-disciplinary boundaries, while moral questions became viewed as belonging properly to one particular discipline or sub-discipline, cut off from the insights that other areas might provide. This tendency exacerbated the tensions between moral discourse and its application to areas outside the sub-discipline in which it was sanctioned within the academy. The result was a further compartmentalization and erosion of moral debate.

These theoretical reasons for the rather unproductive and denuded forms of current moral discussion are complemented by various social events that were to have a correlative impact. These factors relate more directly to the loss of genuine communities that has also compromised our ability to discuss sensibly the social meaning of democracy.

As a society we have to a very large degree lost a sense of history. Not only is our understanding of previous events incomplete or even non-existent, though this is surely a part of the problem. We have also lost a sense of historical continuity — the notion that past, present, and future cannot be fragmented. This is as much a personal and local problem as it is a national one.[38] A part of the reason for this lack of historical perspective has to do with the incessant drive for novelty, future-oriented schemes of material reward, production, and distribution, and a certain fascination with the future generally.[39] As a culture we emphasize goal-directedness and linear thinking, believing (or hoping) that the future will be an improvement upon the present. The fascination with a future more rewarding than the present is also furthered by the dismissal of authoritative traditions and the embrace of individualism:

> The American understanding of the autonomy of the self places the burden of one's own deepest self-definitions on one's own individual choice ... the notion that one discovers one's deepest beliefs in, and through, tradition and community is not very congenial to Americans. Most of us imagine an autonomous self existing independently, entirely outside any tradition and community, and then perhaps choosing one.[40]

This negligence toward history and tradition has been accompanied by the drive for commodification and the massive production and consumption of non-durable goods.[41] Beginning with the rise of factory capitalism and increasing with the expansion of more corporate forms, we have found ourselves increasingly surrounded by 'things' from which a large part of our identity is derived, as Christopher Lasch has recently emphasized:

> Both as a worker and as a consumer, the individual learns not merely to measure himself against others but to see himself through other's eyes. He learns that the self-image he projects counts for more than accumulated skills and experience. Since he will be judged, both by his colleagues and superiors at work and by the strangers he encounters on the street, according to his possessions, his clothes, and his 'personality' — not, as in the nineteenth century, by his 'character' — he adopts a theatrical view of his own 'performance' on and off the job ... the conditions of everyday social intercourse, in societies based on mass production and mass consumption, encourage an unprecedented attention to superficial impressions and images, to the point where the self becomes almost indistinguishable from its surface.[42]

Surrounded by non-durable objects from which our identity in no small way springs, goaded by images that promise health, happiness, sexuality, wealth, and social respectability virtually in an aerosol can, modern Americans have lost a sense of permanency and belonging. Everything becomes disposable — to be purchased, used, and discarded. Personal and social commitments, pursuit of non-emotivist principles, and political involvements alike become harder to understand, let alone justify. 'Freedom', in such a society, 'comes down to the freedom to choose between Brand X and Brand Y, between interchangeable lovers, interchangeable jobs, interchangeable neighborhoods'.[43] In a society enamored with the latest fads, 'revolutionary' breakthroughs, and the dogged pursuit of commodity consumption through advertising, the larger historical context that might lend meaning to human life becomes obscured.

The lack of historical perspective is also attributable to contemporary forms of barbarism that virtually defy understanding and response. The horrors of the Holocaust, other genocidal practices during this and the preceding century, and the constant threat of total annihilation through nuclear attack or accident, present situations for which communal recognition and moral response seem equally implausible. The most that we seem able to do is promote various coping strategies that have survival as their ultimate end.[44] Given the unprecedented and all but incomprehensible atrocities of the past, we can understand how a society such as ours might be compelled to seek a more future-oriented perspective. Yet not only does an ignorance of history condemn us to a repetition of past mistakes, it also makes the articulation and development of alternative futures more problematic. A society that denies historical continuity is one that also makes implausible a sense of genuine community.

The breakdown of moral discourse and the demise of genuine communities fostering visions of the social good, virtue, and commitments that are larger and more enduring than individuals, has resulted in the appearance of two distinctively American 'character types' that, in social practice, subvert discussions of what is entailed by democracy. Generated by those processes detailed above, the therapist and the manager/administrator form a substantial part of our current cultural foci, embodying perspectives and orientations that capture contemporary society.[45]

As a part of the larger bureaucratic structure of our economic and social worlds, the manager embodies those proclivities toward technical rationality that have come to dominate our world. As Bellah *et al.*

express this:

> The essence of the manager's task is to organize the human and
> non-human resources available to the organization that employs
> him so as to improve its position in the marketplace. His role is
> to persuade, inspire, manipulate, cajole, and intimidate those he
> manages so that his organization measures up to criteria of
> effectiveness shaped ultimately by the market ... The manager's
> view of things is akin to that of the technician of industrial
> society par excellence, the engineer.[46]

As the ultimate expression of what the authors call 'utilitarian
individualism', the manager thus captures something of the essence of
modern America's economic and social heart. As character type, the
manager has come to symbolize economic situations, and larger social
and cultural patterns as well. Within education the contemporary trend
toward deskilling of teaching is one manifestation of this emphasis on
management, technical control, and functional utility, as these values
have infiltrated cultural as well as economic practices. The craft of
teaching, as with the art and intrinsic value of work generally, is
sacrificed to the technical display of managerial competence. Importantly, this reliance on technical rationality means that moral discourse,
religion, and art alike tend to be relegated to the sphere of the
subjective, the relative, and the emotive, and to the domain of 'the
feminine' as well.[47]

Again, as Bellah *et al.* document, 'with the coming of the managerial society, the organization of work, place of residence, and social
status came to be decided by criteria of economic effectiveness ... The
older social and moral standards became in many ways less relevant to
the lives of those Americans most directly caught up in the new
system'.[48] The manager symbolizes not only the ascendancy of the
economic and the utilitarian in American life, but the near replacement
of moral discourse by those more technical, consumptive, and
bureaucratic work and life styles that accompany the adoption of that
character type.

The reaction to the dominance of the manager has taken several
forms. The therapist, as the second American character type, captures
our culture's fascination with psychologized life patterns and choices.
In some ways the job of trying to reunite a self deluged with the
demands of the managerial character has fallen to the therapist.
Committed to 'personal satisfaction', 'self-actualization', 'psychic
wholeness', and the like, the therapist represents attempts to heal an

assaulted psyche. Yet, 'like the manager, the therapist takes the functional organization of industrial society for granted, as the unprob-lematical context of life'.[49] Keyed to a notion of proper 'adjustment' of individuals to a personal and social context that is regarded as largely immutable, the therapist seeks individualized accommodation of clients to those contexts. 'Its genius is that it enables the individual to think of commitments — from marriage and work to political and religious involvement — as enhancements of the sense of individual well-being rather than as moral imperatives'.[50] Like the manager whose work and social lives involve the furtherance of patterns that undermine moral discourse, the therapist — in individualizing people's choices, commit-ments, and actions — personifies our culture's hostility to forms of moral and communal life.[51]

Given these cultural and social propensities, it is not surprising that our vision of democracy has often been clouded and confused. Unable to conceptualize moral commitment within a system continually deni-grating — at both a theoretical and a more day-to-day level — historical tradition, extra-individualistic commitments, and communal involvements emphasizing the social good, democratic possibilities are short circuited. Since democratic possibilities and some set of value commitments are essentially conjoined, as indicated earlier, the former are theoretically clouded and all but impossible to put into practice because of our inability to engage in authentic, meaningful moral discourse. It is not surprising that discussions of the possible role of educational institutions in fostering democracy have been accompanied by so much confusion. As a central thrust of alternative possibilities, it is crucial that we generate ideas that build new communal and moral practices.

Schooling and the Culture of Democracy

Communities and Moral Value

In contrast to the development of what Bellah *et al.* refer to as 'life-style enclaves' in which the manager and therapist take up an individualized residence (in their utilitarian and expressive guises, respectively) these authors pose the reestablishment of genuine com-munities — 'communities of memory':

> Communities, in the sense in which we are using the term, have
> a history — in an important sense they are constituted by their

past — and for this reason we can speak of a real community as a 'community of memory', one that does not forget its past.

The communities of memory that tie us to the past also turn us toward the future as communities of hope. They carry a context of meaning that can allow us to connect our aspirations for ourselves and those closest to us with the aspirations of a larger whole and see our own efforts as being, in part, contributions to a common good.[52]

One of the central functions of schooling, in helping rebuild those contexts within which discussions of democracy can be meaningfully instigated, must be the rebuilding of such communities of memory. At the same time, we must work to regain the authenticity of moral discourse and principles as they provide the grounding for the enactment of democratic participation.

These twin goals entail what I shall call the reconstitution of schooling for the culture of democracy. With the renunciation of authentic moral discourse, the abandonment of communities in favor of lifestyle enclaves, and the emergence of the cults of managerial competence and therapeutic adjustment, democratic ideas have been relegated to smaller and less meaningful realms of civic life. To a large extent the meaning of democracy has been reduced to pulling the appropriate levers of a voting machine on election day. And even this minimalist interpretation of what democracy means in social practice is being currently acted upon by something less than one-half of the eligible participants in the US. Two aspects of this situation are remarkable. First, what constitutes 'civic responsibility' and democratic involvement is becoming more and more narrowly circumscribed. The fact that some recent reports have concluded that a central problem of modern industrial nations is an excess of democratic participation perhaps epitomizes the conceptual confusion and ideological roadblocks surrounding the practice of democracy.[53] At the same time, second, the domain of participation has become increasingly restricted. As the cult of technical expertise has gained momentum in contemporary cultural and social life, the possibilities for active input and involvement in our daily work, recreation, and family lives have decreased. While the meaning of political democracy has been reduced, other social spaces for the enaction of participatory possibilities have been precluded.

In rebuilding a commitment to democracy as a cultural form, the notion of participation becomes a key. In order for democracy to be a living, viable force in modern society, people must be provided opportunities — in their daily actions and involvements — to engage in genuinely participatory ventures. As Carole Pateman has argued, 'for the operation of a democratic polity at national level, the necessary qualities in individuals can only be developed through the democratization of authority structures in all political systems'.[54] Democracy as participation in life decisions, institutional configurations, and daily activities points to the need to see our commitment to democracy as a cultural force — one that has legitimacy within a wide range of settings.

Pateman makes a distinction between full, partial, and pseudo-participation that is quite useful. Pseudo-participation occurs in those cases when people are provided the *feeling* of participation without the reality, usually accompanied by various stylistic or human relations devices offered to help us feel soothed or placated. This is reminiscent of the therapeutic ethos of lifestyle enclaves as characterized by Bellah *et al.* Partial participation results when people are able to offer input into a course of action, but there is a power differential affecting the ultimate resolution of the process. This is perhaps the typical mode of organization in work situations — even in those that purport to foster greater worker involvement. Full participation, on the other hand, is a 'process where each individual member of a decision-making body has equal power to determine the outcome of decisions'.[55] In working for democracy as a cultural form, it is the model of full participation that must guide our efforts.

It might be objected that such broadly defined participation is inconsistent with the development of communities of memory that emphasize tradition, collective consciousness, and principled action. For, it could be argued, to be 'democratic' implies giving equal weight to all points of view and disregarding traditions that are authoritative, resulting in intellectual relativism and social paralysis. Fully participatory democracy that emphasizes human agency on the basis of moral principles, certainly, is only possible within a context in which alternative, divergent perspectives may be articulated, expressed, and openly debated. Yet while allowing for the expression of divergent points of view, such a context must also include participants' challenging and defending their positions. In the process, judgments will necessarily be made about the range of alternative positions discussed, so that the possibility of enlightened action may be realized. Within these processes of expression, challenge, and defense of positions, the importance of communal traditions will be apparent, as tensions between stated positions and received traditions come to the fore. Such traditions are not to be uncritically superimposed, however. Rather, they are to be appropriated — as intimately connected with who we are as people, a culture, and a collective — reflectively, and examined and modified where necessary. Thus the development of authentic communities capable of genuine moral discourse implies neither the acceptance of all viewpoints as equally valid (thereby disallowing judgment as to their suitability as a basis for action within that community), not the potentially autocratic superimposition of traditions that are unreflectively internalized.

Within the context of education, the culture of democracy must include these elements: first, a commitment to moral discourse, and the development of moral principles, as guides for decision making and action; second, the building of communities of memory that provide the social and historical context within which such discourse can be realized; and third, the enactment of full participation in a variety of settings, allowing morally principled, participatory agency to blossom as the key to democracy. It is important to clarify the normative framework that ought to underly a conception of schooling that promotes the culture of democracy. It is also crucial that we at least begin the task of articulating guides to moral action within educational institutions.

Values for Schooling

Equality and autonomy, as well as democracy itself, embody central moral principles for the reconstruction of educational practice. These principles can guide the rejuvenation of educational inquiry and classroom life.

Three criteria were utilized to identify central, grounding moral principles. First, such principles must arise from on-going moral discourse without relation to class or status. This propels a second criterion, the consistency of these principles with a critical analysis of our cultural heritage. This heritage is not only a part of the most recent cultural history of the U.S., linked with such documents as the Declaration of Independence, the Constitution, and the like, but is a continuation of the Enlightenment Tradition in Western thought. This gives rise to a third criterion, the necessity of moral principles that are aligned with what Habermas has called an 'emancipatory' human interest.[56] What Habermas claims is that the basic human project since the Enlightment has been human emancipation from 'ideologically frozen relations of dependence'.[57] This necessitates the continued expansion and promulgation of moral principles that can promote emancipatory projects. How do equality, democracy, and autonomy satisfy the foregoing criteria?

Equality is perhaps the most contested of these principles. As deLone among others has pointed out, our current cultural definition of the concept is locked within the framework of equality of opportunity.[58] This social substitution of equal opportunity for equality is a substitution which is rejected in order to reclaim the moral strength of the principle of equality. The rejection of equal opportunity is based on the grounds that it is an historical substitution designed primarily to limit equality and justify disparities of wealth, income and power.[59] As such it violates the necessity of moral principles not being grounded in the rationale of narrow class interests. Further, abandoning equality for equal opportunity violates the very Enlightenment, human project. It suggests that we meet in communities not as equals, but rather as unequally entitled to social shares of status, wealth, and power. Equal opportunity is not a substitution for equality, it is in fact a repudiation of it.

What is meant by equality? First, this concept does not embrace the neoconservative notion of equality of results. Such a concept would only function well in a totalitarian state, where means and ends can be dictated, violating the second and third of the criteria for moral principles identified above. Rather, equality means nothing more, nor less, than it means when used as follows:

> We hold these truths to be self-evident: that all men are created equal, that they are endowed by their creator with certain unalienable rights, that among these are life, liberty, and the pursuit of happiness.

Taking the term 'men' in its generic sense, I agree with William Ryan's argument that the claim to equality means 'the right of access to resources as a necessary condition for equal rights to life, liberty, and the pursuit of happiness'.[60] Thus, equality means that as human beings, we all share equally in certain basic rights. To obtain these rights we must also equally share the physical, political, spiritual, and cultural resources that make such rights possible. 'If the idea of a right is to have concrete significance, it must be possible to exercise that right'.[61] To have a right to life means that we all have a right to food, shelter, clothing and other life sustaining necessities. A right to liberty assumes equal access to political resources that make the exercise of liberty significant in the forming of social governance. A right to pursue happiness assumes equal access to spiritual and cultural resources that enrich life and enhance human happiness.

It is only when we see equality in this sense, as the equality of access to our 'inalienable rights', that it fulfills the criteria of a central moral principle. This is because an understanding of equality fulfills the universality criteria by resting upon the grounds of applicability to all people without reference to position, status, age, or gender. The very notion of equality as so defined strikes at the heart of social privilege and differentiation. Finally, it is only in a universe of equal communicative power that human emancipation from myth and misery, and the possibility of dialogue and social action, can be contemplated. Such a universe is required to engage in the hermeneutic, political, and social activities that are the central concerns of this monograph. When we face one another as equals in terms of access we have the potential of being free — a concept further explained below with regard to autonomy — and thus being autonomous social and political actors. Equality is a central moral principle.

Protectionist democratic theory is based upon a concern for social efficiency and stability. Rather than embracing broad popular participation, limited participation through interest group formation is central. Such interest groups' actions are limited to choosing political elites to represent (protect) their interests, verifying their choices at each election. The absence of direct participation or widespread political engagement is justified by appeal to the alleged fact that the attitudes or capacities for self-government are simply not to be found in the public at large. Thus, such participation would be ill-formed and lead only to social chaos.

In opposition to such a protectionist understanding of democracy, an on-going movement to recapture the classical, participatory nature of democratic theory has arisen. Drawing from Rousseau, Mill, and Cole, this understanding of democracy embraces the broadest possible participation in direct public decision making, an understanding that is close to the sentiments of the pursuit of the culture of democracy discussed above. Democracy is seen as an evolving life-form in which participation leads to more participation through the development of personal political efficacy. Not a static model by any means, participatory democracy argues for expanding direct political decision-making at the local level, which would lead to expanded participation on the state and the national levels. In fact, evidence suggests that when participatory democracy is practiced in a manner consistent with its three fundamental conditions — political participants having equal access to requisite knowledge, being the actual makers of decisions, and having equal power — the political process becomes more efficient[62] and participants gain an enhanced sense of political efficacy.[63]

This participatory notion of democracy is invoked for more fundamental reasons than the empirical evidence, however. Participatory democracy is not dependent upon meeting the needs of any one class for its legitimacy. It embraces the needs of all cultural groups for political access without violating the needs of any similar group. Further, this sense of democracy holds us closer to the notion of democracy that was called upon in drafting our shared political conventions. Finally, if human emancipation is to be possible it necessitates a system of political organization that both empowers individuals and creates the psychological characteristics needed to utilize such power. Participatory democracy, as a form of evolving social life, opens up the possibility of human emancipation unbounded by class and consistent with our cultural heritage.

In defining human autonomy, the third proposed central moral principle, the assumption of individualism discussed above is expressly rejected. Such a notion of people as totally 'free' social agents has long since been discredited by Marx and others as has the notion of 'free' psychological agency by Freud. Freedom occurs, as Dewey and others have argued, within the context of human rules, social conventions, and psycho-sociological development.[64] In fact, it is only within limitations on what might be proposed as 'absolute' freedom that we find ourselves free to act within a social group. 'Communities of memory' foster freedom.

An emancipatory notion of autonomy implicates freedom in its strong or positive sense as opposed to its weak sense. The weak sense of freedom is cast as the individualistic 'freedom from restraint' perspective. Individuals are to be free to do those things of which they are capable or have the power to perform. This argument has recently been taken up by libertarians such as Robert Nozick in philosophy[65] and Joel Spring in education.[66] There is a wide array of formidable critiques of this position, exposing the often ahistorical notions of justice, political naivete, and confused logic it embodies.[67] For our purposes the most striking of these critiques is framed in the contradictory nature of the very claim for autonomy made. That is, freedom from restraint for one individual often depends upon the restraint of others. Nothing prevents someone in a superior position, by means of wealth or power (political or material) from limiting the autonomy of another through the sanctions of negative freedom. For example, the father of starving children might conceivably 'freely' sell himself into slavery to an individual with money or access to food. While nothing has occurred here to violate the 'freedom from restraint' principle, the autonomy of at least one of the two individuals is lost.

The notion of human autonomy advocated here is found in the positive or 'freedom to do' concept. The premise is that social structures should be designed so that individuals are both free from coercion or forces beyond their control and are empowered to take those actions which they believe will yield positive results. Each member of the social group is to be secure from forces that would limit his/her actions, be they economic, political, or social. Further, no member would have the right to impose an action upon another member of the social group. This implies certain social limits. Each individual is under restraint not to act in ways that will restrain or coerce another. And, the collectivity may decide that some social, political, or economic actions, say the forming of racial barriers, are not permissible in that these limit human autonomy.

Perhaps it is important to conclude this discussion of moral principles by pointing out their inter-relatedness and their heritage. As to the first, it is virtually impossible to imagine any of these principles operating independently of the other two. Each is a necessary, though not sufficient, condition for the others. This seems apparent when we consider the following questions: is it possible to conceive of truly autonomous individuals who are free from coercion and do not have equal access to economic, political, and cultural resources? Is autonomous human judgment meaningful in any context short of participatory democracy? Is democracy genuinely participatory if citizens do not function in an autonomous and equal manner? Does equality for equality's sake have any meaning or is it understood best as a means of self-determination? Is equality possible under any social structure which does not value autonomously participatory political action? The inter-relatedness of the moral principles of equality, democracy, and autonomy is demonstrated by the negative answer each of these queries necessitates.

One of the three criteria involved in identifying central moral principles was their necessary nature in relation to the advancement of human emancipation. This project has been overshadowed by the dominance of technical rationality, administrative competence, and therapeutic adjustment. Rejecting the commitment to critical reflection, the tradition of positivism and objectivism assumes that theory is removed from the world. Thus we are to do what we can do and all knowledge and political/social action takes on an instrumental sheen. As an example, workers are reduced to the mere nature of machines as they are 'retooled' for new demands of industry. Political discourse is abandoned in favor of absolute, value-free knowledge.

Such technical rationality indeed pervades schooling and has led to 'action guides' within education that are non-moral and anti-human. Since we 'can' measure some 'abilities,' the school is a center for sorting, classifying, and ultimately segregating students; knowledge becomes a commodity, the possession of which leads to high status positions. The very possibility of self-reflection is negated as the dogma of technical rationality is asserted. It is only when we place ourselves firmly within the traditions of community, hermeuentic understanding, and normative inquiry that education can be directed to the enhancement of the culture of democracy. Reflection on these matters can only operate effectively within educational practices consistent with the values of equality, democracy, and autonomy.

Moral Values and School Practice

Earlier in this chapter we noted that in order for people involved in critical inquiry in education to speak with other concerned educators in a variety of academic traditions it is necessary to establish a set of moral principles that both strengthen, and move us beyond, our critique. Three central moral values have been presented to help such a project. Now attention is turned to practicing those values by offering a tentative set of guides that can help generate our own programs and plans. Curricular recommendations are implied here as are some pedagogical and organizational ramifications for schooling. These enable us to act not in the name of one group of students but for all our children:

1   *Equal access to knowledge*: Primary to all the action-guides is this one, which insists upon the equal access by every student to school knowledge. Any curriculum which is designed to appropriate knowledge on the basis of class, sex, or race, or that has this as a consequence, is explicitly rejected. This does not merely mean that every child is to be exposed to the same lectures, tests, drills, etc. Rather, support mechanisms need to be created that assure all students will be able to enjoy

engagement with all forms of knowledge in the classroom. Only by doing so will we begin to approximate the goal of equal access; moreover, both participatory democracy and autonomy are founded upon individuals having the access to knowledge upon which personal and political actions are based. In addition, 'equal access to knowledge' must ensure that the forms of knowledge contained in school practice will not inculcate — as they often now do — messages and ideas that are politically biased and ideologically laden.[68]

2   *Images of human equality*: Much of what we now teach seems designed to celebrate human inequality. Certainly some strides have been made to eliminate sexual, racial and cultural stereotypes from educational materials. However, each of these steps has been undertaken with an eye toward equality of opportunity, not access. If the curriculum is to play a truly emancipatory role, the images it generates must be of our equal rights and what is necessary to obtain such rights.

3   *Critical consciousness*: Schooling is too often a laundry list of givens — facts to be memorized and restated. An emancipatory curriculum should focus on the nurturing of 'why?' questions in children. Children often ask 'why?' as soon as they recognize the word's meaning. On one hand, 'why' is just an interesting device to evoke repeated verbal comments from parents and teachers. Yet on a deeper level 'why' questions attempt to make sense of the world. 'Why' challenges all which went before, the very essence of our actions. The curriculum must be designed to nurture such questions — continually focusing on the rationale for our social relations.

4   *Self-Reflectivity*: As a complement to critical consciousness, emancipatory curricula must foster self-reflectivity. For the notion of human action, reflective practice is central. We are, argues Habermas, essentially reflective beings. Yet this reflectivity is too often abandoned to a technocratic rationality where decisions are based solely upon what 'works' as opposed to what we 'ought' to do. Assumptions such as these should be challenged and the primacy of human reflection restored. Reflection upon the human condition, one's own condition, and the consciousness/ideology of the age, should be encouraged.

5   *Creativity*: An emancipatory curriculum has to abandon the over-riding logic of right and wrong answers in favor of critique and the production of alternatives. If we are claiming to

assist children in becoming equal, autonomous, democratic decision-makers, we must realize, as Dewey did a half century ago, that the very problems they will face (let alone the answers to them) may not even be on the horizon. To attempt to teach students frozen bits of knowledge that will resolve these problems defies reason. What is needed is an embracing of their most creative and critical powers in the face of new problematics.

6   *Cultural acceptance*: A democratic culture demands cultural tolerance and acceptance. An emancipatory curriculum needs to locate the arts, both 'high' and 'popular', within our shared social lives.[69] This will help us see when culture merely reinforces dominant/subordinate social relations and when it genuinely serves to further a vision of human fulfillment.

7   *Moral responsibility*: Are we obliged to one another or merely to ourselves? Our technocratic, emotivist, and individualistic commitments infiltrate much of our schools' curriculum and are located in the latter assumptions. We are locked into a structure that leads us to believe that acting only in our own interests is the key to our freedom. In fact, we enslave ourselves to larger social forces by freeing ourselves of obligation to our neighbors. Emancipatory curricula will focus on a sense of shared social responsibility. Our obligations to one another, to the culture, are empowering forces of social transformation.

8   *Democratic empowerment*: The curriculum should be designed so as to give students an experience with self-government — thus leading to a belief that such action is both possible and useful. The curriculum should be organized in a manner that would increase every child's stock of cultural capital, in that the values, perspectives, and beliefs of students become respected and a source of dialogue (even when they are normally objectionable from our point of view). The knowledge that she/he is a member of a vital and worthwhile cultural tradition and as such has a right to act politically, needs to be encouraged. As well, alternatives to current social practices must be offered in order to demonstrate the possibly meaningful results of democratic action. This involves establishing possibilities in our classroom for genuine participation.

9   *A pedagogy of caring*[70]: Rather than the establishment of hierarchical, one sided, and often technicist and individuated social relations in classrooms, we need to understand the world from

the point of view of our students. This means coming to place ourselves within the perspective of those whom we teach, no matter how outlandish this perspective may seem. This does not entail sharing our students' presuppositions, of course, nor that we necessarily attempt to further them; critique, discussion, and dialogue are often transformative. Yet we do need to be able to accommodate other perceptions of events, even when (perhaps especially when) we do not share them.

This list of action guides is of necessity incomplete. It outlines some of the parameters of educational practices that are consistent with the moral imperatives of democracy, autonomy, and equality. To offer an elaborate plan of implementation that details all of the steps necessary to achieve our stated aims would be to violate the very emancipatory, empowering, hermeneutic project that is central. Thus many of the details of this approach must be worked out collaboratively with those teachers, students, parents, and others who are involved on a daily basis with classroom practice.[71] The usual impositional model of educational reform violates the spirit of the culture of democracy and the normative framework underlying it.

It is useful, however, in making the ideas and directions discussed here more meaningful, to look at one of our proposed action guides more fully. Consider, for purposes of illustration, the implications of 'cultural acceptance' as an action guide for altered educational activity.[72]

Consider the role of the arts in American society generally, and the domain of art and aesthetic education in schools in particular. While it is a truism to note that 'art' of one form or another has been universally prized by all societies, or that 'art' is itself an honorific label, these observations are worth keeping in mind, as they may reveal something essential about the domain of art. This approval of 'art' in the abstract is apparently a part of contemporary society as well. For we spend large amounts of time listening to, watching, and otherwise interacting with art forms.[73] Moreover, numerous business organizations in the US spend large sums of money in support of the arts, which are increasingly available to the public at large.[74] Television, film, literature, music, and painting seem especially available to greater numbers of people, at lower cost.

Yet there are important ambiguities here as well, which testify to the cultural differentiation and elitism that affect aesthetic appreciation. In 1978, the median income in the US was $14,476. Yet if we look at figures for art museum visitors, we find that their medium income was $18,000. For opera goers, the figure was $21,000. Further reinforcing the elitist nature of the 'high arts,' 80 per cent of those visiting art museums had attended college, those whose education did not go beyond high school comprised only 15 per cent of these visitors, and those who did not complete high school comprised only 5 per cent of this population.[75] There exists in US society a 'cultural elite', whose income, education, status, and leisure time make the 'proper' appreciation of the fine arts possible.

At the level of schooling, other ambiguities are evident. We often applaud art as the 'highest achievement of humankind' while dismissing it as a 'frill' in times of school budget cutbacks. Almost always art courses in secondary schools are elective, lacking the status of more 'intellectual' or 'academic' courses. At the elementary school level, 'art' is often associated with 'play', something to be allowed after 'work' has been completed. Even in primary grades, artistic activities are frequently valued for their instrumental value — in facilitating the development of fine motor skills, for instance. The relatively small amount of time and resources afforded art and aesthetic education further testifies to the contradictions inherent in our interaction with art in educational settings.

These social and educational ambivalences reflect the distinctions we have created between 'high' and 'popular' arts, and the value and significance of representative examples. The high arts tend to be perceived and appreciated by one class or segment of society, while the popular, craft, or folk arts are enjoyed by others. The result is a dual cultural formation, with distinctly different rewards for members.

If we take the culture of democracy seriously, such a dual system cannot be allowed to persist. Within educational settings, the distinction between the 'fine' and 'popular' arts must be dismissed. Works of art that are exhibited in galleries, performed in concert halls, and applauded at opera houses are not different in kind from the more popular forms that we often casually dismiss. We must include both kinds of art in classrooms, as we uncover the moral force of the artistic image.[76]

In addition, the separation of art in classrooms — as a frill or 'special', needs to be rejected. This entails not only the increased availability of courses in the arts, but a change in their orientation as well. Art courses currently tend to emphasize the performance or constructive nature of art — as exemplified in the creation of paintings, drawings, poetry, dramatic performances, and so on. While such creative ventures are obviously crucial for aesthetic education, it is equally important for students to develop appreciative and evaluative capacities with respect to the arts. Not only do the arts serve as a vehicle for the expression of one's own ideas, emotions, and perspectives, they also create opportunities for investigating the perspectives and values of others.

An important part of broadening the significance of the arts and overcoming our cultural dualism is tied to their communicative potential. While works of art can be regarded from a number of vantage points, it is their capacity to communicate a particular point of view, set of values, or perspective on the world that is most telling if we are to reveal their social and ethical connotations. Through a variety of symbolic arrangements, they communicate something to their audience that can enhance, modify, or transform the way we see and understand ourselves, others, and existing social arrangements. Paying attention to the communicative nature of aesthetic forms means, then, understanding how they make a statement about some aspect of our and others' lived experiences, and can serve to highlight their moral value.

Inasmuch as works of art provide a kind of communicative agency, their latent connection to our actions outside the aesthetic encounter must be emphasized in schools. It is crucial that students see the aesthetic image, social consciousness, and ethical conduct as conjoined. There are at least two possible avenues for this expanded perception. On the one hand, the aesthetic image can become a crystallized vision of what is true, good, or proper — a representation of society, personal relationships, or political practices in what is regarded as their proper light. Such visions offer alternative conceptions of what ought to be — conceptions that, in their illumination and insight, may prove existentially provocative. On the other hand, works of art can provide a critique of current situations and predicaments — a way of challenging the accepted order of things. Our students need encouragement to use aesthetic forms to illuminate or challenge a contemporary issue — the patterns of sexism, racism, or social class exclusion, for example; their visions of justice and fairness may become the framework for artistic ventures, exploring them with the insight provided by symbolic forms which the arts provide. Such activities would serve to propel educational activity beyond critique, toward alternative possibilities.

This revised conception of aesthetic education entails a withering of the divisions between the arts and other curricular areas. Not only do we need to infuse the arts with greater social and ethical significance, we need also to investigate the aesthetic components of the language arts, social studies, the humanities, and the natural sciences.[77] Integrating aesthetic expressions into the other curricular areas of schools is, of course, fraught with peril. For it is all too easy to regard the arts as an instrumentally useful tool with which to articulate preconceived ideas from the sciences and humanities — e.g., the occasional visual display of an abstracted idea or concept, the use of the arts as depicting central themes, etc. Instead of such instrumental uses of aesthetic forms, what I am urging is the development of our awareness of how scientific, social, and humanistic enterprises all have aesthetic components or aspects. For example, we might show how the patterns of geometric shapes in nature have both mathematical and aesthetic qualities; or how the development of historical trends is related to developments in the arts of a particular society. The basic notion here is to increase our understanding of how aesthetic, humanistic, and scientific matters are intertwined.

Much more could be said about the changes that are necessary in terms of promoting cultural acceptance. It should be clear that the changes outlined here would further the pursuit of the culture of democracy. In rejecting the division between 'fine' and 'popular' arts, we work against the elitism that this division fosters and reinforces. In urging that art become valued for its communicative potential, we are giving voice to its democratic value in promoting dialogue. In promoting art that encourages social and moral values, we are encouraging the meaning of art as praxis.

The moral principles and normative actions outlined here illustrate ways to move beyond the theories of social reproduction and resistance that have uncovered the ideological and political meanings of education. The ideas presented here indicate the contours of practices that generate alternative worlds. The implications of these ideas for teacher preparation are the subject of the following chapter.

Notes and References

1 B. PAUL KOMISAR and JAMES E. McCLELLAN, 'The logic of slogans' in *Language and Concepts in Education*, Edited by B. OTHANEL SMITH and ROBERT H. ENNIS (Chicago: Rand McNally & Company, 1961).

2 RAYMOND WILLIAMS, *Problems in Materialism and Culture* (London: Verso Editions and New Left Books, 1980).

3 I am indebted to Professor Philip H. Steedman for discussions of this and related issues. See his, 'Should Debbie do Shale?' *Educational Studies*, Volume 13, Number 2, Summer, 1982.

4 Examples of 'debates' of this sort are quite numerous. See, for example, PHILIP W. JACKSON, 'Curriculum and its discontents', invited address to

Division B of the American Educational Research Association, San Francisco, California, April, 1979; DANIEL TANNER and LAUREL N. TANNER, 'Emancipation from research: The reconceptualist prescription', *Educational Researcher*, Volume 8, Number 6, June 1979; BARRY FRANKLIN, 'Reply to Landon Beyer's "Ideology, Social Efficiency, and Curriculum Inquiry"', *Curriculum Inquiry*, Volume 13, Number 4, Winter, 1982; and PETER MCLAREN, 'Review article — Postmodernity and the death of politics: A Brazilian reprieve', *Educational Theory*, Volume 36, Number 4, Fall, 1986, especially p. 399, note 25.

5   LANDON E. BEYER, 'Ideology, social efficiency, and curriculum inquiry', *Curriculum Inquiry*, Volume 12, Number 3, Summer, 1982.

6   See LANDON E. BEYER, 'The parameters of educational inquiry', *Curriculum Inquiry*, Volume 16, Number 1, Spring, 1986; and chapter 3 above.

7   PAUL WILLIS, *Learning to Labour: How Working Class Kids Get Working Class Jobs* (Westmead, Farnborough, Hampshire, England: Gower Publishing Company Limited, 1980).

8   *Ibid.*, p. 121.

9   *Ibid.*, p. 122.

10 MICHAEL W. APPLE, 'Old humanists and new curricula: Politics and culture in *The Paideia Proposal*', *Curriculum Inquiry*, Volume 15, Number 1, Spring, 1985.

11 *Ibid.*, p. 98.

12 KENNETH A. SIROTNIK, 'What you see is what you get: Consistency, persistency, and mediocrity in classroom', *Harvard Educational Review* 53, number 1, February, 1983.

13 Apple, *op. cit.*, p. 98.

14 *Ibid.*, pp. 98–99.

15 *Ibid.*, p. 99.

16 SAMUEL BOWLES and HERBERT GINTIS, *Schooling in Capitalist America* (New York: Basic Books, 1976).

17 For an interesting, alternative analysis of this issue, see STANLEY ARONOWITZ, 'Academic freedom: A structural approach', *Educational Theory*, Volume 35, Number 1, Winter, 1985.

18 MARCUS SINGER, 'Moral skepticism', in ANTONY FLEW *et al.*, (Eds.) *Skepticism and Moral Principles* (Evanston, Illinois: New University Press, 1973).

19 KURT BAIER, *The Moral Point of View* (New York: Random House, 1965).

20 WILLIAM FRANKENA, 'The principles of morality', in ANTONY FLEW *et al.*, (Eds.) *op. cit.*, p. 53.

21 Baier, *op. cit.*, p. 96.

22 CARL WELLMAN, *Challenge and Response: Justification in Ethics* (Carbondale, Illinois: Southern Illinois University Press, 1971).

23 JoANNE PAGANO, 'The myth of cultural reproduction', presentation to the Sixth Annual Conference on Curriculum Theory and Practice, Dayton, Ohio, October, 1984.

24 Williams, *op. cit.*, pp. 238–239.

25 See, for example, GORDON C. LEE, (Ed.) *Crusade Against Ignorance: Thomas*

Jefferson on Education (New York: Teachers College Press, 1961); LAW-RENCE A. CREMIN, (Ed.) *The Republic and the School: Horace Mann on the Education of Free Men* (New York: Teachers College Press, 1957); and THE NATIONAL COMMISSION ON EXCELLENCE IN EDUCATION, *A Nation at Risk: The Imperative for Educational Reform* (Washington, DC; U.S. Government Printing Office, 1983).

26 Contemporary examples include desegregation efforts, a number of 'compensatory education' efforts such as Head Start, and more recently, the enlistment of schools in regaining lost economic and military ground. On this last point, see especially the National Commission on Excellence in Education, *op. cit.*

27 Consider this issue within the context of recent reform proposals. Again the National Commission on Excellence in Education provides an important parameter here. See also MORTIMER ADLER, *The Paideia Proposal* (New York: Macmillan Publishing Corporation, 1982), for an oppositional view of what democracy might entail. Other contrasts can be found in the series entitled, 'Educational reform: A dialogue', in *Curriculum Inquiry*, beginning with Volume 15, Number 1, for which I served as special editor.

28 See ALASDAIR MACINTYRE, *After Virtue: A Study in Moral Theory* (Notre Dame: University of Notre Dame Press, 1984).

29 See ROBERT N. BELLAH, RICHARD MADSEN, WILLIAM M. SULLIVAN, ANN SWIDLER, and STEVEN M. TIPTON, *Habits of the Heart* (Berkeley: University of California Press, 1985).

30 See CHRISTOPHER LASCH, *The Minimal Self: Psychic Survival in Troubled Times* (New York: W. W. Norton & Company, 1984); and BENJAMIN BARBER, 'A new language for the Left: Translating the conservative discourse', *Harper's Magazine*, November, 1985, pp. 47–52.

31 My colleague George H. Wood and I have been working in collaboration on these issues for the past few years. See, for example, our article, 'Critical inquiry and moral action in education', *Educational Theory*, Volume 36, Number 1, Winter, 1986; readers can also contact the Institute for Democratic Education at Ohio University, which Professor Wood has organized, and The Public Education Information Network in St. Louis, organized by Harold Berlak.

32 See BARBARA FINKELSTEIN, 'Thinking publicly about civic learning: An agenda for education reform in the '80s', in *Civic Learning for Teachers: Capstone for Educational Reform*, edited by ALAN H. JONES (Ann Arbor: Praken Publications, 1985). For an analysis of the relationship between technicism, education, and community, see MANFRED STANLEY, *The Technological Conscience: Survival and Dignity in an Age of Expertise* (New York: The Free Press, 1978), especially Part III, 'Toward the liberation of practical reason: The problem of countertechnicist social practice'. Also see LANDON E. BEYER, 'Beyond elitism and technicism: Teacher education as practical philosophy', *Journal of Teacher Education*, Volume XXXVII, Number 2, March–April, 1986.

33 Finkelstein, *op. cit.*, p. 15, emphasis added.

34 RICHARD L. MORRIL, 'Educating for democratic values', *Liberal Education*, Volume 68, 1982, p. 367.

35 In putting forward this conception of democracy, I realize that many issues have been neglected and alternative conceptions and disagreements overlooked. In particular, some may find this conception suitable for some situations or institutions, and illegitimate for others — for example, the family, the school, or the workplace. The fundamental epistemological question here is what status to provide the judgments, positions, and points of view of those involved in decision-making processes. The underlying fear often stated or implied is that democracy as broadly conceived as is the case here may devolve into epistemological relativism, emotivism, or anarchy. That this is not the case will be clearer in the discussions of the importance of moral principles and the notion of 'communities of memory'. Suffice it to say here that the culture of democracy mandates broad, value-based participation leading to action, but does not sanction any position, belief, or point of view; the exercise of judgment within communities must be brought to bear in ways that expose the injudicious, immoral, and unwise.

36 MacIntyre, *op. cit.*, p. 2.

37 For examples, see JONAS SOLTIS, (Ed.) *Philosophy and Education: Eightieth Yearbook of the National Society for the Study of Education* (Chicago: University of Chicago Press, 1981); and R. F. DEARDEN, *Theory and Practice in Education* (Boston: Routledge & Kegan Paul, 1984). More than other philosophers, however, Dearden is aware of some of the difficulties of ordinary language analysis I am pointing to here. See LANDON E. BEYER, 'The practice of philosophy', *The Review of Education*, Volume 11, Number 2, Spring 1985.

38 There are, of course, counter examples of this tendency toward ahistoricism. The recent success of *Roots* as a mass media production, the emphasis on local and oral history in some social studies programs, and the Foxfire and Highlander alternatives, provide some of the more well known exceptions to our dominant orientation. We have much to learn from such efforts.

39 There are many contradictions involved here. To cite one such irony, our fascination with the future is taking place at the same time that we are placing the survival of the human species and the planet itself in jeopardy. Our recent record in nuclear proliferation, contamination of ground water, destruction of wildlife habitat and numerous animal species, and a wide array of toxic waste and other pollution problems, provide disturbing evidence of our actual callousness toward the same future that we long for culturally.

40 Bellah *et. al.*, *op. cit.*, p. 65.

41 The classic essay on the subject of commodification of art is WALTER BENJAMIN, 'The work of art in the age of mechanical reproduction', in his book *Illuminations*, translated by Harry Zohn (New York: Schocken Books, 1969).

42 Lasch, *op. cit.*, p. 30. There are important issues of gender in how people

learn to see themselves through the eyes of others. See JOHN BERGER, *Ways of Seeing* (New York: Penguin Books, 1977).

43 Lasch, *The Minimal Self, op. cit.*, p. 38.
44 See *Ibid.*, Chapter III, 'The discourse on mass death: "Lessons" of the holocaust'.
45 Bellah *et al.*, *op. cit.*, p. 65.
46 *Ibid.*, p. 45.
47 See the discussion of feminist epistemology at the end of chapter 2 above.
47 Bellah *et al.*, *op. cit.*, p. 46.
49 *Ibid.*, p. 47.
50 *Ibid.*, p. 47.
51 For a similarly psychologized view of art, see DAVID BLEICH, *Subjective Criticism* (Baltimore: The Johns Hopkins University Press, 1978).
52 Bellah *et al.*, *op. cit.*, p. 153.
53 See MICHAEL J. CROZIER, SAMUEL P. HUNTINGTON, and JOJI WATANUKI, *The Crisis of Democracy: Report on the Governability of Democracies to the Trilateral Commission* (New York: New York University Press, 1975).
54 CAROLE PATEMAN, *Participation and Democratic Theory* (New York: Cambridge University Press, 1970), p. 35.
55 *Ibid.*, p. 71.
56 JURGEN HABERMAS, *Knowledge and Human Interests*, translated by Jeremy J. Shapiro (Boston: Beacon Press, 1971).
57 *Ibid.*, p. 310.
58 RICHARD DeLONE, *Small Futures* (New York: Harcourt, Brace, Jovanovich, 1979).
59 See WILLIAM RYAN, *Equality* (New York: Vintage Books, 1981).
60 *Ibid.*, p. 8.
61 *Ibid.*, p. 8.
62 See ARTHUR WIRTH, *Productive Work — In Industry and Schools: Becoming Persons Again* (New York: University Press of America, 1983).
63 See G.A. ALMOND and S. VERBA, *The Civic Culture* (Boston: Little, Brown, 1945); MARTIN CARNOY and DEREK SHEARER *Workplace Democracy: The Challenge of the 1980's* (White Plains, NY: M.E. Sharpe, 1980); Wirth, *op. cit.*
64 See JOHN DEWEY, *Experience and Education* (New York: Collier Books, 1938), especially Chapters 4 and 5.
65 ROBERT NOZICK, *Anarchy, State, and Utopia* (New York: Basic Books, 1974).
66 JOEL SPRING, *The Sorting Machine* (New York: David McKay, 1976); and *Educating the Worker-Citizen: The Social Economic and Political Foundations of Education* (New York: Longman, 1980).
67 See JEFFREY PAUL, (Ed.), *Reading Nozick* (Totowa, N.J.: Rowman and Littlefield, 1981); and GEORGE H. WOOD, 'The theoretical and political limitations of deschooling', *The Journal of Education*, Volume 164, Number 4, Fall, 1982.
68 See MICHAEL W. APPLE and LOIS WEIS, (Eds.), *Ideology and Practice in Schooling* (Philadelphia: Temple University Press, 1983); GEOFF WHITTY

and MICHAEL YOUNG, (Eds.) *Explorations in the Politics of School Knowledge* (Nafferton, Driffield, England: Nafferton Books, 1976); and the discussion in chapter 3 above.

69   LANDON E. BEYER, 'Art and society: Toward alternative directions in aesthetic education', *The Journal of Curriculum Theorizing*, Vol. 7, No. 2, 1987.

70   NEL NODDINGS, *Caring: A Feminine Approach to Ethics and Moral Education* (Berkeley: University of California Press, 1984).

71   LANDON E. BEYER and MICHAEL W. APPLE, (Eds.) *The Curriculum: Problems, Politics, and Possibilities* (Albany, New York: State University of New York Press, in press).

72   I have discussed the issues outlined here in more detail in Landon E. Beyer, 'Art and society,' *op. cit.*

73   Following are figures listed in *The National Income and Product Accounts of the United Stated, 1929–76*, Table 2.4, 'Personal Consumption Expenditures by Type of Expenditure: Annually, 1929–76.' For 'Books and maps', figures for selected years are as follows (in millions of dollars): 1950: 674; 1960: 1,139; 1970: 2,903; and 1976 (the most recent year for which data are available): 3,866. For 'Radio and television receivers, records and musical instruments', the figures are: 1950: 2,421; 1960: 3,003; 1970: 8,436; and 1976: 15,631. For 'admissions to legitimate theatres and opera, and entertainments of nonprofit institutions (except athletics)', the figures are: 1950: 183; 1960: 342; 1970: 501; and 1976: 777. Interestingly, these figures are listed under the heading 'Recreation'.

74   Corporate contributions to 'Culture and Art' productions for 1983 (the latest year for which information has been compiled) were $145.2 million, or 11.4% of total corporate giving. Dollar figures and percentages of the total for previous years were: 1982: $145.8 million, 11.4%; 1981: $139.6 million, 11%; 1980: $108.7 million, 10.9%. See *Annual Survey of Corporate Contributions, 1985 Edition* (New York: The Conference Board, Inc.).

75   LAURA H. CHAPMAN, *Instant Art, Instant Culture: The Unspoken Policy for American Schools* (New York: Teachers College Press, 1982), pp. 171–172.

76   See Beyer, 'Art and society,' *op. cit.*; and LANDON E. BEYER, 'Aesthetic experience for teacher education and social change', *Educational Theory*, Volume 35, Number 4, Fall, 1985.

77   See, for example, ELLIOT W. EISNER, (Ed.) *Reading, the Arts, and the Creation of Meaning* (Washington: National Art Education Association, 1978); PETER ABBS, *English Within the Arts* (Toronto: Hodder and Stoughton, 1982); MASHA KABAKOW RUDMAN, *Children's Literature: An Issues Approach* (Toronto: D.C. Heath and Company, 1976).

5
Beyond Training: Teacher Education as Praxis

The vision of teacher preparation developed here emerges from ideas and issues discussed in the preceding chapters. The central themes of these chapters will be synthesized in articulating an alternative view of the appropriate ways to educate future teachers, and to counteract some of the current proposals for the reform of teacher preparation.

This synthesis will include a discussion of the major ideas and perspectives that constitute an advocacy for teacher preparation based on the unity of theory and practice, an understanding of the social and ideological role of schooling, and the need for a normative framework that, in emphasizing social and moral values, will alter both the internal dynamics of schooling and the larger social world to which they contribute. We will flesh out this conception of teacher preparation, and discuss the policy and programmatic emphases in teacher preparation these ideas entail. The final chapter will include a discussion of attempts to develop and implement specific programs of teacher preparation based on the ideas developed in this and earlier chapters. It will detail the challenges and possibilities of the ideas and policies advanced as well as some of the practical, institutional, and procedural difficulties that attend their enactment. Having begun with the problem of how to reconcile theory and practice in education, we end with a discussion of policies and programs that take the central activity in teacher preparation to be based on praxis. Of course there are a number of problems to be faced in implementing such a program. Yet such difficulties can no longer be seen — in keeping with the spirit and substance of this volume — as merely 'problems of practice'.

The Nature of Teacher Preparation

The most applied wing of educational studies, teacher preparation is often thought to consist in vocational preparation, where 'neophytes' are inducted into a profession with standards, activities, norms, and cultural attributes that need to be internalized and acted upon. The proper course of study for such professionals is one that emphasizes the attainment of both appropriate types of knowledge, skills, and techniques, on the one hand, and various forms of demeanor, dispositional tendencies, and what we might loosely call 'style', on the other. The curriculum is, accordingly, weighed heavily toward the provision of courses that inform students of these techniques and skills, experiences that highlight the proper dispositional and cultural attributes, and evaluations that attest to the competence or 'fitness' of the neophyte as an aspiring professional. A variety of 'methods and materials' courses (especially at the elementary level), courses in behavioral psychology emphasizing the practical need for classroom management and control together with developmental theories of human growth, experiences in classrooms before and as a part of student teaching that foster professional socialization, and a clear separation between 'general' and 'professional' education are crucial aspects of this course of study. Teacher preparation programs are somewhat isolated, as a result, within institutions of higher education.

It is no wonder that liberal arts advocates have often been so adamant in their rejection of educational programs thus conceived. Driven by rather immediate concerns and convictions about professional standards, competencies, and techniques, teacher training emphasizes the practical, the applied, and the illiberal.[1] Its aims arise not from the demands of inquiry and scholarship, but rather from the perceived needs of a profession whose interests lie outside those of the academy. The point is not to encourage scholarly inquiry but to train professionals to meet the challenges that await them.

This vision of teacher preparation as technical and vocational training is not tenable. It misconstrues the role of professionals as people who make decisions on the basis of technical rationality and what we have in our culture largely construed as 'problem solving'.[2] Teachers must not be reduced to technicians whose commitment is to competence, isolated proficiency, and the skillful manipulation of means and ends. There are at least three general reasons for rejecting this technicist view of teaching and of teacher training to which it leads. First, it overlooks the complexity of actual classroom experience. The teacher is simply not in a position, most of the time, to articulate a 'scientific' rule that fits the immediate situation at hand, deduce the appropriate ideas that follow from it, and apply them in an orderly, consistent, 'rational' way. By the time such a procedure is concluded, the situation that gave rise to the need for a response may well have evaporated — replaced by new situations and problems that just as urgently require a response. The immediacy and complexity of classroom life undermine the possibility of technical rationality as a dominant force in the fluid, dynamic environments that classrooms exemplify.

Second, teacher preparation as vocational training actually curtails possible growth and development for teachers. Such an approach, following Dewey, is 'miseducative', as it tends not to lead to experimentation, further inquiry, and growth-promoting experience.[3] Consider what happens, for instance, when technically oriented methods courses are a dominant aspect of teacher training. At their most technical, such courses offer students a 'tricks of the trade' list of guidelines with which they can make practical choices (e.g.,'10 "handy hints" for teaching addition to 7-year-olds'), anecdotal accounts of 'real life' in schools, and procedures to introduce, implement, and follow up on lessons — keeping in mind, of course, the 'ages and stages' of the pupils involved. As such guidelines and patterns become stylized through repetition and reinforcement, fostering a technical view of teaching, the beginning teacher finds it understandably difficult to respond meaningfully to novel or unanticipated classroom events. As problems are categorized and dealt with in standardized or routinized ways, other interpretations of a problematic situation are obscured, as are possible alternative responses. Teaching then becomes more and more deskilled, with fewer opportunities for autonomy and creative engagement with students, ideas, and materials. More committed to standardization of outcomes and activities, and to formalized, ready-made procedures, the opportunities for personal fulfillment and meaning through teaching dwindle as technicism prevails. The 'proletarianization' of teaching — and, at the same time, the gender relations and realities of domination they support — diminish the act of teaching and its value for students and teachers.[4] What is commonly referred to as 'teacher burnout' tends to be misperceived as something that may be rectified solely through the provision of merit salary increments, career ladders, greater incentives for entry into teaching, and improvements in the professional status of teachers.[5] Efforts to combat the problem of why so many teachers leave the arena of teaching must address the gender, political, and ideological pressures that shape teaching and schooling. Technicism and vocationalism in teacher preparation fail to address and thus ultimately strengthen the patriarchal control that exists in schools, narrowly constraining what teaching is and stunting its value; as well, technicism avoids a critical view of schooling.[6]

This leads to the third reason for rejecting a technical and vocational approach to teacher preparation. As we have seen, the domain of education is hardly neutral. Some of the most commonplace, seemingly innocent activities of classrooms — from segregating students by 'ability' to discussing US Presidents in high school history to 'individualizing' the curriculum in elementary schools — promote political and ideological interests that must be challenged and overcome. Yet in taking an uncritical, apolitical, 'neutral' view of such commonplace activities — in seeing political and ideological questions as irrelevant to the concerns of future teachers and extraneous distractions to programs that prepare them for work in schools — we tacitly encourage and transmit the values that lie behind them (such as the 'legitimacy' of inequality and the marginality of work by women, Blacks, and Native Americans). In confining teacher preparation to a technical domain, the role of schools in promoting social and cultural reproduction is actually aided, in the process cutting short the possibilities of more democratic school practice and social transformation. As technicist approaches to teacher preparation avoid critical engagement with large issues, they tacitly support the political and ideological interests schools tend to promote.

For persuasive personal, institutional, and political reasons, teacher preparation must be more than a technical and vocational domain. This is not to deny the importance of education as involving 'practice', but to argue for an expanded view of what meaningful practice entails.

At the same time, a rejection of teacher training should not lead us to an embrace of liberal inquiry, as normally conceived. As we have seen, the traditions of positivism and their incorporation into theories of knowledge arrived at through the 'structure of disciplines' in higher education have led us to value allegedly objective, value-free, rational, and decontextualized forms of inquiry. Reciprocally reinforcing perspectives from capitalist, masculine, and bureaucratic institutions and practices have also infiltrated the contemporary view of liberal study. It has kept hidden its own social, ideological, and gender affinities, while serving as a gatekeeper for 'respectable' scholarship — in the process excluding issues and people whose perspectives undermine its own presuppositions. Liberal inquiry could thus serve a regulatory, norm-ative, and self-affirming purpose, under the guise of neutrality and certainty. In rejecting vocationalism and technicism as guides for teacher preparation, we must not fall back on images of knowledge and scholarship that rely on traditions of rationality and objectivity that cannot withstand philosophical and moral scrutiny.

In rejecting both the view of teacher preparation as vocational and technical training and the view of liberal inquiry as committed to the attainment of objective, value free knowledge, I am not proposing some 'middle ground' between them that escapes their shortcomings; it is not clear that there is any such middle ground nor how it could be constructed. Likewise, I am not rejecting all the attributes and orient-ations of these views in saying we must transcend them. Rather, I am suggesting that the dichotomization between liberal and applied study, theory and practice, is itself the result of epistemological, political, and institutional pressures and patterns that we must transcend; this pattern of producing polar opposites has led us to assume that we must choose between the linearity of training and the abstractions of 'pure inquiry'. Yet 'knowledge' and 'inquiry' must become phenomena we prize and attend to not because they lead us closer to an abstracted, asocial, and largely manipulated Truth, but because they permit us to become people who are morally just, to live in worlds that are decent, aesthetically pleasing, and robust, to interact with others in the elimination of inequalities and toward personal and social fulfillment, and to construct realities that emphasize caring, democratic partici-pation as a cultural form, and moral and social responsibility. Neither is the domain of action to be commended for its exclusion of reflection and introspection, but cherished for the opportunity to enact those very processes that point us toward the aims listed above. If action without thought is blind, thought without action is empty. Reconceiving educational studies and teacher preparation must begin with a realiz-ation that either of these without the other is incomplete. Each fully exists only in conjunction with the other, as a whole that eclipses each in isolation.[7]

Education as a field of study, hence, is advantaged in some important ways. Unlike other disciplines, the questions addressed by educators are at some level prompted by a concern with the predica-ments of flesh and blood people, and the actions that are appropriate within a social and moral context. Unable to content ourselves with the delights of 'pure' discovery and analysis, those concerned with educa-tional matters embody a 'field of play' as part of our identity. At the same time, those committed to liberal inquiry hold values and orientations that can enlarge the domain of educational practice: a capacity and proclivity toward careful introspection, reflection, and sustained analysis, and a general commitment to ideas, are central for the thoughtful, engaged actor.

There is another important way in which education as a field is advantaged in comparison with other disciplines. With the growing movement toward specialization of academic study, the tendency for areas of inquiry to become more and more isolated and esoteric — separated from the ideas and insights of other domains — is intensified. We find it harder to talk with scholars outside our own rather limited range (if not depth) of expertise, more 'hemmed in' by the perceptions, values, and assumptions shared by those within our specialty. If the 'structure of the disciplines' is only a modern myth promoted and sustained by positivistic pretensions, and if the separation of institutions of higher education into divisions and departments is only an administrative, bureaucratic convenience, we will need to amplify precisely those areas that are most synoptic, integrative, and multi-dimensional. While Jacob Bronowski's view that all great advances in philosophy came from people who were not professional philosophers may be a bit overstated, the general point is worth emphasizing.[8] Often advances in a field — new intellectual discoveries, solutions to anomalies, the solving of seemingly intractable puzzles — occur when multi-disciplinary 'cross-fertilization' gives birth to a new hybrid.[9] Education is synthetic and open textured in this way. It integrates ideas and methods from a variety of fields. Educational analysis frequently incorporates and blends the work of historians, philosophers, psychologists, sociologists, artists, and others, in the course of clarifying an issue or action. As such, educational inquiry transcends not the concrete of time and place, but the limitations of more specialized, isolated domains, suggesting an inter-disciplinary approach to knowledge and action.

Teacher preparation must combine these advantages as it embodies both theoretical and practical work, integrating areas of inquiry that do not rely on a specious 'structure of the disciplines' but instead regard knowing and acting as homologous. Such a view of educational studies and teacher preparation has much to commend it as it moves away from the elitist, removed, masculine forms of inquiry we have inherited from modern conventions in philosophy, the natural sciences, and social science; and as it goes beyond efforts in teacher training.

We might summarize these comments by saying that this approach to teacher preparation sees it as a species of 'practical wisdom', affiliated with the Aristotelian notion of 'phronesis'.[10] As William M. Sullivan has recently recounted the heritage of this idea:

> one does not, indeed, cannot 'rest' from applying one's sensitivities about how to live ... a person is who he or she is only through exhibiting a kind of practical understanding and skill. Practical knowledge forms the personality of its practitioner and so is inseparable from his [/her] identity. Aristotle concluded from this that the possibility of coming to understand a form of cultural life requires competence in moving within that life. Practical involvement is the precondition for reflective clarification, which in turn plays its role in deepening the person's comprehension of how to live his [/her] life.[11]

Because certainty, theory- and value-free description, and discipline-based pronouncements of truth are no longer supportable, what we are left with is the proliferation of communities within which conversations that lead to understanding take place, arguments are mounted and challenged, moral actions are debated and undertaken, and character formed. To be a member of such a community, we must develop the sort of 'ethical know-how' discussed by Aristotle.

In Book VI of *The Nicomachean Ethics*, he clarifies the search for purely intellectual truth and how this differs from practical wisdom where judgments need to be made about courses of action. Unlike lower animals that only utilize sensations in making *movements*, people are capable of exercising reason and desire in ways that lead to right *action* and virtue. Becoming morally virtuous, Aristotle says, involves combining reason and desire in the making of choices about practical actions:

> ... this kind of intellect and of truth is practical ... [in the mind that is both practical and intellectual] the good state is truth in agreement with right desire.
>
> The origin of action ... is choice, and that of choice is desire and reasoning with a view to an end ... good action and its opposite cannot exist without a combination of intellect and character.[12]

While reasoning is clearly central in Aristotle's account of action, as a central part of what makes us human, it is reason and desire leading to moral choice that is to be facilitated. This conjunction of reason and desire emanates in practical wisdom, leading to virtue.

Rather than searching for absolute truths, participants in activities encouraging practical wisdom ground knowledge within the community of actors. In the last instance, it is those actions of people that are made possible, rather than the assimilation of allegedly universal truth, that has epistemological precedence. In essence, phronesis emphasizes the practices of people embedded in interpretive communities. In rejecting the traditions of positivism, more contemporary versions of practical wisdom see ethical and political debate as central to such communities. The crucial question becomes what kind of world we ought to construct with our fellow human beings — hence the centrality of ethical and political understanding.

In some ways this view of practical wisdom is allied with the conception of the university as an association of scholars committed to questions of the general, social good. Yet three distinctions are important: (i) practical wisdom has a pointedly democratic, anti-elitist orientation — the aim of establishing interpretive communities is to foster dialogue and understanding among all members of society and to consider vastly discrepant points of view; (ii) consistent with the collapse of positivism, disciplinary boundaries, and differences in status among them, tend to dissipate; and (iii) the isolation of scholastic studies is abandoned as real actions within existing institutions and communities are highlighted.

Unlike other areas, education contains both communities (and divergent ones at that) and an emphasis on practical wisdom. Education by its very nature involves dialogue, interpretation, a commitment to understanding, and the exercise of judgment. As opposed to other disciplines, education has inherent tendencies that are conducive to the development of practical wisdom. Yet too close an identification with current or accepted practice, especially through technical approaches to teacher preparation where the school becomes the site for determining acceptable practice, violates the emphasis on virtue, deepened understanding, and communication over desirable aims that are central to practical wisdom.

Teacher preparation as practical wisdom, synthesizing knowledge and action, has important implications for the current clamor for reform. As we have seen, many proposals advocate an extension of time for teacher preparation, so that a fifth or sixth year would be required for certification.[13] Usually such proposals are accompanied by pleas to expand the number of courses in liberal education, whose knowledge and structure can then be applied to problems of teaching. Assumed in these discussions is that 'professional education' courses are unlike those in general or liberal education, and must await the completion of the latter before they may be commenced. Another consequence of such views — especially clear in the writings of The Holmes Group — is that 'education' is not a legitimate academic major; since it lacks a liberal orientation and is concerned only with the application of genuine knowledge, it is not a bona fide member of the undergraduate curriculum. Both these assertions are faulty, in view of the arguments and ideas presented here. Education as a field of study may indeed be seen as a partner in liberal studies — indeed one that goes beyond the pretentions and illusions of traditional liberal inquiry.

A foundationally oriented approach to teacher preparation contradicts many reform proposals in yet another way. One of the aims of these proposals is to elevate the status and prestige of teacher preparation, and the position of teachers as well. To accomplish this, several groups have been addressing the problem of how to identify an appropriate 'knowledge base' for education that will authenticate its status as a profession. Most notable in these attempts is The Holmes Group, who reassures us that 'the science of education promised by Dewey, Thorndike, and others ...' will be accomplished through the efforts of researchers to employ the 'behavioral sciences' in schools.[14] Several ideas contained in these proposals are worth pondering.

The conflation of the work of Dewey with that of Thorndike in pursuing a 'science of education' is curious. While there are some similarities between these two people, their views on education and teaching are hardly compatible, for the most part. Even to assume that Thorndike and Dewey meant at all the same thing by a 'science of education' is implausible. More importantly, the search for a *science* of education is misguided. There are two principal reasons for this. First, the critique of positivism and its consequences for social and human studies presented in chapter 2 makes an allegiance to generating a science of education wrong headed. The privileged epistemological and ontological status afforded the ideology of scientism in our culture simply cannot be justified. Thus it is of little value to insist on the articulation of such a science, for even if we were to locate one, it would hardly put us in any more secure position, or elevate the status of education as a field. It is ironic that The Holmes Group is advocating such a pursuit at the same time that recent critical investigations into science have overturned its privileged status.

Second, basing our field on a science of behavioral psychology is, obviously, hardly a new idea. There are many objections one could bring to bear on this recurring suggestion, though some are especially relevant to the notion of teacher education advanced in this volume. At the turn of the century, there were attempts made by many academics to save the notion of 'community' from the threat of immigrants and others who were culturally and politically different. These 'scholars':

> viewed the immigrants as a threat to American civilization until they came 'to think about, and act on, political, social, economic, sanitary, and other matters in the approved American way'. ... Edward L. Thorndike ... viewed Blacks in the same way ... He not only doubted their ability to adjust to democratic institutions, but he saw them as an undesirable element within the population of most American cities. [15]

Within schools, the response to such 'undesirable elements' was to emphasize the ideology of genetic meritocracy, and a system of curriculum differentiation and individualization that would Americanize the immigrants, segregate minority populations, and socialize the working class. Socially, such educational processes confirmed cultural and racial prejudices at the same time that they justified inequalities. Nor should we forget the racist views of Edward L. Thorndike specifically, and his involvement in the eugenics movement earlier in this century. [16]

More generally, we need to remember that the field of educational psychology Thorndike helped form has led educators to construct elaborate systems fostering managerial control and measurement of 'learning outcomes' in schools and, as in the case of the testing movement, social control through education. It thus has served to promote forms of social reproduction that need to be overturned as we initiate programs of teacher education built on a commitment to equality, democracy, and autonomy, and that utilize practical wisdom in the pursuit of an empowering praxis. A behaviorist science of education is one of the least desirable and legitimate bases for teacher preparation.

Third, a 'science of education' of whatever orientation (behaviorist, Deweyan, or other) may have eluded us since proposed at the turn of the century for a quite substantial reason — namely, that education and teaching can not be reduced to 'scientific' endeavors in any important sense. Understanding education, being adept at the craft of teaching, is not aided by thinking about them as scientific enterprises (even if 'science' no longer has a special epistemological status, and even if we embrace forms of it that are less manipulative than behaviorism). Teaching is much closer to political, deliberative/interpretive, moral, and aesthetic acts. [17] Attempts to make schools more 'scientific' or 'rational' serve only to flatten the human, social, and intellectual dramas that unfold there. Far from assisting in the elevation of teacher preparation, holding out for a 'science of education' seems to draw on precisely the wrong traditions at a time when they are being dismantled, and to misperceive the nature of educational inquiry and the practice of teaching.

One of the confusions that needs to be addressed is the assumption that both teacher preparation and educational studies generally are narrowly concerned with problems of schooling (especially teaching and learning) in their present forms. This seems to be implied in many of the current proposals for reform in teacher preparation. Yet the distinction between 'education' and 'schooling' and their relationship to 'teacher preparation' need to be carefully analyzed, lest we assume that schools are only educational institutions devoted to 'learning' (in addition to, or combined with, political, economic, and cultural centers that carry ideological meanings); and to prevent us from simply assuming that the aim of teacher preparation is the maintenance of current realities of schooling. Issues and ideas in education are much broader than the domain of schooling per se, though the former are often crucial for understanding the dynamics and possibilities of teaching. An illustration will clarify the relationships involved among educational studies, schooling, and teacher preparation.

The critical perspective in educational studies, in rejecting the functionalism of some research, has begun to argue for the articulation of alternative possibilities that reverse the tendencies toward social reproduction through schooling. They highlight the political nature of the choices that confront teachers and others in our day to day work lives. Consider, as a concrete case in point, the perspective we take on historical events and ideas in secondary schools. Frequently the names of people (mostly men), places, dates, events (mostly related to wars and other conflicts) are presented for students to memorize, with unit tests and semester exams given to evaluate students' acquisition of this 'factual' material. Textbooks are the central curricular focus, with chapters often organized chronologically. Pedagogical relationships follow from this curriculum, with the textbook and the teacher (who in some way authorizes the text) controlling interactions that lead to rather one-dimensional, passive, uninterested responses from students.[18] Several things are worth noting about this situation. The content of history texts, on critical examination, often reveals ideologically based emphases and exclusions, reflecting larger patterns of inequality — especially by gender, race, social class, and ethnicity.[19]

The pedagogy of this approach to the study of history reinforces the habits of passivity, dependence on authority, and half-heated involvement for students that typify much of the hidden curriculum of schooling. The reliance on 'objective testing' — multiple choice exams, evaluation of straightforward recall ability, 'essay questions' that ask for little more than a summary of the dates and people covered in the text — restrict our view of the importance of history at the same time it is provided legitimacy through an identification with positivistic emphases on quantification, objectivity, and certainty. The approach to history sketched here views the past only as a succession of people and events that have little or no contemporary relevance or meaning. Historical phenomena become indicators of a process of development that seems extra-social and impersonal, negating the view of history as part of the present, actively constructed by people who have struggled to shape and reshape the world in particular ways.

Consider an alternative view of history for secondary schools. We might, instead of the above scenario, teach our students about the important contributions made by women, Blacks, Hispanics, Native Americans, Asian Americans, and others, in the formation of contemporary US society. Instead of disregarding the efforts of such people, we might highlight their struggles against dominant interests and groups who felt their position threatened, celebrating their actions and victories; at the same time, we could help our students reflect on the dynamics of power that have resulted in oppression, enslavement, and denial of fulfillment for many. Along with this, we might encourage high school students to become actively involved in historical projects and research related to a topic or issue of personal significance. Such projects could be shared by students and engaged in cooperatively, with the teacher participating as a joint collaborator. Activities could be presented to the rest of the class, with evaluation taking a different orientation — e.g., the extent to which students were able to cooperatively engage with a topic, to connect past, present, and future, and to discover the 'hidden realities' of history.

To the extent that teacher training is concerned only with a technical understanding of the current realities of schooling, we might expect proponents to advocate the former view of secondary school history, as it is functionally related to current classroom practice in a number of cases — though many teachers work hard to put together curricula more closely resembling the second scenario. Preparing future teachers would then proceed in such a way as to promote the development of 'professionals' who could take over the teaching of history in this form. On the other hand, the more critically oriented landscape of history sketched as an alternative would necessitate the redefinition of teaching and teacher training, even though there may be a tension between this landscape and the current domain of schooling for many. Pursuing forms of education and teacher preparation that are oriented toward extant patterns of schooling is to accept those patterns as they exist, marginalizing educational inquiry and prohibiting an approach to teacher education as praxis.

This points toward a major claim about the nature of teacher education as this is advocated here. The aim of such programs is not to 'train professionals' who will only be competent to take over the demands of teaching as these are currently defined and enacted. Rather, teacher education must be committed to the development of critically oriented, compassionate and impassioned, reflective and socially engaged practitioners who can aid in the process of educational improvement and social change; the encouragement of critical reflection on our own situations and those of our students, our futures, and our social possibilities, that leads to actions favoring empowerment of teachers and a commitment to democracy, equality, and autonomy. A part of this idea is captured in Dewey's discussion of the relation between theory and practice, and the role of teacher preparation; institutions responsible for such programs, Dewey tells us:

> do not perform their full duty in accepting and conforming to present educational standards ... educational leadership is an indispensable part of their office. The thing needful is improvement of education, not simply by turning out teachers who can do better the things that are now necessary to do, but rather by changing the conception of what constitutes education. [20]

Beyond this, prospective teachers must see work in classrooms and issues of social justice as part of the same phenomena. Since school practice cannot be separated from larger social, political, and ideological realities, they must be reflective about the full range of consequences of their actions. [21]

One of the conventional categories of educational studies is helpful in refining the role of praxis in teacher education. Courses in the foundations of education emphasize the importance of critique and reflection, and are thus important programmatic components of teacher education.

Against Technicism: The Role of Educational Foundations

One caution must be noted about the role of 'educational foundations' in teacher education. We discussed in chapter 2 the ways in which the dominant traditions in epistemology are misguided, and need to be abandoned in favor of a more contextualized, hermeneutic, feminist, and interactive view of knowledge. The view of epistemology — and of the natural sciences and philosophy — as 'foundational' in the sense of providing avenues to certain, value-free, objective truth that transcends personal, social, and historical processes was accordingly rejected. Foundationalism in epistemology is a rather different matter from pursuits in the foundations of education, however. The rejection of positivism and its foundational claims regarding knowledge should not be confused with the 'foundations' of education, as the latter do not make claims regarding the status and value of knowledge generally.

There is a sense, however, in which educational foundations are often considered basic or fundamental in teacher preparation. Conventionally thought of as dealing with the history, philosophy, sociology, and psychology of education, courses in the foundations of education precede other areas of study in education, and provide some sort of base on which more specific practices and investigations can be built. While they do not claim to validate transcendent, grounding principles for knowledge (either inside or outside of education), they do claim to provide a basis for further study. And even this more modest claim is frequently the source of problems. For once the largely theoretical work of the foundations is complete, the 'practical,' more detailed work of curriculum development, pedagogical decision making, and classroom evaluation may be regarded as superceding the earlier study of foundations. Again we see the tendency for 'theory' and 'practice' in education to be separated into mutually exclusive domains.

Rather than tying educational foundations to specific areas within educational studies, and separating them from other aspects of teacher preparation, I propose that we regard as foundational any area or course of study that critically examines the underlying ideas, assumptions, and principles of that area, making them a subject for scrutiny; and that considers how the issues in that area are related to broader normative questions and possibilities. Such courses offer an important element of criticism and self-criticism, as they leave no aspect of their body of inquiry unexamined (at least in principle). They take a normative approach to investigations, refusing to be limited narrowly to 'questions of fact' about, for example, 'what works' in schools. Such courses inquire into the proper relationship between the specifics of education and the larger interests and realities they contribute to. Given this depiction of the foundations of education, the four areas mentioned above do not necessarily exhibit a foundational orientation; for example, a course in the sociology of education that emphasized a structural/functionalist perspective exclusively would not be foundational, while specific courses in curriculum or pedagogy that critically examined both the assumptions of those areas and their relationship to other issues and debates would be foundational in the sense being employed.

The foundations of education recognize the nature of schooling, education, and teacher preparation as political, moral, and ideological practice, and make such questions a focus of discussion. They generate just the sort of questions about the short and long term consequences of schooling and teaching that were illustrated in our discussion of approaches to high school history. Courses in educational foundations do not begin by assuming a particular system of education is 'natural' or inevitable or the best — the way that those advocating technical and vocational teacher training do. Instead, foundationally oriented courses raise questions such as: what kind of educational institutions are most appropriate or justifiable; what are the possibilities for teaching as a moral, political, and social act; what kind of world am I helping build by the environment I construct in my classroom; and what moral principles and action guides should I use in making educational choices. Maxine Greene, in defense of foundations teachers, suggests:

> there must always be a place in teacher education for 'foundations' specialists, people whose main interest is in interpreting — and enabling others to interpret — the social, political, and economic factors that affect and influence the processes of education. It is not of incidental interest that the proponents of the 'competencies' orientation favor elimination of the 'foundations' component in the teacher education curriculum and have already succeeded in eroding it.[22]

There is an important tension between those who advocate 'competencies' in education and those who argue for a foundational perspective, just as there is more generally between teacher training as technical and teacher education and as a kind of praxis.

This is not to suggest that the questions that characterize

educational foundations are dealt with in a similar way by those working in these areas, nor that the establishment of some consensus is a reasonable aim of such courses of study. Such an aim is in fact at odds with a primary purpose of practical wisdom and communal action: the continuation of dialogue that, in 'breaking the crust of convention', continually probes the conventional, the taken for granted, and the settled. Both the approach to particular questions as well as their resolution often vary within a foundational area of study. Yet those who investigate a topic or issue foundationally will be engaging in the sort of critical, reflective, integrative, and empowering work that is central to teacher preparation as praxis. Students enrolled in teacher preparation programs that take a foundational perspective will come to look at educational issues and possibilities in a way that contradicts the orientation to more technical and vocational programs.

The foundations of education provide the sort of inter-disciplinary, multi-dimensional inquiry that is required to reverse the trend toward overspecialization and isolation. By looking at educational issues and ideas with a variety of lenses, the foundations convey to students the importance of analyzing situations from multiple perspectives. Consider, for example, how we prepare future teachers to engage in curriculum development. A foundational approach to this area would include several components. First, the history of the curriculum field would be an important area to investigate, as we encourage students to engage in conversations with those who preceded us. This would allow students to see patterns of continuity in the curriculum field, as well as to understand how competing interest groups have vied for control of public school curricula.[23] Second, a foundational approach to curriculum would investigate the variety of models, theories, and approaches that have been utilized by those involved in curriculum work. Current approaches to curriculum that stress standardized outcomes via behavioral objectives, the articulation of means to accomplish those objectives, and organizational strategies fostering privatized individualization need to be clarified and understood. Yet equally important to understand are the alternatives to these systematic, rationalized models, as we encourage creative and divergent possibilities. Third, in order to fully appreciate these alternatives, we must analyze the larger social values and meanings that these curricular models draw upon, and how they lead to the development of specific traits, dispositions, and values in students as they interact with this curriculum. Instead of thinking about curriculum design and development as a technical problem of matching efficient means to largely taken for granted ends, the foundations of curriculum would stress the linkages between the particularities of curriculum form and content and broader historical, social, political, and cultural realities. Fourth, this approach to curriculum would insist on the union of reflective inquiry and practical action that defines teacher preparation as praxis. Opportunities for both critique, reflection, and inquiry, on the one hand, and practical engagement, on the other, would have to be provided.

We can see how a variety of orientations and forms of language would be employed in the articulation of an approach to curriculum within a program of teacher preparation committed to praxis. Historical, philosophical, and sociological investigations would be crucial, as would a critical analysis of the role of language as it shapes teaching, schooling, curriculum, and education.[24] Yet if left as merely interesting, abstract ideas, such courses would fail to fulfill the promise of teacher education. Equally important is the provision of experiences in which ideas can be enacted. While the aim of such experiences would be quite different from the provision of experiences in a technically oriented program — a point I shall return to at greater length below — they are essential in the sort of program being advocated.

Beyond the critical and inter-disciplinary focus of educational foundations, they also provide the sort of normative framework that allows us to go beyond social reproduction through schooling. In *Understanding Education*, Walter Feinberg concludes with the claim that there are two general social functions of schooling. The first involves instruction in acquiring knowledge and skills that have an exchange value in the marketplace. A critical approach to this function would involve inquiry into the specific content and form of the school's curriculum, and into the habits and forms of demeanor that are emphasized through the hidden curriculum. The second function of schooling, 'is concerned with those forms of instruction primarily intended to further social participation as a member of the public through the development of interpretive understanding and normative skills'.[25] As detailed in chapter 4, the normative principles of democracy, equality, and autonomy form a core around which such normative skills and understanding can be developed.

Within teacher education, these normative principles can be usefully employed in creating courses and experiences based on the unity of reflection and action. At one level, a commitment to democracy and participation within the foundations is important for thinking through problems and prospects for classroom activity. What the instructional and curricular consequences are for a normative commitment to democracy have already been briefly discussed, in our discussion of curriculum as a foundational area of study. Beyond this, there are implications for the relationship between college and university faculty and programs, and regional public school classes and teachers. Existing within an institutional structure that is hierarchical, patriarchal, and impositional, the reform and control of teacher preparation have remained largely within the confines of higher education. Academics enunciate reform measures that have more or less direct implications for public school teachers and administrators. Typically these reforms are introduced to (or imposed upon) teachers who have little or no say in their conceptualization. Understandably, such efforts — for example, the 'new math' and science reforms of the early 1960s — are often met with resistance by teachers. A foundationally oriented program of teacher preparation guided by the normative principles of democracy, equality, and autonomy and committed to practical wisdom would alter this pattern.

Instead of a hierarchical model of reform and organization, teacher education would insist on inclusion of public school people as collaborators on a common project. The ideas, perspectives, and interests of teachers and others would provide input into the creation and operation of teacher education. The integration of theory and practice would be facilitated by a closer working relationship and affinity between college and pre-college teachers, whose divergent views and values might inform each other's work. Moreover, such collaborative possibilities would further the development of dialogue while encouraging communities that oppose the social pressures toward individualism in contemporary cultural life. There is, then, much to recommend the enlargement of teacher preparation communities, that are dedicated to continued discussion, moral engagement, and the role of teaching within a normative framework.

Many of the same observations apply to educational research. Typically planned and organized by academics who 'invade' a school or classroom for a relatively short period of time, collect data, and then analyze it as a way of answering their own questions, we can understand why researchers might be met by teachers with less than open arms. Often it seems as if educational research is conducted primarily for the benefit of the researcher rather than to illuminate some idea or practice that is valuable for schooling and teaching. When this happens the teacher becomes a tool to achieve ends proposed by the researcher. Discontent about being used in this way is easy to understand and empathize with. Such research is not likely to generate the sort of insight that will significantly improve school practice.

A program committed to praxis and practical wisdom, on the other hand, would include research (conceptual, historical, and empirical) that could be either undertaken in conjunction with teachers, or at least discussed and evaluated in concert with them. In the case of classroom research especially, it is crucial that teachers become instigators of research problems, and that such research be carried on collegially among school teachers and college professors. This is one area where some recent reform proposals seem more sensitive.[26] Organizing research agendas democratically, including teachers as researchers,[27] would help expand the nature of teacher preparation, moving it in the direction of a reflective and engaged praxis.

The foundations of education are thus a key to fostering teacher preparation as praxis. They provide ways of looking at issues and ideas in education and other fields that critically examine what is and point us toward what might be. Conceived as lenses through which education can be viewed and debated, such courses are invaluable aids with which to critique, challenge, and question the taken for granted in schooling.

We noted above how materials and methods courses within technically oriented programs of teacher preparation promote stylized, context specific recipes for teacher decision making that disempower teachers and avoid a critical view of schooling. Yet, the argument often goes, such courses are crucial if students are to be adequately prepared to deal with a classroom of 30 or more pupils. How would a foundationally oriented program differ in this respect, and what sort of teacher and orientation to teaching are implied?

The view of the teacher within such a program would not be one in which she or he is a technician, dispensing knowledge, skills, and rewards in ways that are thought effective, where the purposes or aims of schooling have already been decided by others. While it is important to maintain some level of classroom decorum, and while we need to help beginning teachers make reasonable decisions about teaching methods, these concerns must not be so paramount that they hide the deeper questions that lurk beneath these goals.[28] In keeping with the normative center of teacher preparation as praxis, our commitment must be to democratically empowering teachers who are creative, autonomous, reflective people. This means that we must provide opportunities for them to develop their own curricular, teaching, and evaluative practices. For example, experience in putting together ideas and issues around which a specific curriculum could be built in literature, and which could be introduced in a school setting, would be imperative. A part of this experience would involve the selection of a curriculum model(s) that would be investigated as a part of a foundations course within this program; the normative contours of this model, and its ramifications for larger social structures, would obviously be ingredients of such a course. In addition, students would be responsible for developing and justifying an approach to pedagogical relationships, and for integrating these with other aspects of school life.

Yet another distinctive trait in a teacher preparation program based on praxis is that it encourages students to form communities in which they learn from and support one another. All too often coursework is completed individually, and evaluated only by the instructor, with little attention paid to cooperative learning and community building. For both pedagogical and political reasons it is important for students to engage in projects cooperatively, sharing ideas where appropriate and learning new possibilities from others in the cohort group. Also, such communities of encouragement and support could assist in the process of critical reflection as this continues as a part of field experiences in schools. If a communal identity can be established early on in the program, it can be extended through subsequent courses and in student teaching. The process of forming such a communal identity is an important part of developing teaching as an empowering, creative, critical praxis—one in which the virtue of caring is significant.

While technical approaches that result in teacher training discuss 'methods and materials' in isolation, teacher education incorporates normative questions, educational decisions (like those regarding teaching methods and the selection of materials) and classroom strategies as interdependent. A foundational emphasis augments the development of the teacher by clarifying the decisions that must be made, tying them to moral, political, and social principles and consequences, and linking these to the possibilities of teaching. It helps prepare people for a 'calling' (with its moral and social overtones) rather than for a 'profession'.

A foundational approach to teacher preparation must, then, include an attention to possibility in actual and future practice. There is clearly a tension here. If the foundations only challenge current assumptions, uncovering connections between educational and other spheres, without also considering carefully the construction of alternative possibilities, little productive change will result. Emphasizing the replication of current realities, on the other hand, produces conformity with those realities, with political and moral consequences that are not justifiable.

Yet to be totally disengaged from school practice, to remain distanced from problems of schooling and teaching, is to withdraw from the articulation of possibilities that go beyond current limitations. While a focus for our actions that accentuates practical wisdom, dialogue, and engagement is central, a singular focus on what now happens in classrooms is detrimental. 'Practice' cannot refer exclusively to things as they are, but equally to how they might become. Thus the aim and value of field experiences in programs of teacher education deserve sustained attention.

Critical Reflection, Praxis, and Field Experience[29]

The student teaching experience has become an almost universally accepted part of teacher preparation. As typically the final portion of the prospective teacher's professional program of study, it is expected to provide sufficient 'real life' experience to allow students to explore teaching methods and styles, connect 'theory' (chiefly learned in the college classroom) and 'practice' (mostly as experienced in a school setting), become familiar with the demands of teaching, and acquire the necessary skills and values needed to function adequately in that setting. Since the classroom is the arena within which students will presumably spend a major portion of their work lives, it seems reasonable to include substantial experience of this sort as a prelude to their full time, professional activities.

Additional field experiences are also being suggested or mandated by colleges and state departments of education. In Ohio, for example, students must spend some 300 hours in field experiences prior to student teaching.[30] Similarly, the state of Illinois requires 100 hours of 'clinical experiences' as a prerequisite for student teaching and ultimately for state certification in elementary education.[31] The general consensus seems to be that the greater the number of hours a student spends in the classroom — observing, assisting the teacher, teaching in formal and informal settings — the better prepared she/he will be. As with the student teaching experiences, this seems like a sensible idea; the more experience people have in schools, the more proficient they will presumably become, and the more comfortable they will be once the full responsibilities of teaching are undertaken. No doubt a part of this concern for early field experience may be traced to the general concern expressed by parents, public officials, and others about the presumed decline in teaching excellence, the perceived downturn in standardized test scores, and the decline in teaching 'basic skills'. The message seems to be that if what we want are better trained, more competent and able, more well-adjusted teachers, increased time in school settings provides one fruitful means of assuring these things. Field experiences thus seem worthy of inclusion in programs of teacher preparation.

Yet there is a tendency for prolonged field experiences to produce and perpetuate strategies that are congruent with existing institutional and professional expectations. The possibility that immersion in field settings will promote patterns of socialization, and the development of meanings, values, and commitments, which are compatible with the educational status quo, is a serious concern. Thrust into the existing culture of the school, and having less than the professional status of paid teachers and administrators, students may tend to accept existing conditions, patterns, and relationships as forming the boundaries beyond which one need not, or should not, trespass. This is especially the case in situations where instructional and other activities seem to proceed smoothly and with little pupil resistance — where, that is, the teacher is composed, the atmosphere is non threatening, and the pupils are consistently 'on task'. The student teacher, as a prospective initiate into the profession, quite naturally wants to 'succeed' and become accepted as a professional; and seeing others 'succeed' can lead to an imitation of 'successful' practice, with definitions of success taken from the situation as experienced. Couple this with a supportive teacher who is anxious to assist the student in becoming accomplished, and a pattern of uncritical uniformity and cultural maintenance may unconsciously become established. Such patterns may serve to replicate and make more uniform practices of schooling and teaching.

As we accept current situations and practices as 'natural', the experienced environment is objectified — perceived as embodying a permanence and validity that is not to be challenged. This leads in turn to a devaluation of critical analysis and interpretation, and the curbing of alternatives in classrooms. Through the development of utilitarian and survival oriented teaching perspectives, current situations may become accepted as a part of the educational 'given', and thus unchallengeable. Such a process of uncritical acceptance is indefensible even were we to develop criteria for teaching effectiveness of the sort that have so far eluded us. Field experiences which lead to such uncritical, disempowering, and functionalist results oppose the spirit and substance of teacher education as praxis.

The paradox of providing early and prolonged field experiences within programs which attempt to foster a more critical approach to education, schooling, and teaching is clear. While exposure to classroom situations is increasingly mandated for students in education, this process — while apparently justified and appealing to common sense, almost at face value — can lead to a duplication of existing procedures and activities that are both miseducative and ideologically suspect; such exposure, in any case, curtails or even opposes a critical, foundational approach to teacher preparation programs. Since state departments of education and institutions of higher education are moving in the direction of expanding such field experiences, we shall now turn to the question of how these pejorative tendencies of field experience may be mitigated, so that they become valuable components of the sort of program under discussion.

The central problem here involves the tendency for students to accept existing classroom situations almost as if they are discovered rather than created, essentially unalterable, and beyond criticism or reform. Maxine Greene has captured this general sense of the taken for granted, and its deficiencies, rather well:

> In spite of doubt and cynicism, the public appears to remain convinced that existing social arrangements are perfectly 'natural'. ... The schools ... play an important role in reinforcing this conviction. It is not that teachers consciously mystify or deliberately concoct the positive images that deflect critical thought. ... Often submerged in the bureaucracies for which they work, they simply accede to what is taken for granted ... they are likely to present the world around as *given*, probably unchangeable and predefined. [32]

Once the world of schooling is accepted as predefined and unchangeable, the aim of field experience revolves around adjustment, containment, and accommodation. The result is educational stasis within which alternative possibilities and critical reflectiveness are seen as dysfunctional, unresponsive, and irrelevant to student 'needs'. We may counter these tendencies by remembering that: (i) both knowledge and institutions responsible for its dissemination are socially constructed rather than organic processes that lie beyond human intention; (ii) commonsense perceptions, observations, and attitudes, through the use of critical theory and practice, can be turned into problematic situations requiring analysis and debate; (iii) the development of alternative principles and approaches around which transformative theories and practices may be built is a central part of teacher education; and (iv) school practice and social, economic, and political exigencies are fundamentally intertwined. Each of these four ideas is central to a foundational approach to teacher preparation.

To illustrate, a part of seeing that knowledge is socially constructed, and that social institutions neither develop out of thin air nor are constructed out of whole cloth, involves situating schools, curricula, and pedagogy within their sociohistorical contexts. Understanding what schools do, then, involves seeing what they were designed to do historically. This kind of understanding is of no small moment in education, especially since our field tends to be seen through excessively ahistorical lenses.[33] Despite our commonsense understandings, schools were created partly to serve as a vehicle for social control within a society that was facing the pressures of an industrialized, capitalistic, urbanized nation whose numbers were swelling, partly due to notable increases in immigration.[34] What this history of education documents is that schools were not as dedicated to the ideal of equality of opportunity or the development of students' individual capacities as we have commonly supposed. To the extent that recent scholarship in the history, philosophy, and sociology of education indicates that schools have historically served as a social safety valve, and as a mechanism for reproducing social, cultural, and economic inequality, students may begin to question their basic assumptions about what is *given* within the world of schooling, and the legitimacy of its origins.

The development of alternative principles and practices is a part of the process of critical reflection that together generate a commitment to praxis. Recognizing that knowledge and schooling are socially informed, and turning commonsensical perceptions into problematic ones, includes, coincidentally, seeing that schools, curricula, and teaching could be other than the way they now are. While students must be familiar with the current domain of schooling, and learn when to accommodate and when to stretch its boundaries, their vision of education can not be limited to schools as they happen to function currently. Reflectivity is not 'just' an analytic tool or based on some abstract ideal, but can lead to intervention strategies that work toward changing the experiences of teachers and students. In the process, reflection and action, thought and action, theory and practice, and continuity and change, become unified.

The inclusion of field experiences in a program of teacher preparation emphasizing critical reflection and normatively guided action can be justified, finally, on a number of grounds. First, such experiences can demonstrate many of the more theoretical points that are made in foundations courses. For example, by placing students with a sensitive and critical eye in classrooms, they can see for themselves the patterns of bias by gender, social class, and race that may be found there. Again, analyses of curricular and pedagogical practices can be undertaken in field experiences that illustrate how choices made by teachers are related to issues in curriculum and teaching discussed in other aspects of the students' program. Classroom observation (guided by an appropriate framework that acknowledges both commonsense definitions and alternatives to these) provides a forum within which critique and practice can co-mingle, in the formation of practical wisdom. Second, and just as important, field experiences can lend insight into how, concretely, teachers work to overcome such biases. Even though schools as social institutions reproduce both inequalities and forms of consciousness that tolerate them, numerous teachers are actively involved in trying to reverse those reproductive tendencies. Aspiring teachers (and college professors) have much to learn from the efforts of classroom teachers in this regard. Third, a similar point may be made about the actions of public school students. Frequently pupils act in ways that redirect or subvert the dominant ideological messages of the school. Seeing how students creatively respond to the demands of the hidden curriculum of their classroom is a useful pedagogical and political lesson for would-be teachers. They may learn how to restructure classrooms so that different hidden curricula are obtained — ones that are more consistent with the values of democracy, equality, and autonomy. Fourth, teacher preparation as praxis must encourage an awareness of current realities while not allowing them to become objectified. Despite the shortcomings that a given classroom may reveal, students must be able to deal with that classroom situation at the same time that they seek to transform it; a critical approach to teacher preparation can not result in outright rejection of current practice, nor an inability to see it as connected to the development of alternatives. Fifth, seeing a multiplicity of classrooms, especially those that differ in crucial respects — e.g., in curriculum content and pedagogical relations — will reinforce the important point that schools are socially constructed institutions that represent a variety of perspectives and values. Observing and analyzing these differences in practice will enhance the critical process of understanding that schools are not natural or given but variable and susceptible to change.

Some readers may see these proposals as giving rise to a 'reformist' perspective that may not generate the kind of global transformation both inside and outside of schooling that is required if their ideological

consequences are to be overturned. While this is obviously a complicated issue, a few brief comments are necessary in the current
context. The central point of contention is the relationship between
reform and transformation in schooling, on the one hand, and between
alterations in patterns of schooling and the larger social order, on the
other. While I am in strong agreement with those who seek substantial,
far reaching economic, political, and cultural changes, it does not seem
likely that these will come about through sudden, revolutionary shifts
that sweep away what has gone before. Part of the reason for this is
purely pragmatic. The structures of power and control that now exert
an influence on both the society generally and schools in particular will
not quickly be altered or suspended; changing these will necessitate
protracted, complicated dialogue and action that will be measured not
in months but in years and decades. Moreover, the very political project
at the center of this monograph — expanding opportunities for the
democratic development of social and cultural spaces for knowledge
and actions that reverse the patterns of inequality and oppression that
are evident currently — entails collaborative, collective engagement
with people within and without education that will be time consuming
and often frustrating. Thus the fact that the proposals identified here
seem 'reformist' is hardly, from my point of view, a criticism; it reflects
an assessment of both the realities of power and what is normatively
required of us as democratic actors.

A foundationally oriented program of teacher preparation committed to critical reflection and action based on normative principles
and practical wisdom would significantly alter policies and programs of
teacher preparation. It would also require of its practitioners a background and set of interests that diverge from those associated with
technical and vocational approaches to the preparation of teachers.
They would have to be equally responsive to inquiry and school
practice, theoretical analysis and purposive actions. In addition, programs and practitioners of them would need to be more fully integrated
with other aspects of the college or university culture than they now
tend to be. Caught in an environment stressing alternatively a scholastic, elitist tradition, a research and development, technical mission, and
a professional/vocational set of values, educational studies and teacher
education seem to fall neatly within none of these higher education
orientations.

The Institutional Contexts of Teacher Education

The study of education and the preparation of teachers must involve a synthesis of several other disciplines, in order that its parameters can be fully appreciated and investigated. Prospective teachers must similarly be prepared to take a variety of coursework in fields that are not now commonly emphasized in programs of teacher preparation — for example, in philosophy, history, sociology, women's studies, and the arts. We might say that the most appropriate course of study for future teachers would be a strong, diversified, and protracted liberal education. Students preparing to become teachers would be encouraged to become scholars, to actively inquire into a variety of fields, and to develop the traits of intellectual curiosity, engagement, and excitement.

At the same time, educational studies itself benefits from this broad pattern of liberal inquiry. As we move beyond vocational and technical pictures of education, it is clear that there are issues and ideas in educational studies that are inextricably related to other domains. Issues in the philosophy of education, for example, can be amplified by examinations in epistemology, aesthetics, moral theory, and the history of philosophy, to name only a few possible areas. Again, courses in the fine arts, especially art and music appreciation, the history of these areas, and a variety of studio courses, would be invaluable for the prospective teacher.

Yet educational studies has a good deal to contribute to the general intellectual life of institutions of higher education. One way to suggest how this might be so is to remind our colleagues that the study of education is not synonymous with the technical preparation of teachers. There are a variety of issues and debates in education that are of general value and benefit to students, whether they are contemplating a career in teaching or not. Regardless whether one chooses to work in schools or elsewhere, we are all involved in educational enterprises (inside and outside of schools) for which the insights of educational analysis and theory are useful. To take one example, while we may not all become public school teachers, we would all benefit from an understanding of how the historical development of educational institutions and practices were influenced by systems of administration and control that originated in the early twentieth century development of systems management. Within higher education programs, understanding the educational thought of Socrates, Rousseau, Dewey, and Peters makes as much a contribution to liberal or general education as other courses outside the department of education.

If educational studies is to be a legitimate area of inquiry within higher education, then, it must be synthetic and integrative in both directions. On the one hand, for students contemplating work as teachers, we must utilize the insights of other disciplines and areas of study as these provide important avenues for inquiry and the discovery of ideas, and for a career and life long commitment to reflection and investigation. In this regard the curriculum for teachers must be as broad based as we can reasonably make it. At the same time, the study of education must be integrated with the other areas of study, so that students and faculty see it as a legitimate academic field in its own right, rather than simply a vocational training ground for a smaller number of interested students.

One of the ways this integration of educational studies could be facilitated is through the offering of cross-listed, interdisciplinary, and team taught courses. There are many interesting possibilities here. For example, faculty from the education and philosophy departments might cross-list a course in the philosophy of education, and even collaboratively teach it occasionally, as a way of sharing possibly divergent insights and perspectives. Or a course might be developed dealing with values in education that would include faculty from education, philosophy, the arts, literature, and political science. Such courses could serve to illustrate the forms of interdisciplinary study that, as we have seen, can assist in the creation of new forms of understanding, breaking down the artificial barriers that make it difficult for us to communicate with colleagues in other disciplines.

Other forms of collaboration are possible and desirable that would further integrate educational studies with other areas of higher education. Many faculty have interests in schooling — sometimes associated with their own subject matter interests — that could be drawn upon in programs of teacher education. Two kinds of possibilities come to mind. First, professors might work with students on developing ideas about how their own interests and ideas could be incorporated into a curriculum for the public schools. Perhaps a music teacher with a special fondness for Baroque music could assist education students in thinking about how this music could be integrated into an elementary or secondary classroom — possibly in conjunction with other areas of the curriculum. Or a professor of history with a special interest in the civil war period could prove valuable for a secondary social studies teacher who wants to explore a topic related to that era. Such interactions could go a long way toward encouraging the view that education is not reducible to teacher training.

On the other hand, college and university faculty share an important identity that is often overlooked (even sometimes scrupulously
avoided): we are all teachers. For all of us except perhaps those who
work in the most elite, research-oriented institutions, a major portion
of our responsibilities in higher education concern teaching and interacting with students. Here it seems to me education faculty might be
able to play a more direct, service-oriented role for our colleagues.
While problems and possibilities of teaching are not usually included in
graduate programs, they are often discussed and debated by faculty
once they begin teaching, and some colleges and universities have
inaugurated summer sessions to discuss the improvement of college
teaching. As people who have thought about issues and possibilities in
curriculum, pedagogy, and evaluation, professors of education may
have ideas that would be of use to our colleagues. This is not to suggest
that education faculty have 'inside information' that is unavailable to
others, but merely to suggest that study in education — like that in any
other field — may result in insights and prospects that can be profitably
shared. This too might integrate education with the other areas of the
institution, and help foster a greater degree of community.

These suggestions for integrating educational studies with the
other aspects of higher education are intended to resolve two major
problems regarding the institutional context that confronts faculty in
education. Often departments or schools of education are removed
from the general cultural life of the institution, with little interchange
between education and other faculty. A substantial part of this is due, of
course, to the philosophical ideas regarding knowledge and liberal
inquiry, the historical development of institutions of higher education,
and the technical orientation of teacher training that were discussed
earlier in this book. Overcoming these sources of isolation entails a
good deal of intellectual and political work that allows our colleagues to
surmount the distinction between liberal and applied inquiry that lies at
the core of this isolation. This has to be accomplished through the
reorganization of educational studies itself, along the lines discussed
here. The view of teacher education and of educational studies as an
academic area of inquiry should, over time, contribute to the process of
integration that is so important (for epistemological and psychological
reasons).

If the isolation of educational studies weren't difficult enough, a
compounding factor is that departments and schools of education are
often regarded as intellectually inferior domains within the college or
university. Since 'real intellectual work' allegedly takes place in the

'pure' disciplines, education finds itself in an inferior role in the academy. Such a situation is not only difficult for the faculty involved, of course, but also makes life difficult for students in education. For those who can be swayed by empirical evidence in this matter, the offering of cross-disciplinary courses that represent education as a respectable area of inquiry, the willingness to share curricular and pedagogical ideas, and an openness to incorporate other areas of study into educational programs should assist in the process of integration.

Yet this is only one half of the sort of integration that is necessary, if teacher preparation as praxis is to succeed. In addition to educational studies becoming a partner in higher education, it must also be more closely related to schools and teachers. We noted how the tendency for teacher preparation and curricular reform to be conducted on the basis of an impositional model both continues the deskilling of teaching and virtually guarantees that such reforms will fail in whole or part. The integrating of educational studies and teacher education must include, then, an emphasis on teachers as colleagues who have important ideas to share with college faculty. Discussions of policies, programs, and course offerings can benefit from the inclusion of teachers from the public schools.

This will not of itself alter current school realities, of course, and there is a need just to be honest about this. Those realities in many cases are not congruent with the depiction of teaching as empowering — involving self reflection, critical analysis, moral debate and practical wisdom, continuing opportunities for creativity, autonomy, and academic freedom in the classroom — that is a result of teacher preparation based on praxis. I fully realize that for many people the picture of teaching painted here is one that conflicts with current expectations and patterns.

Perhaps one of the most integrative, supportive actions we can participate in, accordingly, is helping in the restructuring of the teacher's workplace. In the long run it is such a restructuring that is necessary if teaching is to be an empowering, energizing, moral activity. There are of course instances of classrooms that foster the kinds of values and possibilities that are required, and we have much to learn from those environments. While teachers will necessarily have to take the lead in articulating how their work site should be reconceived, there are several considerations that seem central. First, the number of students and classes that a teacher must work with must be drastically reduced. The number of students that can be reasonably taught may vary with the subject matter or grade level, as might the total number of classes taught per day. Yet the current requirement that teachers spend six or seven periods each day teaching 30 or more students is simply miseducative; it precludes the opportunities for reflection, discussion, and creative involvement that are central. Second, the isolation of teachers and teaching must be reversed. Normally teachers communicate only with children or adolescents for most of the day, and the conversations that do take place with other adults in the teachers' lounge are not known for their intellectual stimulation; these places understandably become centers for socializing and, at times, an oasis from the constant barrage of problems and difficulties that sometimes characterize classrooms. Greater collaboration among teachers — sharing ideas, problems, and successes, working jointly on curriculum projects, experimenting with new courses and readings — must be possible within schools. Third, the relations of power and decision making — especially the gender dynamics that run through school governance — must be significantly altered. The fact that most teachers (especially at the elementary level) are women, and that most administrators are men, cannot be dismissed; nor can the reality that teaching, whether done by a man or a woman, is a 'feminine' occupation. This has real advantages as well as problems, of course — an ethic of caring, respect for students' particular difficulties (intellectual, social, and personal), a concern for their special talents and interests — distinguishes the classroom from the masculine, competitive, and distant forms of relationship that dominate in the corporate world. At the same time, the gender dynamics of schools make it that much more difficult to redirect the patterns of power and control that take place there. More democratic, participatory, and collaborative forms of decision making must be worked toward, that empower teachers to make the decisions about teaching practices and curriculum projects that transpire daily. This leads to a fourth area that needs to be addressed as a part of restructuring the workplace of teachers. As curriculum development has become more and more centralized — either in textbook publishers or state departments of education or both — local control and autonomy have been eroded. When decisions about what content to teach, what forms of pedagogical relationships to encourage, and how students are to be evaluated and at what intervals, are made by people removed from the classroom in which these things are enacted, the teacher is reduced to a manager of activities rather than a creator of ideas and environments. Thus one important step toward revitalizing the work of teachers is regaining decision making control at the local level, and giving individual teachers greater responsibility for the educational decisions that must be made. As Aristotle noted, choices are prerequisite for moral understanding and action.

None of these recommendations will be easy to implement. Some will be resisted on financial grounds, some on political and ideological ones. Yet the current climate of reform just may provide an opening for rethinking the work of teachers that can lead to progressive, democratic changes in schools. In any case, our moral obligations require that we work toward such changes as fully as we can.

One final element of the context for teacher education deserves emphasis both because it is of great importance and because it is so frequently overlooked or denied. We have emphasized as a part of teacher education the linkages that exist between the realities of school practice and the larger social world with which they are entwined, and ways to make these linkages more apparent. Our commitment throughout to reflection, critique, and action must extend far beyond our classroom walls. Just so, teacher education must emphasize the similarities between the predicaments of teachers and the struggles of other workers in contemporary society (e.g., secretaries, nurses, and other 'pink collar' employees facing deskilling through unequal gender relations and forms of bureaucratic domination). Out of such similarities alliances can be constructed between teachers and others so that, as we engage in the essentially political efforts that are required to change the material conditions of our lives, we give and get support from groups and individuals outside of schools. This is not to deny the clear need for supportive relations within educational institutions. Yet especially given the importance of democracy as a cultural form, it is imperative that educators become involved with community, labor, and cultural groups with similar interests and prospects. The creation of democratic forms of life demands that we enlarge our conception of 'colleagues' to include those who have long since left the domain of schooling.

We have discussed how the ideas presented throughout this book give rise to policies and programs of teacher education and some of the implications of these for school people, students, and others. Our moral obligation to alternative practice is clear. The final chapter in this book will look more specifically at attempts to take this moral challenge seriously — that is, to implement programs of teacher preparation based on praxis. It is the articulation of such programs in practice — and an honest assessment of their problems and possibilities — that is now urgently required.

Notes and References

1 Throughout this chapter, I will use the more generic phrase 'teacher preparation' when referring to programs for prospective teachers in general. 'Teacher training' will be used to refer to programs that take a technical and vocational approach to such preparation, and 'teacher education' will designate the approach based on praxis recommended in this chapter. Thus 'teacher preparation' provides a conceptual umbrella, with 'teacher training' and 'teacher education' naming alternative avenues for preparing future teachers.

2 See DOUGLAS D. NOBLE, 'Education, technology, and the military', in LANDON E. BEYER and MICHAEL W. APPLE, (Eds.) *The Curriculum: Problems, Politics, and Possibilities* (Albany, New York: State University of New York Press, in press).

3 JOHN DEWEY, *Democracy and Education* (New York: Macmillan Company, 1916).

4 GEOFFREY TABAKIN and KATHLEEN DENSMORE, 'Teacher professionalization and gender analysis', *Teachers College Record*, Volume 88, Number 2, Winter, 1986.

5 See the articles in the special section, 'The Carnegie Task Force Report: Is it the blueprint for the 21st century?' in *Networker*, Volume 2, Number 3, 1987.

6 See THOMAS S. POPKEWITZ, (Ed.), *Critical Studies in Teacher Education: Its Folklore, Theory and Practice* (Lewes: The Falmer Press, 1987).

7 This does not mean that any given experience must include both reflection and action in equal amounts simultaneously. Rather, to form a harmonious whole, there must be opportunities for each to inform and reform each other. Certain actions preclude preparatory reflection — for example, when we must decide immediately which of two options is best 'for now' — just as reflective activities may not lead to immediate action. Yet 'knowledge' and 'inquiry' cannot form their own ends, and action cannot be divorced from reflection.

8 See JACOB BRONOWSKI, *Science and Human Values* (New York: Harper and Row, 1965); cited in RICHARD A. QUANTZ, 'The "new" scholars in philosophy of education, 1976–1986', presentation to a joint session of the Ohio Valley Philosophy of Education Society and the Mid-Atlantic States Philosophy of Education Society, Pittsburgh, Pennsylvania, November, 1986.

9 See THOMAS S. KUHN, *The Structure of Scientific Revolutions*, second edition, enlarged (Chicago: University of Chicago Press, 1970).

10 I have discussed some of these ideas in LANDON E. BEYER, 'Beyond elitism and technicism: Teacher education as practical philosophy', *Journal of Teacher Education*, Volume XXXVII, Number 2, March–April, 1986.

11 WILLIAM M. SULLIVAN, *Reconstructing Public Philosophy* (Berkeley: University of California Press, 1986), p. 66.

12 ARISTOTLE, *The Nicomachean Ethics*, translated by David Ross (Oxford: Oxford University Press, 1980), p. 139.

13 See chapter 1 above, 'Teacher training and professionalism'.

14 THE HOLMES GROUP, *Tomorrow's Teachers* (East Lansing, Michigan: The Holmes Group, Inc., 1986), p. 52.

15 MICHAEL W. APPLE, *Ideology and Curriculum* (Boston: Routledge & Kegan Paul, 1979), p. 74; the quotation within this citation is from CHARLES C. PETERS, *Foundations of Educational Sociology* (New York: Macmillan Company, 1924), p. 25.

16 See, for instance, CLARENCE J. KARIER, *Shaping the American Educational State: 1900 to the Present* (New York: The Free Press, 1975).

17 See, for example, ELLIOT W. EISNER, *The Educational Imagination: On the Design and Evaluation of Educational Programs* (New York: Macmillan Publishing Company, Inc., 1979); ALAN R. TOM, *Teaching as a Moral Craft* (New York: Longman, 1984); ROBERT V. BULLOUGH, JR., STANLEY L. GOLDSTEIN, and LADD HOLT, *Human Interests in the Curriculum: Teaching and Learning in a Technological Society* (New York: Teachers College Press, 1984); and Landon E. Beyer and Michael W. Apple, *op. cit.*

18 See KENNETH A. SIROTNIK, 'What you see is what you get: Consistency, persistency, and mediocrity in classrooms', *Harvard Educational Review*, Volume 53, Number 1, February, 1983.

19 See MICHAEL W. APPLE and LOIS WEIS, (Eds.) *Ideology and Practice in Schooling* (Philadelphia: Temple University Press, 1983)

20 JOHN DEWEY, 'The relation of theory to practice in education', The Third Yearbook of the National Society for the Scientific Study of Education, Part I, *The Relation of Theory to Practice in the Education of Teachers* (Chicago: University of Chicago Press, 1904).

21 LANDON E. BEYER, 'Curriculum deliberation', in ARIEH LEWY, (Ed.) *The International Encyclopedia of Education* (New York: Pergamon Press, in press).

22 MAXINE GREENE, *Landscapes of Learning* (New York: Teachers College Press, 1978), p. 59.

23 HERBERT M. KLIEBARD, *The Struggle for the American Curriculum 1893–1958* (Boston: Routledge & Kegan Paul, 1986).

24 See DWAYNE HUEBNER, 'Curricular language and classroom meanings', in WILLIAM PINAR, (Ed.) *Curriculum Theorizing: The Reconceptualists* (Berkeley: McCutchan Publishing Corporation, 1975); and LANDON E. BEYER, 'Theory, ideology, and school practice', *Teaching Education*, Volume 1, Number 1, February, 1987.

25 WALTER FEINBERG, *Understanding Education: Toward a Reconstruction of Educational Inquiry* (New York: Cambridge University Press, 1983), p. 228.

26 For example, see LYNN OLSON, 'Network for renewal: Goodlad seeks stronger school-university alliances', *Education Week*, Volume VI, Number 25, March 18, 1987, which discusses John Goodlad's work in trying to encourage the 'two cultures' of the school and university to interact.

27 'Action research' promises one avenue for helping accomplish this.

28 See JESSE GOODMAN and SUSAN ADLER, 'Critical theory as a foundation for methods courses', *Journal of Teacher Education*, Volume XXXVII, Number 4, July–August, 1986.

29 I explored this idea initially in LANDON E. BEYER, 'Field experience, ideology, and the development of critical reflectivity', *Journal of Teacher Education*, Volume XXXV, Number 3, May–June, 1984.

30 See R. MACNAUGHTON, F. JOHNS, and J. ROGUS, 'When less seems like more: Managing the expanded field experiences of the 80's', *Journal of Teacher Education*, Volume XXXIII, Number 5, September–October, 1982.

31 ILLINOIS STATE BOARD OF EDUCATION, *Minimum Requirements for State Certification*, 1980.

32 Maxine Greene, *op. cit.*, p. 56.

33 See HERBERT M. KLIEBARD, 'Persistent curriculum issues in historical perspective', in William Pinar, *op. cit.*

34 See, for example, Karier, *op. cit.*; DAVID B. TYACK, *The One Best System: A History of American Urban Education* (Cambridge, Massachusetts: Harvard University Press, 1974); DAVID NASAW, *Schooled to Order: A Social History of Public Schooling in the United States* (New York: Oxford University Press, 1979); and PAUL C. VIOLAS, *The Training of the Urban Working Class: A History of 20th Century American Education* (Chicago: Rand McNally College Publishing Company, 1978).

6
Critical Scholarship and the Practice of Teacher Education

In keeping with the spirit of this book, it would be impermissible to conclude with an exclusively theoretical discussion of the ideas and issues on which an alternative direction in educational inquiry and in programs of teacher preparation can be based. Critique and analysis have of course been essential in developing the arguments of the preceding chapters, and in articulating proposals for change. Such arguments and proposals reach their culmination, though, in the enactment of concrete programs, courses, and classroom actions that embody, extend, and modify them. 'The practice of possibility' necessarily goes beyond static and removed analysis, as we work out our theoretical visions in practice, and recalculate actions in ways that better align them with our beliefs, values, and convictions.

There are a number of ways we might augment this discussion of practice: by analyzing examples from research studies that either encompass, alter, or reject the ideas presented here; by discussing in greater detail the current trends in teacher preparation and their relation to the alternatives discussed above; or by developing hypothetical models that extend these ideas and perhaps discuss their implications for educational and governmental policy. All of these approaches have merits. Yet they fail to fully integrate theory and practice in the way that is crucial if we are to understand teacher education as praxis. For these strategies could not include within them the dynamic, on going, personal accounts of the possibilities and difficulties associated with the task before us. They lack the 'flesh and blood' realities that are so necessary as we attempt educational (and hence social and cultural) transformation. It is time for analysis and argument to be accompanied more directly by descriptions of attempts to specify how things might be, how we can work toward them, and the problems we will confront along the way.

For these reasons, this chapter will discuss two specific attempts to develop teacher education programs and courses that I have been personally involved in, and that seek to further the ideas discussed previously. This is not to imply that these programs are necessarily the most representative or the best embodiments of the ideas they seek to instantiate; nor is it to suggest that other programs and institutions may not provide additional evidence of the kind of alternative practices described here — clearly they can and do.[1] Rather, I utilize these examples for other reasons. First, they obviously involve activities and predicaments with which I am intimately familiar, having been involved in both cases in their genesis and operation. While there are some potential problems associated with such familiarity, my first hand acquaintance with the actual creation of these programs may generate insights that would not otherwise be possible. Second, the relative success or failure of any program depends to a large extent on the institutional, interpersonal, communal, social, and political contexts within which it functions. Even the most well conceived, thoughtful, and stimulating program will not flourish in situations where the surrounding environments are hostile or belligerent. A part of the description that follows depends on a familiarity with the context of these programs that may not be possible in cases where participation is more removed and indirect. Third, the programs described below contain instances of successes, failures, and uncertainties that need to be further analyzed as we consider possible future redirections. An important part of such an analysis is a rather close-up view of microenvironments and practices, as these often mediate more general trends and commitments. Including a discussion of these close-up realities is an important part of thinking through new possibilities and ultimately acting on them. Fourth, the programs described here are in a real sense examples of 'work in progress'. They will, I trust, convey something of the lived experience of acting on knowledge and values as this unfolds in actual situations.[2]

I discuss below my experiences at Knox College in Illinois and Cornell College in Iowa. In describing the activities at these colleges in the order in which they occurred, I will spend considerably more time on the situation at Cornell. This is primarily because the alternatives being considered there are more extensive than those undertaken previously at Knox, and because the outcome of the efforts at Cornell are not completely certain at this point. Before describing these programs separately, however, it is worth noting some of the characteristics of these colleges that are held in common. Despite some significant differences between institutions and the communities in which they are located, there are important similarities that may illuminate the successes and failures of the alternatives that were undertaken in these colleges' education programs.

Knox and Cornell Colleges are similar in size, general mission or orientation, and history. They are members of the Associated Colleges of the Midwest, a consortium of thirteen small to medium size, private liberal arts colleges in five midwestern states. The traditions of these colleges are firmly rooted in liberal study, and both began with a religious affiliation that has since diminished in influence (especially at Knox, which is now a secular institution, while Cornell maintains some identification with the Methodist Church). Both colleges have enrollments of around 1,000 students, and each has survived a threatened enrollment decline in the past decade. Like other colleges of this type, Knox and Cornell pride themselves on close and frequent student-faculty interactions, a commitment to teaching, and a general provision for broad based liberal learning in a variety of disciplines.

In addition, Knox and Cornell take seriously their ties to the local community, and frequently seek ways to reinforce or extend these ties. 'Town and gown' distinctions sometimes can be seen, to be sure, but to a lesser degree and severity than is frequently the case with respect to larger universities and communities. This may be the case in part because both colleges are located in small town, rural, somewhat isolated areas of the midwest, so that each institution has attained a measure of community identity. My own association with these colleges occurred at a time when the agricultural crisis was at or near its peak. During this crisis both colleges were more or less stable institutions (though they suffered some of the consequences of the decline in agriculture, certainly), offering economic advantages to the townspeople and local government. Both colleges also continue to provide substantial cultural and social opportunities for local citizens, many of whom take advantage of artistic, political, and social activities that would otherwise be unavailable in communities of their size.

More particularly related to education and teacher preparation programs, each college was in the process of rethinking its Department of Education at the time I was employed there. Some sense of dissatisfaction was in evidence at the time my associations began, as was a more general sense that the Department could be doing better — even if what constituted 'doing better' was not always clear to those who were dissatisfied. This meant that alternatives to current or previous programs were not only possible but actively encouraged and, to a large extent, supported.

The Department of Education at both Knox and Cornell is very small, consisting in each case of two full time, tenure track faculty positions, with a varying number of part-time adjunct faculty employed to teach specific courses. As one might imagine, this is a mixed blessing in many ways. While program coherence and compatibility are clearly more attainable than is typically the case, individual faculty members also find themselves teaching courses and being responsible for activities for which they have little experience (which is itself a mixed blessing, often).

At the same time, the liberal arts orientation of these institutions made the place of the Department of Education something of an anomaly. As I discuss in more detail below, education had been seen as something closer to a vocational training area than to an academic area of study and investigation. Yet a department of education was, at both institutions, not only accommodated but rather actively supported. There were several reasons for this. Both Knox and Cornell have historic interests in pre-college education and teaching, and see their own interests as at least related to those of the public schools. In addition, many individuals on the faculty and administration had personal commitments to public schooling; some had been public school teachers themselves, while others were active in local school board activities, and many had children who were pupils in the public schools of their communities. Education was thus considered an important area in the lives of many women and men associated with the liberal arts traditions embodied by Knox and Cornell. Lastly, and especially at Cornell, the Department of Education enrolled a substantial number of students in its programs, many of whom enjoyed a strong personal identification with education programs. Especially at a time when enrollment declines were a reality at similar institutions and a threat at these colleges as well, such identifications were not taken lightly.

The environment in which teacher preparation was conducted was, in sum, a complicated and somewhat contradictory one at both Knox and Cornell. There was support for education, as one might expect, as a generic activity, at the same time that teacher preparation was seen by some as a less than full partner in the liberal arts tradition that was central to the identity of both institutions; the interests of the colleges were seen as overlapping those of schools, and both recognized the contributions of local teachers, at the same time that the 'best students' were at times reportedly encouraged to think about 'liberal studies' rather than 'education'; and an openness to alternatives was generated at least partly by discontent over current courses and programs. At each college the situation was ripe for an approach to educational studies that went beyond training, helped integrate the department with other units of the college, and that might reinforce or extend the colleges' presence in the local community. Underlying many of the contradictions noted above was the perceived schism between 'liberal' and 'applied' or 'professional' fields — a schism fostered, as we have seen, by the very legacy of liberal inquiry.[3] The fit between the liberal arts and educational studies thus formed the center of the picture of education at these colleges.

The Practice of Teacher Education and Liberal Inquiry

Educational Reform at Knox College

As half of a Department of Education existing within a distinctively liberal arts institution, the value and purpose of teacher preparation programs was not obvious, to say the least. Upon my arrival at Knox in the fall of 1981, I found a teacher preparation curriculum that included the more or less standard fare: in the elementary program, an introductory course, 'Issues in Education', courses in educational psychology, child development, philosophy of education, special education, methods of reading, an assortment of other methods courses, and student teaching; while the secondary education program included the introductory and educational psychology courses, general and special methods courses, philosophy of education, special education, and student teaching. Moreover, as in other small, liberal arts colleges, several parts of the education program were taught by adjunct professors and others — for example, in the elementary education sequence, someone from the natural sciences taught a mini-course on science methods, another person taught a section on social studies, and so on. These faculty members' primary affiliation was not in education, of course, but in other academic disciplines or other institutions. While many of these people enjoyed the teaching responsibilities associated with the education department, and performed admirably, such additional responsibilities were extraneous to their primary duties. At another level, the prestige of the department, and its programs, again as in many other colleges of this type, was not all one might hope for. At least some academics with degrees in other disciplines saw the education department as something like a vocational preparation program, where certain students could thrive who might not succeed in the more rigorous, demanding disciplines. The academic respectability of education faculty was, for some, also an open question.

Lest this picture be painted too bleakly, though, it is important to see that such an image was itself contradictory. One of the results of the relatively low status of education as a field was that members of the administration and faculty at Knox were almost completely open to any revisions in departmental courses and programs that were consistent with the requirements of the state department of education. Thus the lack of prestige afforded education in practice actually made significant change more attainable. And since state requirements at the time were minimal, there were few significant obstacles to such change. In addition, I was early on able to develop personal and professional relationships with faculty in other departments (especially sociology, anthropology, philosophy, and history) who had intellectual interests which overlapped my own. After both private discussions and presentations at public forums, several faculty made a point of discussing issues of mutual interest. The discovery that there were substantive, complex issues in educational theory and practice that required sustained analysis was a pleasant surprise for many. Thus the originally rather anomalous picture of education began to gradually change, with the aid of a generally supportive or at least non-obstructionist administration and faculty.

Before beginning my duties at Knox I had reviewed the current programs and course offerings. In talking with both faculty members and administrators I was assured that there was ample room for alteration of those programs, and that this was in fact expected. My general intent was to introduce areas of the curriculum that had been generally de-emphasized or excluded altogether. Principally this meant introducing a number of foundations courses, especially covering issues in the sociology, history, and philosophy of education, and in curriculum theory and history. In addition, I wanted to alter the nature of the methods courses and student teaching experiences so that they would reflect a more critical (rather than technical) orientation. This was designed to accomplish at least three things. First, to emphasize important areas of educational studies whose ideas and concepts would help revitalize the teacher education programs. Second, to help change the perception of educational studies, so that it might be seen by the

Knox students, faculty, and administration at as a valuable asset, and a member of the academic community. And third, to develop courses that would be of general interest to the student population, rather than exclusively to education majors.

The college as a whole supported these ideas, though precisely what it meant to be a 'member of the academic community' was not especially clear — either to me or others. There was a clear sense in which these ideas were seen as appropriate and at least headed in the right direction, by the faculty at large and the members of those committees that approved program and course changes. Had this not been the case the changes that were advocated could not have been implemented, especially as quickly as they were.

Shortly after my arrival I had begun thinking about specific revisions in the elementary education program, for which I had the major responsibility. After lengthy discussions with various faculty members, school people, and others who were directly or indirectly involved, a revamped program emerged. In addition to relatively minor changes in general education requirements, the revised Department of Education program leading to elementary education certification included the following courses:

1 *School and Society*, offered as the first course in the sequence leading to certification, and to non-education majors interested in issues related to the content of the course. Significantly, this course was given 'distribution credit' in the social sciences, which meant that students enrolling in the course did not necessarily do so because of an interest in the teaching profession *per se*.

2 *Philosophy of Education*, which enrolled mostly students interested in teaching as a career, and occasionally students majoring in philosophy as well.

3 *Education of Exceptional Children*, a special education course required by the state for certification in elementary education, taught by an adjunct instructor.

4 *Educational Psychology*, also given distribution credit in the social sciences and drawing students from outside of education, though in fewer numbers than *School and Society*.

5 *Reading and Language Arts Instruction*, taken exclusively by elementary education majors, and created in response to the mandates of the state department of education.

6 *Knowledge and Power: Perspectives on the Curriculum*, also given

distribution credit in the social sciences, though in part because it was a new and advanced level course, few non–majors enrolled.

7 *Curriculum Development and Elementary School Teaching*, an advanced course for majors, which included a substantial field experience component. This course was taken exclusively by elementary education majors.

8 *Student Teaching-Elementary*, and *Seminary in Elementary Student Teaching*, obviously taken only by majors, almost always during their senior year.

One of the consequences of teaching in a small department is that, with the exception of the educational psychology and special education offerings, I taught all the courses which comprised the elementary education sequence. This did two things simultaneously. First, it meant that, to a greater extent than may be possible in larger universities and colleges, general principles might be created that could shape the contours of the program. Since inter-disciplinary disagreements could not arise, the freedom afforded the creation of such principles provided an important sense of personal and programmatic autonomy. As a result, second, the sense of there being an overall coherence to the program was enhanced. Having the opportunity to teach the six primary areas of coursework in the sequence made such coherence at least more possible than might be the case in larger, more diversified and specialized, departments.

More important than the specific courses in the program is the general orientation or approach to education within which they were embedded. Essentially there were four guiding principles that were involved in the operation of this teacher preparation effort, that relate directly to the discussion of foundationally oriented teacher preparation programs as discussed in the previous chapter. These include, first, a recognition of the socially constructed nature of what counts as 'knowledge' in general, and 'school knowledge' in particular, and educational institutions responsible for its distribution; second, the ability and need to question commonsensical ideas and perceptions, thereby turning them into problematic phenomena; third, the development of alternative approaches for educational theory and practice; and fourth, the continual reminder that educational action is a part of larger institutional frameworks and patterns of meaning.[4] The guiding ideas which flow from these basic principles are that students see the current world of schooling as only one among many possible such worlds, engage in critical dialogue over both the normative issues of classroom phenomena and their wider social consequences, and actively engage in the process of reconstruction within the extant framework of the school system. It was this last point, of course, that frequently gave rise to particular anxieties and frustrations, and which I will comment on shortly.

Against this background of ideas and concepts, I was fortunate to have students who, in enrolling in a liberal arts institution, were probably less tied to a notion of education as vocational training than may be the case in other kinds of institutions. Faculty could presume that students attending the college had an interest in intellectual inquiry and academic involvement, and that the matter of job preparation was at least secondary. And indeed I generally found this to be the case. Thus the fact that the courses in the new program had a strong theoretical component, and that 'methods courses' in the traditional sense of that term had been eliminated, did not generate the sort of discontent that might have been manifested at institutions with a different orientation. I found students generally willing, and able, to engage the rather complicated arguments which the new courses embodied.

Returning to the three aims of this revised program as outlined above, the new courses did serve to introduce previously excluded areas of the curriculum, principally the foundations areas, and to reorient the general program to one based on reflection, critique, and transformation. In addition, the new courses (especially the introductory one) were taken by large numbers of non-education students, so that they became seen as of more general value than apparently had been the case previously. The Knox community also acknowledged these changes in various ways, and were often openly supportive of the new courses. One of the events that had a noticeable impact in this regard was the team teaching of the philosophy of education course with a member of the Philosophy Department, whereas this course had been taught exclusively by a member of that department for a number of years. More generally, the positive responses from students also helped to increase the level of faculty support for the new courses and programs. It should also be noted that both members of the Department of Education taught sections of an introductory humanities course required of all freshmen, *Perspectives on Being Human*, which further assisted in the integration of faculty in the department with the rest of the college.

One of the requirements for state certification was that students spend at least one hundred hours in schools before undertaking student teaching. This requirement, the student teaching experience itself, and the more general nature of teaching in contemporary society, provided the backdrop against which the ideas discussed above were to be implemented. This created certain tensions within the programs, as experienced by our students. First, as student teachers and earlier as observers, researchers, and participants, they had to somehow accommodate the ideas they were exposed to, the values they held, and the perspectives they developed, to the world of practice as embodied by the public schools. This was an especially difficult situation in the context of the program under discussion since the local school system tended to be rather conservative in its educational policies and practices. For example, there were reports of corporal punishment in some schools, despite objections by certain parents. In addition, the school board had mandated the use of one particular basal reading series for the K–6 school system. And in at least one elementary school where student teachers worked, the principal asked for a monthly report on the progress of each pupil, in terms of which reading unit, skills area, etc., she/he was working on at the moment. Such strict accountability measures served to constrict what was considered educationally appropriate in the local school district.

Second, the schools in which students were placed had developed characteristically standardized, systematic, and deskilled practices. While the kind of system which resulted was typical of many American schools, the degree of standardization and deskilling may have been uncharacteristic. At the level of classroom phenomena and architecture, a fair generalization is that the typical classroom was one in which teacher proof curricula were continuing to dominate more and more (the basal readers were but one example of this), manufactured and stylized displays typified what attention to aesthetics there was, classroom discipline was strict, with attention paid to 'time on task' measures, teacher–student interactions were mostly teacher initiated, and classroom schedules were relatively rigid and carefully adhered to.

Third, what developed within the general confines of the elementary teacher preparation program was a rather deep-seated antipathy between the critically oriented, foundational perspective embodied in the principles of this program, and the particular work context with which students were faced.[5] While frequent attempts were made throughout the program to remain mindful of the current realities of curriculum, teaching, and professional ethos of schools, and to occasionally insert the sort of distance from these that could allow for critical reflection and analysis, the actual contours of schools and the work of teaching were always something of a culture shock for students. Perhaps a couple of short vignettes can illustrate the difficulties and contradictions embedded in the operation of this program. Let us look at the experiences of two students, whose names have been changed to protect their anonymity.

'Sally'

Sally was a 'non-traditional' student who had decided to return to college and obtain a teaching certificate, having become dissatisfied with the profession in which she was working. Sally was on the whole a more mature, self-assured, and committed student than many with less extensive experiences. She was hardworking, friendly, and open to the kinds of issues covered in the new teacher education program, though, like most students, such issues required a good deal of effort and time. Sally had taken some teacher education courses at another college several years previously, but the bulk of her preparation was received in courses at Knox.

Sally's warmth, sense of humor, and dedication were reflected in the approach she took with the third grade students in her student teaching experience. She wanted to treat the students with respect, to get to know them as people who could make important contributions to their own learning, and to refrain from being the traditional authority figure in the classroom. The room in which Sally taught was representative of the local school district, with a relatively small number of minority group students (mostly Black, with a few Hispanic children). The morning schedule consisted of reading, recess, math, and 'special' classes (learning center, art, music, or physical education [twice], on alternating days), while the afternoon was taken up with reading, spelling, English, and either social studies or science (though the latter was pursued only sporadically). On one of my visits to Sally's classroom, about midway through her student teaching experience, I observed the following reading activities:

1   As part of the lesson for that day, Sally distributed a worksheet on following directions. She played a phonograph record that accompanied the worksheet, as prescribed for that particular lesson. The voice on the record asked the class questions about following directions, after which there was a short pause, and Sally turned the phonograph off. After the pupils wrote their answers on the worksheet,

Sally turned the phonograph back on, and the voice on the recording provided the correct answers. The students were then to see how well they had done in writing the correct responses, as measured by their match with the disembodied voice on the record. The only responsibilities Sally had were to introduce the lesson (by following the printed instructions in the teacher's manual), and to turn the phonograph on and off at the appropriate times. The final activity Sally engaged in was the distribution of another worksheet on following directions that was assigned as homework for the next day. The entire lesson took about twenty minutes.

2   The subsequent activity was another reading lesson, this time to a different group although in the same classroom (there were always at least two reading groups meeting simultaneously). This activity consisted of the group checking problems they had worked on during the first part of the reading class. Individual students read the selections aloud, while the rest of the group checked their own workbook pages. Sally spent this lesson calling on individual pupils, telling them how to score each page, and exhorting the other group of students to get to work, be quieter, and the like. At the end of the lesson Sally asked each student to tell her the grade he/she had gotten on each of the pages. As the students reported their numerical scores, Sally used a 'computer wheel' to calculate letter grades for each page, which she then recorded in the grade book. This activity took about twenty minutes from beginning to end, after which the students had recess.

3   From the end of recess until lunch break, Sally's activities consisted of reading problems from a math text, illustrating them with a story problem she had composed herself, and then helping individual pupils who had problems with the homework assignment for the next day. The math activities lasted about thirty minutes, after which the class was given time to work on their homework. Throughout the morning, Sally was uncommonly patient with the pupils, and her sensitivity and caring attitude were obvious.

I offer this vignette not to disparage the teaching Sally was engaged in but to provide an illustration of what were in many ways typical classroom phenomena. I could sense that Sally was frustrated and bored by the activities in which she was engaged but felt compelled to carry them through nonetheless. During my observations that morning I noted several pupils having difficulty paying attention, keeping 'on task', and understanding the meaning of classroom activities.

Within the teacher education sequence, the notion of deskilling of teaching had been discussed at length, as had the history and consequences of teacher proof curriculum, the trivialized and impersonal knowledge often taught in schools, and the values that become manifest through social relations sanctioned by the hidden curriculum. And, as I intimated before, Sally was more able than many to understand such issues, and had developed alternatives that might diverge from current practice. The fact that she changed little from the prescribed program of this classroom was, in short, not due to a simple lack of enthusiasm on Sally's part, nor the absence of conventional methods courses in the teacher education program. Rather, the interactions described above were undertaken out of a desire to 'fit in' to the established patterns and routines of the school — to become, in brief, an *accepted professional*.

After observing the lesson described above, I had a rather long conversation with Sally, in which the morning's activities were analyzed and critiqued. I asked about her thoughts and feelings regarding these activities, and shared with her my own observations. In particular, we discussed at length the reading lessons during which she basically acted as an appendage to a machine (the phonograph), followed by her duties as a record keeper/accountant, while at the same time trying to retain order in the classroom. We talked about these things in relation to the deskilling of teacher's work, the tendency for administrative, record keeping, and technical activities to prevail in schools, and the hidden curriculum fostered by the 'teacher as keeper of order'. She felt guilty about having done those kinds of lessons (for herself, and especially for her students), but believed there was really no effective alternative in that situation (though she knew of other activities and had developed strategies that could be used to implement them). One of the reasons for Sally's sense of 'being caught' had to do with the very sense of caring, desire to be open and responsive to her class, and genuine fondness for teaching that had characterized her initial interactions. What she found was that, quite predictably and understandably, her students had in some ways taken advantage of her openness and good humor, by failing to do the work Sally asked of them, being disruptive, occasionally rude (from Sally's point of view, at least), and generally unresponsive. Indeed the students used the opportunities Sally provided as an opening to resist the structures, activities, and interactions that the regular teacher, and the school culture generally, sanctioned. While we might see such resistances as provocative or even valuable,[6] for Sally they made life more complicated, agonizing, and personally painful. Indeed at one point during her student teaching experience Sally had contemplated ending her program, an idea she later rejected.

'Angela'

Like Sally, Angela was a non-traditional student who had decided, after raising three children of her own, to resume her college career and obtain a teaching certificate. Angela was very mature, self assured, and intense, with a strong desire to change school practices, in part because of the experiences her own children had undergone. Angela was particularly interested in political activities, had participated in local peace and anti-nuclear weapons demonstrations, and was anxious to convey these ideas to elementary school students. In addition, she had a strong spiritual but non-sectarian sensitivity, and frequently tried to express those sentiments to myself and others. Angela, like Sally, was among the most committed, dedicated students with whom I have worked.

The kindergarten classroom in which Angela student taught was in the same school district as Sally's. Angela taught a group of about 25 students in this classroom, and to an unusual extent tried to implement her own ideas, values, and commitment. Two specific incidents are revelatory.

1   I entered Angela's classroom during one of my visits to find a half dozen children seated around Angela on the floor. She was talking with this group of children about the morning's activities, though at first the tenor of her remarks was unclear. I soon realized Angela, and at least a couple of the children, were visibly upset, crying intermittently, and close to the point of breaking. The particular group sitting on the floor included those who had been most offensive that morning, running around, pushing and shoving children, yelling, and generally making life painful and difficult for the pupils and for Angela. She was attempting to understand the students' behavior, and to get them to discuss the situation with her. In spite of her most patient efforts, however, the children were for the most part silent and uncooperative. The session ended when the rest of the class returned from recess.

2   On another occasion I observed a part of a unit dealing with Japanese culture, during which Angela had attempted to talk with the class about Hiroshima, the issue of nuclear armaments, and the like. The activities I actually witnessed on this day had to do with the construction of Japanese kites. Most of the pupils worked diligently and quietly on their projects, but there was still in evidence the nucleus of the disruptive group that resisted Angela's efforts. In general, though, the class responded favorably to this activity, though getting there had been an evident struggle.

Angela was committed to providing alternative activities for her pupils, to getting to know her students on a more personal level, and to conveying to them the sense of her own political and spiritual convictions. She rejected the typical forms of control, order, and authority that existed in that kindergarten, and in most elementary school classrooms. To a greater extent than Sally, Angela attempted to incorporate those ideas and activities that were of personal significance to her in her classroom, and to an extent was successful at doing so. On the other hand, the toll such attempts took on Angela's self esteem, confidence, and sense of commitment to the profession were very extensive and disheartening. She frequently felt that the sacrifice demanded was too much, and several times contemplated quitting. Angela often left the school in tears, and felt frequently exasperated by the experience. Like Sally, she was quite able and willing to discuss her experiences in light of the critical literature and analyses that were familiar parts of the program.

The stories of these two students are in many ways typical of the conditions and experiences of students I had contact with in the teacher preparation program at Knox College. While most students have been able to find teaching positions of one sort or another, and have pursued teaching as a career to a greater extent than either Sally or Angela, I did not include these two particular vignettes as a way of justifying an attitude of pessimism. Such an attitude is not, in my view, justifiable. Rather, in pointing out some of the fundamental dilemmas and contradictions involved in trying to organize and operate a program based on an affiliation with critical theory and practice, I wanted to illuminate some of the ethical dilemmas of such a program.

I especially want to emphasize, first, that these are not technical problems that can be solved solely through the adoption of higher admissions standards for students, the creation of better courses, the finding of better field placements, or the attraction of brighter students to the field. While each of these ideas has received considerable attention in the media, and though each may have some relevance for programmatic reconsiderations, they do not comprise the core of the issue. Rather, the central problem — as entailed in the contradictions between critical theory, personal reflection, social and political sensitivity, on the one hand, and a deskilled, routinized, administrative, patriarchal, and intellectually uninvigorating cultural environment in which work is carried out, on the other — is an ideological one.

One of the ethical issues growing out of this problem concerns the extent to which teacher educators who want to foster critical reflection, a political consciousness, and a sensitivity to social issues in students, can expect such tendencies to flourish in their teaching practice, in ways that do not professionally or psychologically jeopardize them. The duplicity involved here is extensive, and since the curricula, pedagogy, and evaluative practices that currently dominate in schools do, in some way, have to be reckoned with, there is a point one reaches where students may be unfairly compromised. It is not that I think we should refuse to put students in positions where they are challenged, critiqued, or even emotionally strained. Such situations can be professionally and personally gratifying for students and those whom they teach. Yet it does seem to me that there is a point where they also become counter-productive and ethically questionable.

I also want to reject, second, the notion that effective action and change in schools must await transformations of a more general sort. While this is the view of some analysts of educational policy and practice — not surprisingly, especially of those whose primary affiliation is outside the educational arena[7] — it is not a tenable one. It misconstrues the nature of social change, I think, and insists upon a mechanistic model of alienation, domination, and resistance that is over determined and a-cultural. Insofar as schools are fertile ground for ideologically impregnated cultural practices, there may be no more important forum from which, along with our institutions, social change may spring. In addition, such an attitude fails to recognize the plight of students, teachers, and others who are caught in a network of interactions that are frequently injurious. We cannot wait for broader social changes before acting.

Of course the examples of Angela and Sally came from a new program whose consequences were only just beginning to be felt. Their possible long term effects, and the changes that might be made as a result of findings like those reported here, can only be imagined. Yet they were a part of the reexamination of education at Cornell College, to which we now turn.

Educational Reform at Cornell College

Like the situation at Knox College in the early 1980s, Cornell College has embarked on a reassessment of its programs in the Department of Education — a reassessment that continues as of this writing. Contemporary discussions of the department's programs commenced because of numerous factors that, while similar in many respects to the reasons for reform at Knox, seem more formalized, widely debated, and matters of frequent public discussion. These factors form the institutional and conceptual bases for current discussions of educational reform. They all predate my arrival at Cornell.

First, members of the faculty were animated by the spate of national reports regarding the state of public schooling and teacher preparation in the US. Many faculty had read at least a few of these reports and were concerned about the role of liberal arts colleges in assisting in educational reform. In particular, many faculty were familiar with at least the outline of The Holmes Group's recommendations, and worried about their consequences for colleges like Cornell. Many correctly perceived this as a largely political debate, and wondered how (and if) such colleges would become actively engaged in that debate. While there was nothing like consensus on campus regarding calls for educational reform, the publication of scores of studies critical of American public schooling and programs of teacher preparation at least gave cause for concern, and in some cases furthered doubts and suspicions that were already held.

Second, such national concerns were shared regionally in a conference sponsored by the Associated Colleges of the Midwest in the fall of 1985. Several colleges reportedly expressed concern at that conference about the relationship between the liberal arts and education on their campuses, and spoke about the isolation of programs of teacher preparation. These concerns were further voiced in a report of the Committee on Academic Affairs at Cornell, completed in the Spring of 1986. This report cited certain national trends that were alarming — the shortage of teachers in several areas of secondary education, the proper balance between education and liberal arts courses, the failure to attract the best students into education programs, and the like — as well as local concerns of Cornell faculty. Among the latter were concerns about the lack of breadth in the academic program, grade inflation in education courses, the number of students who avoided the distribution requirements of the BA degree in favor of the more individualized, less restrictive requirements of the Bachelor of Special Studies degree,[8] the number of education courses that those involved in certification programs were required to complete, and the isolation of such programs from the rest of the campus.

Third, the Iowa Department of Education was in the process of reformulating certification requirements, in response to calls for educational reform both inside and outside the state. There was some faculty concern about this, especially since a number of neighboring states had implemented or were contemplating changes in certification rules. These rules often seemed to further compromise the role of the liberal disciplines as the state departments of education expanded the number of required courses in education. The national call for exclusively graduate level programs in teacher preparation exacerbated the state situation, since there was undoubtedly pressure from some groups to mandate graduate level programs in Iowa as well.

Fourth, there were particular personnel questions and opportunities that also were involved in the push for reform in the Department of Education. In the fall of 1985 it became clear that both full time people in the department would soon retire. As it turned out, the chair of the department retired at the end of the 1985–86 academic year, while the other full time member of the department retired one year later. This meant that within a one year period there would be a 100% turnover in Department of Education faculty. Many in the faculty and administration saw this as providing Cornell its own 'window of opportunity', as it were, and such personnel shifts gave further impetus to the reform of the department's programs and courses.

Having been apprised of these and related events and perceptions by faculty and administration members, I accepted the position as Chair of the Department of Education at Cornell, and began work there in the fall of 1986. I saw this position as not only providing an opportunity to implement the ideas and principles outlined in the previous chapters of this book, but to do so in an environment that appeared supportive and encouraging of education at the same time that it was willing to generate alternative approaches. The intersection of national debate, regional and state discussion, and local concerns and faculty changes, combined with a long held sensitivity and concern for public schooling by many in the Cornell community, provided a rather special opportunity. Moreover, my previous experiences at Knox provided me with a basis for reform of education that would more closely align it with many of the values of liberal inquiry.

Early in September, I sent a memorandum to all members of the Cornell faculty, indicating that a reassessment of the department and its programs would take place. I indicated that the discussions that would take place would be wide ranging, involving both the internal workings of the Department of Education as well as its relation with other units of the college. This memo invited interested faculty to volunteer to serve on an ad hoc committee that would be making recommendations regarding the future of the department. Within one week, eleven faculty members (out of about 70, or roughly 16 per cent) had volunteered to serve on this committee, representing the following departments and offices of the college: Art, Biology, the Dean's Office, Education, History, the Library, Music, Psychology, Sociology, and Theatre and Speech. Still other faculty, unable to serve on this committee because of other assignments and responsibilities, from time to time conveyed ideas, perceptions, and suggestions to the committee. In addition, two staff people were invited to become members of the committee because of their experience within the department and the college as a whole.

The membership of this committee was further expanded to include two current Cornell students and two local public school teachers (one elementary teacher and one secondary history teacher). In all, then, the 'Ad hoc Committee on Education' consisted of eighteen quite diverse individuals, united by a concern for education and the programs supported by Cornell. Needless to say, the discussions that ensued were frequently wide ranging, protracted, and rather stimulating. The intent was to expand the dialogue as much as possible (consistent with the commitments of contextualized, human inquiry, democratic participation, and the expression of contrary perspectives and presuppositions, as outlined in earlier chapters) so that we might create some understanding of current practices and future possibilities.

From our first meeting in September of 1986 until the first of the year, eight meetings of the ad hoc committee were held, with discussions generally going from more general philosophical questions and concerns to more specific issues of policy and programmatic impediments and possibilities. The initial meeting of the committee concerned the status of education as a field, whether it was a genuine discipline or not, and its conceptual relationship to other departments and areas of study. While the discussions were intense and expansive, there emerged a general consensus that while education is a more open ended or integrative area than other subjects, it should be seen as having equal status with other departments in the college. I frequently made the claim during this and subsequent meetings that if this point of view was not generally held by college faculty, and if they did not perceive educational studies to be a full partner in the liberal arts tradition of the college, then the department should not continue in operation. Stating the issue in this way I believe laid bare the essential conceptual and political question, and helped clarify the consequences of the faculty's view of the department.

The next general question then became, given the desirability of education becoming a full partner in the liberal arts tradition of the college, how do we facilitate this through the revision of programs and courses. One of the persistent attempts to help with this was to argue that 'education' and 'teacher preparation' are connected but not identical. That is, that there are a variety of issues and ideas in education that, though they may be important for those planning a career in teaching, are of more general value and relevance. This meant that 'education' should be seen and respected as an academic area of inquiry, with its own questions, disputes, history, and literature. This being the case, it is important that courses in the department be perceived as useful and 'liberating' for virtually all students, and not just prospective teachers.

Another way to convey the perspective of education as an area of inquiry was to offer courses that would highlight their academic nature and intellectual depth. This meant, in essence, creating new courses that would replace current ones. The program then in operation included the following 'professional education' courses:

I. Elementary Education
   1 'Education and the Role of the Teacher' (half credit)
   2 'Principles of Human Development'
   3 'Multimedia Methods' (half credit)
   4 'Introduction to Special Education'*
   5 'Human Relations in Teaching'
   6 'Student Teaching' (4 credits)
   7 'Teaching of Reading and Language Arts'
   8 'Social Studies in the Elementary School' (half credit)
   9 'Children's Literature'
   10 'Mathematics in the Elementary School' (half credit)
   11 'Science in the Elementary School' (half credit)
   12 'Teaching Writing in Elementary School'* (half credit)
   13 'Music Education in the Elementary School' (half credit)
      — taught by Department of Music faculty

II. Secondary education
   1–6 as above
   7 'Principles of Learning' (half credit)
   8 a specialized methods course in the area(s) in which certification is sought.

* indicates a strongly recommended but not required course

Even more than the programs replaced at Knox College, the

elementary and secondary education offerings at Cornell lacked foundational offerings, emphasizing instead a mostly psychological, technically oriented methods course orientation. There were no course requirements in the history, philosophy, or sociology of education, and the methods courses as outlined did not contain the critical, reflective approach to curriculum and teaching discussed earlier. In addition, the student teaching experience included only a one hour per week meeting, which required little or no reading and instead focused on classroom problems and themes. The then current programs in education were indeed quite far removed from the foundationally oriented perspective described in chapter 5.

Before discussing specific course changes, it is important to note that the committee discussed at length another means of altering the perception of the department on campus, so that it could become a respected area of inquiry rather than an avenue for job preparation exclusively. This was the possible creation a new major, 'Educational Studies', that would not lead to certification but would be an area of emphasis for those interested in educational issues and ideas. The committee responded favorably to this idea, though for reasons that I will detail below it has not as yet been approved. In any case, this new major would assist in moving away from the notion that 'education' and 'job preparation' are synonymous, and might encourage more students to explore education as a field of study.

Over the course of our discussions during the fall of 1986 we became increasingly concerned about the time constraints associated with generating proposals for curriculum change, as well as with their approval and implementation. Because of recent changes in certification rules in Iowa, a completely revamped program would have to be submitted and approved as part of a more general evaluation to ensure compliance with the new rules; this would likely take several months. In addition, the committee structure at Cornell is fairly elaborate, as is the process for approving curriculum changes. The ad hoc committee provides suggestions, on an advisory basis, to the Teacher Education Committee (consisting of 8 faculty members from around the college; there were 4 people who served on both this and the ad hoc committee). This committee then reports its recommendations to the Academic Programs Committee who can alter, support, or disapprove the recommendations made to it. Its findings are then sent to the Committee on Academic Affairs (of which Academic Programs is a subcommittee). Recommendations to this committee have to reach them shortly after the first of the year, so that any course changes could be acted on in time to be printed in the following year's publications. After deliberating on the recommendations of its subcommittee, Academic Affairs distributes in writing to each faculty member its decisions. Any member of the faculty can dissent from any of these decisions, and request (within 10 days) that they be discussed by the faculty as a whole. If no such request is received within the 10 day period, they are approved as distributed and become a part of the curriculum of Cornell College.

Because of the rather elaborate (especially for a small institution) and time consuming procedures for curriculum changes, and the requirements for review mandated by new state certification rules, it became apparent that the expansive changes anticipated in the Department of Education could not be negotiated in one year, as we had originally intended. Instead, the ad hoc committee agreed to submit a number of changes to both the committees of the college and the state department about the first of the year. These recommendations would meet the time requirements of the internal committee structure and would not necessitate a full review by the state department, as they were presented as a one year interim proposal, while a plan for compliance with the new certification rules would be submitted the following year.

At the center of the changes proposed was the development of 4 new courses that would fulfill a number of functions within the department and college. First, these courses would provide instruction in the foundations areas that had been excluded from the current programs. This is important not just because it filled certain conceptual gaps in our department but also because it broadened the sort of work that could be conducted in the rest of the program as well (e.g., in student teaching and field placements that encourage reflective teaching[10]). Second, the courses identified would provide a common core around which both programs in elementary and secondary teacher education, and the prospective Educational Studies major, might revolve. In addition to altering the substance of our programs, this core would help unify education offerings, whereas in the current programs there were few shared courses and experiences for elementary and secondary students. Third, the core courses would highlight the academic integrity of education as a field of study, as they symbolized the movement away from a more technical and vocational orientation. They would make clear the new direction of the department as they involved issues, subject matters, and ideas previously excluded from our courses. Fourth, the separation between the Department of Education and other areas of the college, a major concern of many, would begin to be bridged by the installation of foundations courses that were intimately related to the offerings and interests of other departments and faculty members.

After a good deal of discussion by members of the committee, focusing on these four ideas, the following courses were recommended as part of the alterations for the following academic year:

1 'Educational Psychology'
2 'History of US Education'
3 'Educational Philosophies'
4 'Schooling in American Society'

In addition to the creation of these four new courses, one other course was established, 'Secondary School Curriculum'. This course was designed to replace the more specialized methods courses for secondary students (see the list of courses in the old program above), deal with a number of critical issues in curriculum theory and development, and provide a site for working with students and teachers in a further effort to overcome the division between theory and practice. What turned out to be the most controversial recommendation of the committee was the decision to reduce the amount of required student teaching from 4 credits (16 weeks) to 2 credits (8 weeks). The new programs in teacher education recommended by the committee included, then, the following course offerings:

I. Elementary Education
   1   'Educational Psychology'
   2   'History of US Education'
   3   'Educational Philosophies'
   4   'Schooling in American Society'
   5   'Introduction to Special Education' (recommended)
   6   'Human Relations'
   7   'Reading'
   8   'Social Studies Methods'
   9   'Children's Literature'
   10 'Science and Mathematics in Elementary School'
   11 'Student teaching' (2 credits required; additional 2 credits optional)

II. Secondary Education
   1–6 as above.
   7   'Secondary School Curriculum'
   8   'Student teaching' (as above)

In addition, an adjunct workshop in audio-visual equipment and procedures was created, to be taught by the head of the college's Audio-Visual Aids Department.

The course changes listed above represent the thinking of those associated with the ad hoc committee as it attempted to redirect the department's courses and orientation. They were considered and approved by the Teacher Education Committee in January of 1987, and submitted to the Academic Programs Committee, where these changes received unanimous approval later that month. Before detailing this chronology of events further, it is important to consider in more detail the nature of the courses that were recommended, their place in the overall reform of the department, and their place within areas of instruction offered by the college in general.

Educational Reform and Curriculum Integration

A persistent theme of this book has been the necessity of overcoming the duality between education and other fields, and between theory and practice within education itself. These ideas were clearly in the forefront of the changes discussed and approved by various committees at Cornell College. With respect to the four core courses specifically, several initiatives were undertaken in an attempt to integrate educational studies with other areas of the college.

It is important to note that the curriculum of the college includes two courses with titles and (apparently, at least) contents substantially similar to those contained in the recommended program changes of the Department of Education: 'Philosophy of Education' (included in the listings of the Department of Philosophy) and 'Education and Society' (taught by a member of the Department of Sociology). The overlap between these two courses and the two recommended courses in education was discussed by members of the ad hoc committee, and a number of meetings were held between myself and members of the other two departments. In addition, I had a number of meetings with members of the History and Psychology Departments, to see if faculty in those areas might be interested in contributing to the development of the new core courses in educational psychology and history.

With respect to the courses dealing with the philosophy and sociology of education, both technical and conceptual questions were quickly apparent. The Philosophy of Education course had been taught only sporadically (it had not been offered for several years previously, for example), and the sociology course was being offered only once per year, and its long term scheduling was uncertain. Since it was not possible for members of either department to offer the respective course on a regular or frequent basis, neither course would fulfill the purposes of the education department in its new programs. Also, there was no interest on the part of Department of History faculty to create a new course in the history of US education. A member of the psychology department was, however, very interested in teaching the new course in educational psychology, since her background was in that area. This was readily approved by both departments and the Dean of the College.

My initial discussions with members of all four departments centered on cross-listing the new education courses with each of the affected departments. This would clarify one of the intents of the reoriented study of education — namely, to integrate it as a full partner in the liberal arts tradition of the college, and signify the college's commitment to this idea. As one might imagine, the discussions that ensued involved questions of appropriate domain or 'turf', matters of staffing and personnel, the setting of precedents, and general uneasiness about disciplinary boundaries being eroded. One of my surprises during these discussions was that many individuals and departments had a strong departmental and disciplinary identity, and that inter-disciplinary and cross-disciplinary offerings were rare.[11] This was surprising at a small liberal arts college, where all faculty are expected to teach at least occasionally outside their specific area(s) of graduate education, and marked an important difference between the faculties at Cornell and those at Knox. In addition, the lack of enthusiasm for cross-listing new courses with the Department of Education also reflected a question about the status of education within the liberal arts. Given the nature of previous programs and courses, this question was understandable and reasonable. In any event, none of the four departments agreed to cross-listing a new education course. While not completely unexpected, their decisions were disappointing.

The same conclusion was reached with respect to my second inquiry to each department: the possibility of team teaching one of these new courses with a member of the education faculty. This was a somewhat more common occurrence at Cornell, though still not in large numbers. Again, practical as well as conceptual questions arose in response to this request: problems of staffing, disciplinary focus, appropriate audiences, and commitment of departmental resources were all raised. I should note that some departments indicated that they would be willing to reconsider the possibility of team teaching courses

— as well as cross-listing them — at some point in the future. I will return to this topic in the final section of this chapter.

An additional attempt was made to help integrate education courses, and alter their status on campus, that ultimately proved more successful. One of the questions discussed by each of the committees that considered revisions in the education department concerned whether or not the core courses would count toward 'distribution credit' for the BA degree. Courses from around the college could be given credit in one of several categories, including the humanities, the natural sciences, the social sciences, and the fine arts. This was decided on an individual basis, usually as new courses were developed by faculty members. The old programs in the Department of Education included only one course that received such distribution credit ('Principles of Human Development' received credit in the social sciences). If such credit were granted to the new core courses, the image of education, its value for the general student of Cornell, and its integration with other areas of the college — undercut by negative discussions regarding cross-listing and team teaching courses — might be assisted. As the recommendations were forwarded to the Committee on Academic Affairs, it was requested that the new courses in the history and philosophy of education receive distribution credit in the humanities; and that the other two core courses be granted credit in the social sciences.

When the proposals for reform of department courses were reviewed by the Committee on Academic Affairs in early February, 1987, the new courses were debated and discussed at some length. Before voting on them, however, a motion was made to remove the recommendation regarding the granting of distribution credit from all but the educational psychology course (which would, you will recall, be the one course taught by faculty outside the education department). The committee approved that motion on a faculty vote of 6 to 5 (students concurred, on a vote of 2 to 1). The net result was that the curricular revisions in the departments were approved by the committee; yet with the exception of the educational psychology courses, none would carry distribution credit for students graduating with a Bachelor of Arts degree. The memorandum indicating the committee's decision on this and other curriculum changes was circulated on 14 February 1987.

The following day I requested, consistent with formal college procedures, that the faculty as a whole convene to discuss the decision of the Committee on Academic Affairs to deny distribution credit to three of the four core courses that were approved. This issue became the focus of two subsequent faculty meetings. While the issues were discussed and debated at the first meeting, the faculty voted to adjourn without reaching a decision.

At the second meeting called for this purpose, discussion was also extensive and sometimes rather heated. A turning point seemed to be reached when members of the faculty reiterated three fundamental propositions: (i) all subject areas teach courses in the history and philosophy of their disciplines (or if they don't, they certainly should) and the new courses in the Department of Education follow this pattern; (ii) in selecting a new chair of the department, the faculty had mandated a new direction for the department that included as a central commitment its integration with the rest of the college — a commitment that would be significantly eroded if the decision of the Committee on Academic Affairs were not reversed; and (iii) a realization that current (and doubtlessly future) members of the department had backgrounds in the areas comprising the new areas. Many faculty made eloquent, impassioned pleas in this regard, while members of the education department intentionally did not join the debate that ensued. In the end, a motion was made to grant the previously requested distribution credit to the three core courses for which it had been denied in committee. On a voice vote, the faculty overwhelmingly approved this motion, with only three or four dissenting votes.

To summarize the policy and programmatic changes approved at Cornell during the 1986–87 year, the following are worth re-emphasizing: (i) as representative of the movement away from the technical, methodological, and psychological emphases in the department, several courses were deleted from our programs, including:

1 'Education and the Role of the Teacher'
2 'Principles of Human Development'
3 'Multimedia Methods'
4 'Principles of Learning'
5 A variety of specialized, secondary methods courses.

(ii) As an indication of the movement toward a foundationally-oriented program and one committed to praxis, the following courses were created and approved for both elementary and secondary students:

1 'Educational Psychology'
2 'History of US Education'
3 'Educational Philosophies'
4 'Schooling in American Society'.

(iii) To help integrate the new courses in the department, courses 2 and 3 were granted distribution credit in the humanities, while the other two received credit in the social sciences. At the same time inquiries regarding cross-listing and team teaching courses, to help accomplish the same aim, met with resistance. (iv) Another new course, 'Secondary School Curriculum', was created that is expressly concerned with the encouragement of critical inquiry and reflective practice. (v) Further discussions with members of the Teacher Education Committee resulted in changes in entrance requirements for teacher education students. These included raising the minimum grade point average requirements, soliciting evaluations from three faculty members, requiring a writing sample, and requiring a personal interview with members of the Teacher Education Committee. All of these measures were intended, along with the curricular changes already noted, to increase and change the applicant pool for teacher education programs. (vi) At the same time, the idea of altering the orientation of the department, away from a vocational preparation area, toward a respectable academic area of inquiry, was facilitated. The four new core courses in particular, it is hoped, will attract many non-majors and those still unsure about future academic and career directions.

Much work remains to be done. During the 1987–88 academic year, additional changes (especially in the elementary education program, the creation of a major in educational studies, and the further integration of a foundational perspective committed to praxis) will be made. The concluding section of this chapter will briefly discuss these contemplated changes and their significance, and their broader implications for the vision of educational studies discussed in this volume.

Implementing Educational Reform: Praxis, Politics, and Renewal

The commitment to integrating educational studies and teacher education programs with other areas of Cornell College, while facilitated to an important degree by the programmatic and policy changes detailed above, will not take place overnight. This is at one level quite understandable, since the isolation of education as a field is due to both long standing institutional and intellectual traditions (discussed in the first chapter of this book) and to local conditions and patterns within the college itself. Faculty and students will need to learn from experience (as many did at Knox, as outlined above) that the study of education deserves to be a full partner in the traditions embodied by the college, and may indeed have some advantages over liberal inquiry as typically conceived. Several faculty clearly share this view of education already, and their support and encouragement has been of first order importance. The changes already approved by the faculty as a whole will go some considerable distance in allowing the department's programs and courses to become more widely accepted and valued as a part of the college's mission.

The changes that have been instituted, and the additional alterations to be introduced in the near future, counter some of the dominant trends in the reform of teacher preparation that have been discussed in the last few years. In particular, the new programs provide evidence of how teacher preparation might continue to thrive within four year, undergraduate institutions without undermining or diminishing courses in the liberal arts and sciences. As we saw earlier, associations like the Holmes Group have proposed that students' undergraduate education be devoted exclusively to the liberal disciplines, while education — as a 'professional' domain — be pursued exclusively at the graduate level. We have explored the reasons for this false dichotomy and suggested how it might be overcome. The programs discussed here are concrete attempts to promote 'liberal learning' and 'educational studies that are liberating' so that the separation of an allegedly professional domain of preparation can be seen as not only unnecessary but injurious. The ideas and programs discussed here ought to form one alternative to the call — perilously close to becoming the next bandwagon in education, complete with its own slogan system — for exclusively graduate level programs of teacher preparation. This is not to suggest, of course, that graduate programs are not important and valuable, nor that alternatives at that level should be avoided. However, as others have suggested, the reliance on graduate education programs as the panacea for current ills in the field is unwarranted. As a political document, for example, *Tomorrow's Teachers* [12] offers little research and argument to back up its claims. At the very least, programs like the one outlined here ought to be encouraged in an attempt to develop alternative conceptions and policies. In a time of uncertainty such as this, we need a proliferation of well thought out alternatives, not self-serving proposals that limit them. [13]

The programs discussed in this chapter directly confront and reject the search for that 'science of education' that the Holmes Group suggests is now within reach. While it is not entirely clear what this group means by such a science of education — its suggestion of a common legacy from the early twentieth century work of Thorndike and Dewey further clouds this issue — it is clear that *Tomorrow's Teachers* bases its optimism on the ideas and techniques of behavioral psychology and on at least some of the recent research on 'effective teaching'. Such an approach will not bear edible fruit, in my view, since (i) the possible status of education as a 'science' is misguided at root, apparently based on a commitment to empirical certainties through behavior regularities that are both epistemologically problematic and politically suspect; and (ii) as a human, moral, and political phenomenon, teaching is not the kind of activity that lends itself to scientific analysis and procedures (even without their positivistic pretensions). Such a view of education as a science, more generally, tends to overlook the complex social, cultural, and gender-related aspects of teaching that are central for reorganizing and reforming educational institutions. [14]

In contrast to the search for a science of education, the view detailed here stresses the importance of teaching as a reflective, foundational, political act requiring moral judgment and commitment. Teaching is here viewed as something closer to a 'calling' that necessitates commitment, caring, a sense of (political and ethical) purpose, and a desire to work with others (adults and pupils) on a common and important project. It relies not on behavioral regularities that have repeatedly proven inadequate, but rather on an interlocking set of studies that emphasize both the internal dynamics of schooling and a sensitivity to larger historical, social, economic, cultural, and ideological analyses. In part the new program at Cornell (like the one at Knox) reverses the trend toward diminishing the social foundations, as this has been recently discussed. [15] At the same time, the foundational studies need to overcome their own partially self-imposed segregation, so that their value for teacher preparation as praxis can be perceived. This unification, and not a specious science of education based on behaviorism and standardized outcomes and expectations, will serve to reverse the trends toward deskilling of teachers.

Among the remaining work to be done at Cornell College to help with this reversal, three major additional areas for revision are worth noting. First, there is a strong contemporary movement toward greater state control of curricular matters, other decision making processes that can be centralized, and increased pressure on teachers to be 'accountable' for specific and rationalized outcomes. These things need to be recognized as aspects of deskilling, and their class, gender, and racial biases explored, clarified, and acted upon. This entails several programmatic and policy alterations. It is my expectation that further changes in the Department of Education at Cornell will result in a requirement for a course in feminist criticism or women's studies, to help students see the gender dynamics at work historically in schools as well as in current proposals for their reform. The dynamics of class are no less important, as they frequently blend with gender roles in the creation of an ideological synergy.[16] The gender and class dynamics of classrooms, of teaching as a profession (including the workplace itself), and of the larger society which reinforces and is reinforced by these educational patterns, will become a central part of the further changes necessary for teacher education as praxis. While more has been written in the current reports about the problem of recruiting minority students into programs of teacher preparation, the nature of schools as sites for those processes of cultural and racial socialization that might actually deter minority teachers — especially those with a commitment to social activism and change — has been less frequently discussed in the current round of reports. The problems associated with encouraging more minority teachers are complex and far reaching, certainly. Yet teacher education programs must include the racist history of much educational theory and practice, as well as its continued vestiges. If we construe teacher education as praxis that aims at political change and social action, the profession of teaching will become a more friendly haven for minority teachers and their advocacy for racial, gender, and social class equality.

Second, the reforms yet to be considered in Cornell's Department of Education will also center on the need to more fully include local school teachers and administrators both as part of further discussions and, more importantly, participants in a new program for preparing teachers. The concerns of local teachers were taken seriously at Cornell, as noted already, and this marked a change from the earlier reform efforts at Knox. Yet these efforts need to be enlarged, so that teachers may be invited to be participants (and not just advisors) in the final programs that will emerge. For example, it seems possible and valuable for teachers in the local schools to participate in (perhaps teach or team teach) new courses dealing with the particular problems and possibilities of teaching. Such courses, yet to be created, will replace more conventional methods courses, and will more fully integrate the foundational issues and perspectives already discussed, the current realities of schooling, and future possibilities that go beyond those realities. An invaluable aid in this integration would be the inclusion of teachers who, while committed to teaching as a craft, a calling, and a species of praxis, are also personally involved in the daily rigors of public school teaching. Formal relationships between such teachers and college faculty are fully in keeping with the spirit of the Cornell program, and will be urged in upcoming discussions. Such relationships may lessen the tensions between its critical perspective and the demands of schooling, diminishing the tensions faced by students like Angela and Sally.

Third, the further development of a major in Educational Studies will be discussed and, I hope, enacted. This major might include a program constituted by: (i) the four core courses required in both elementary and secondary education programs; (ii) a 'thematic' area of concentration in, for instance, the arts, political and social theory, or the sociology of knowledge or educational institutions; and (iii) a 'senior thesis' based on some topic in the educational research literature (either dealing with schools or a larger area, involving a variety of possible methodologies). Together with the reforms already established and those contemplated, this major will assist in the further integration of education as a field and its attainment of academic respectability.

I realize that some of the accomplishments, setbacks, and concerns expressed in this chapter may be idiosyncratic, related to the specific people, traditions, and perspectives that make Cornell and Knox the colleges they are. No account of the alternatives promulgated at these institutions can hope to be a model for others concerned about articulating a different sort of program of educational studies. On the other hand, there is no reason to believe these colleges are unique, nor that the problems encountered are unusual, the successes unparalleled. The place of education within contemporary academe has a number of common problems, and shared traditions that lie at the root of those problems, that I have attempted to illuminate in this analysis; the specific contexts provided at Knox and Cornell College (and perhaps liberal arts colleges generally) may help us better understand how educators might work to resolve those problems and the traditions that support them. [17] Helping us see the larger institutional and intellectual contexts for the problems we face in education has been a special concern of this book, as we struggle over a number of intricate philosophical, historical, and sociological puzzles.

Yet as important as such struggles are, they pale in significance — if left disassociated from social realities in the way liberal inquiry persists in doing — to other, more human and political struggles. In the end, our judgment regarding the value of teacher preparation programs cannot rest on their ability to graduate 'professionals' who can effect-ively raise students' test scores, increase their 'time on task', generate 'educational excellence', assist in the socialization of pupils so that they display 'appropriate' behavior, or help develop a new class of deskilled managers. On the contrary, the preparation of teachers must be valued to the extent that it promotes a critical consciousness committed equally to (moral, political, and social) reflection and committed action, aimed at a more just, human, satisfying environment. Reform actions that refuse to address such admittedly idealistic possibilities are always suspect; so are forms of inquiry that neglect to consider alternative practices that further this idealism. Educational studies, and teacher preparation, can and must aid in combining knowledge and action in the pursuit of a better world.

Notes and References

1 For example, see Eva Foldes Travers and Susan Riemer Sacks, of the Consortium for Excellence in Teacher Education, *Teacher Education and the Liberal Arts: The Position of the Consortium for Excellence in Teacher Education*, February, 1987.

2 As I detail below, the second example discussed here concerns a program that as of this writing is only half formed. What I want to convey is an understanding of the dynamic, on going nature of the program outlined, and the honest uncertainty of the work that is required to formulate a foundational, praxis oriented attempt at preparing teachers. I will deal with the real prospects and problems associated with this work.

3 In the remainder of this chapter I will use the past tense in describing the programs and courses at Knox College, and the present and future tenses in describing my experiences and expectations at Cornell College. This reflects the actual, lived quality of my experiences, but more importantly how they are interrelated. My current efforts at Cornell are only possible because of my prior involvement at Knox. While my work at Cornell goes well beyond the activities I was engaged in at Knox, I have gained much from the people and ideas that represent the latter institution. I would like to acknowledge especially the support and responsiveness of Steve Bailey, Linda Dybas, Mary Eysenbach, Lance Factor, Henry Houser, and Bruce Strom. While my association with Cornell College has been less extensive, the encouragement and assistance of Ann Blakley, Diane Crowder, Diane Harrington, John Klaus, Susan Laird and Rich Martin has been of immense benefit; Bill Heywood's wisdom, good humor, and social conscience has been of special value, especially at those times when it looked as if the outcomes would not be all we had hoped for.

4 See LANDON E. BEYER, 'Field experience, ideology, and the development of critical reflectivity', *Journal of Teacher Education*, Volume XXXV, Number 3, May–June, 1984.

5   It should be noted that students attending any of the schools that comprise the ACM could elect to complete student teaching (and other, limited coursework, especially in bi-lingual and multi-cultural education) in the metropolitan area of Chicago. This of course created more diverse sites for student teaching, and modified some of the problems discussed here. Yet the number of students who actually took advantage of this option represented a rather small minority. In addition, I present examples of situations in the local schools, with which I was personally and principally involved.

6   See Chapter 3, 'Beyond reproduction ... '

7   See, for example, SAMUEL BOWLES and HERBERT GINTIS, *Schooling in Capitalist America* (New York: Basic Books, 1976); and HENRY GIROUX, 'Marxism and schooling: The limits of radical discourse', *Educational Theory*, Volume 34, Number 2, 1984.

8   Unlike many liberal arts colleges, Cornell offers a number of degree options, including the Bachelor of Arts, Bachelor of Special Studies, Bachelor of Music, Bachelor of Philosophy, and degree programs completed in conjunction with other institutions (e.g., programs in architecture and engineering). The first two are the most frequently chosen, and they differ principally in their requirements regarding distribution requirements. The BA degree specifies a total of 16 courses (half the total needed for graduation), distributed among several areas, including English, the fine arts, foreign languages, the humanities, physical education, the natural sciences, the social sciences, and speech. The BSS degree is essentially an individually designed program (discussed by the student and his/her advisor, and approved by the Dean of the College). It has no college-wide distribution requirements. Historically about three-fourths or more of the students enrolled in education programs have chosen the BSS degree.

9   Cornell has a rather different course structure and calendar — 'One-Course-At-A-Time' (OCAAT) — that is worth mentioning. The nine month academic year is divided into nine blocks, each of which lasts $3\frac{1}{2}$ weeks (with a $4\frac{1}{2}$ day break between blocks). Students enroll in, and faculty teach, one course during these blocks (each faculty member teaches seven courses per year, so that two blocks are non-teaching periods). For the most part, each course earns one credit and lasts one block. The only other college with such a system that I know of is Colorado College, after which Cornell is modeled. The particular problems and assets of this system — and its long term consequences and ideology — must await another volume.

10 See Beyer, *op. cit.*; KENNETH M. ZEICHNER and DANIEL P. LISTON, 'Teaching student teachers to reflect', *Harvard Educational Review*, Volume 57, Number 1, February, 1987; KENNETH M. ZEICHNER, 'Reflective teaching and field-based experience in teacher education', *Interchange*, Volume 12, Number 4, 1981.

11 One exception worth noting is the Women's Studies program at Cornell. Several courses are listed in this program, taught by faculty from several departments. In addition to the value of this program and its course

offerings, it represents a gender-based counter-hegemony within the confines of the college, and is an example from which faculty can learn a good deal.

12 THE HOLMES GROUP, *Tomorrow's Teachers: A Report of the Holmes Group* (East Lansing, Michigan: The Holmes Group, Inc., 1986).

13 See, for example, 'Perspectives on teacher education reform', a special issue of the *Journal of Teacher Education*, Volume XXXVIII, Number 3, May–June, 1987.

14 See MICHAEL W. APPLE, *Teachers and Texts: A Political Economy of Class and Gender Relations in Education* (Boston: Routledge and Kegan Paul, 1986); NANCY HOFFMAN, *Woman's 'True' Profession: Voices from the History of Teaching* (Old Westbury, NY: The Feminist Press, 1981); and JANE ROLAND MARTIN, *Reclaiming a Conversation: The Ideal of the Educated Woman* (New Haven: Yale University Press, 1985).

15 For example, see CHRISTINE M. SHEA, PETER A. SOLA, and ALAN H. JONES, 'Examining the crisis in the social foundations of education', *Educational Foundations*, Number 2, Spring, 1987.

16 See Apple, *op. cit.*

17 JEAN KING, 'The uneasy relationship between teacher education and the liberal arts and sciences', *Journal of Teacher Education*, Volume XXXVIII, Number 1, January–February, 1987.

Index

Abbs, Peter, 171n77
academic achievement, 95
achievement tradition, 95, 96, 101
Adler, Mortimer, 139–40, 168n27
Adler, Susan, 206n28
After Virtue, 147
alienated labor, 100, 102
Allegheny College, 6, 7
Almond, G. A., 170n63
ameliorative tradition in education,
    96
Amherst College, 6
analytic philosophy, 72, 121
Anyon, Jean, 133n34
Apple, Michael W., 43n30, 105,
    132n24, 133n32, 133n46,
    134n86, 139–40, 167n10,
    170n68, 171n71, 205n2,
    206n15, 206n17, 206n19,
    243n14
Aristotle, 179, 204, 205n12
Armstrong, D. M., 89n17
Aronowitz, Stanley, 167n17
art and aesthetics, 74–6, 88, 129,
    162, 163–6, 177, 182, 199, 218
Associated College of the Midwest
    (ACM), 211, 225, 242n5

Baier, Kurt, 167n19
Bailey, Steve, 241n3
Barber, Benjamin, 168n30

Barzun, Jacques, 7, 42n21, 42n22
behavioral sciences, 39, 41, 59–60,
    181
Bellah Robert N., 150, 151, 152,
    154, 168n29, 169n40, 170n45
Benjamin, Walter, 169n41
Berger, John, 169n42
Berlak, Harold, 168n31
Berlin, Isaiah, 89n9
Bernstein, Basil, 106–11, 118,
    133n35, 134n73
Bernstein, Richard J., 66–7, 74,
    90n30
Beyer, Landon E., 41n4, 42n28,
    43n48, 43n49, 45n74, 90n45,
    92n85, 131n3, 132n9, 134n86,
    167n5, 168n32, 169n37,
    171n71, 205n2, 206n21,
    207n29, 241n4, 242n10
Beyond Objectivism and Relativism, 66
Blakley, Ann, 241n3
Bleich, David, 170n51
Bleier, Ruth, 83, 91n71
Bowles, Samuel, 99–103, 105, 111,
    118, 132n18, 140, 167n16,
    242n7
Boyer, Ernest L., 121
Brameld, Theodore, 132n17
Braverman, Harry, 89n20
Bridges, J. H., 89n12
Bronowski, Jacob, 178, 205n8

Broudy, Harry S., 20, 43n43
Brown, G., 44n59
Brown versus Board of Education, 21
Bryant, Christopher G. A., 89n4
Bullough, Robert V., 206n17

Cairns, Huntington, 43n31, 88n1
A Call for Change in Teacher Education, 32, 34
Callahan, Raymond E., 45n71
capitalism, 60–2, 84, 87, 93, 99, 100, 101, 102, 105, 111, 118, 140, 149, 176, 196
Carnegie Forum on Education and the Economy, 27–8, 31, 32, 44n63
Carnoy, Martin, 170n63
Chapman, Laura H., 171n75
Class, Codes and Control, 107
Cole, G. D. H., 157
Colorado College, 242n9
collection educational codes, 108–10
commodification, 112, 145, 149, 169n41
communities of memory, 152, 158
Competency Based Teacher Education, 95, 187
Comte, Auguste, 53–8, 67, 74, 80, 86
Conant, James B., 121
Condorcet, Antoine Nicolas de, 55
Cornell College, 210–13, 224–36, 238, 239, 240, 241n3, 242n8, 242n9
correspondence theory, 99–102, 118, 140
Counts, George S., 98, 132n17
Cremin, Lawrence A., 167n25
Crowder, Diane, 241n3
Crozier, Michael J., 170n53
cultural capital, 162
cultural reproduction, 93, 97, 103–12, 114–15
culture of democracy, 152, 157, 164
curriculum (as a field of study), 98, 107, 108, 110, 111, 112, 116, 188–189

curriculum classification, 107
curriculum differentiation, 104
curriculum framing, 107–08

Dearden, Robert F., 169n37
DeLone, Richard, 157, 170n58
democracy, 19, 56, 78, 81, 87, 129, 144–60, 169n35
–and land grant universities, 8
Densmore, Kathleen, 205n4
Descartes, Rene, 71
Design for a School of Pedagogy, 24
deskilling of teaching, 175, 202, 218, 220–21, 223, 238, 241
DeVane, William C., 9, 10, 42n11
Dewey, John, vii, 2, 39, 41n2, 73, 79, 98, 131n5, 132n17, 158, 162, 170n64, 175, 181, 182, 185, 199, 205n3, 206n20, 238
distribution credit for education courses
–at Knox College, 215–16
–at Cornell College, 234–6, 242n8
division of labor, 80, 100, 106–7, 114, 117, 126
Dreeben, Robert F., 95–6, 103, 132n10
Durkheim, Emile, 53
Dybas, Linda, 241n3

'The 'Ear' Oles,' 116, 117
Ebmeier, Howard, 132n8
economic reproduction, 93, 97, 99–103, 111–12
Eddy, Edward D., Jr., 42n24
Edwards, Richard, 89n20, 132n26
Edwards, Sally, 113
Eisener, Elliot W., 171n77, 206n17
Elias, Norbert, 91n68
Eliot, Charles W., 65
Ellwood, Charles A., 89n7
Ennis Robert H., 20–1, 44n64, 166n1
equality, 146, 155, 156–7, 159, 160–1, 163, 182, 185, 197
equality of opportunity, 121, 156, 161

equality of sudies, 8
Esland, Geoffrey, M., 44n60
ethics, ethical debate, 95, 122, 129, 136
Ethics and Education, 19
Eysenbach, Mary, 241n3

Factor, Lance, 241n3
Feinberg, Walter, 119–131, 133n60, 134n73, 136, 189, 206n25
feminist epistemology, 48, 81–6
Feyerabend, Paul, 79–80, 91n63
field-based experiences, 24–5, 26, 29, 30, 32, 34, 36, 192–8
Finkelstein, Barbara, 168n32
Flew, Anthony, 167n18
Flexner, Abraham, 28
Floud, J., 97, 132n14
foundationalism in epistemology, 1, 29, 48, 66, 71–2, 74, 81, 186
foundations of education, 24–5, 27, 29, 38–9, 44n58, 185, 186–93
Frankena, William, 141, 167n20
Franklin, Barry, 166n4
'French positivism,' 29, 53
Freud, Sigmund, 82, 158
Fuller, Frances, 25, 44n57

Gadamer, Hans-George, 77, 91n56
Galileo, 73
gender and teaching, 175–6, 183, 197, 203, 204, 223, 238–9
Gillin, John L., 58, 89n14
Gilman, Daniel, 64, 90n26
Gintis, Herbert, 99–103, 105, 111, 118, 132n18, 140, 167n16, 242n7
Giroux, Henry, 242n7
Goldstein, Stanley, 206n17
Good, Thomas L., 132n8
Goodlad, John I., 206n26
Goodman, Jesse, 206n28
Grant, Carl, ii, vii, 90n45
Greene, John C., 89n6
Greer, Colin, 121, 133n64

Haber, Samuel, 45n71

Habermas, Jurgen, 91n57, 92n85, 155, 156, 161, 170n56
Hall, E., 44n59
Halsey, A. H., 97, 132n14
Hamilton, Edith 43n31, 88n1
Haraway, Donna, 91n72
Harding, Sandra, 84, 86, 91n73, 92n79
Harper, George Rainey, 65
Harrington, Diane, 241n3
Haskins, Charles H., 42n7
Heath, Shirley Brice, 126–9, 134n79
hegemony, 86, 89n21, 115, 119, 130
Heidegger, Martin, 73
hermeneutics, 48, 69, 73–4, 77–9, 88, 135, 144, 157, 163, 186
Heywood, Bill, 241n3
hidden curriculum, 96, 101, 116, 184, 189, 197, 221
high status knowledge, 105, 106, 125, 139
Hirst, Paul H., 18, 19, 43n37
Hoffman, Nancy, 243n14
The Holmes Group 35–9, 45n82, 181, 206n14, 225, 237, 243n12
Holt, Ladd, 206n17
Hord, S., 44n59
Houser, Henry, 241n3
Huebner, Dwayne, 98, 132n16, 206n24
Human Understanding, 50
Huntington, Samuel P., 170n53

Iannaccone, Lawrence, 44n55
The Idea of a University, 4
ideology, 47, 56, 62, 66, 86, 93, 102, 104, 112, 113, 115, 118, 138, 143, 161, 181
Ideology and Practice in Schooling, 112
Illinois State Board of Certification, 207n31
individualism, 149, 158, 162
'instrumental positivism,' 58–9
integrated educational codes, 108–10

Jackson, Phillip W., 132n11, 166n4
Jefferson, Thomas, 55, 144, 167n25
Johns, F., 207n30
Johns Hopkins University, 64
Jones, Alan H., 168n32, 243n15

Kant, Immanuel, 72
Karier, Clarence, J., 121, 133n64,
    206n16, 207n34
Katz, Lillian, 25, 44n56
Katz, Michael B., 121–3, 133n64,
    134n68
Keller, Evelyn Fox, 81–3, 86,
    91n68, 92n78
Kimball, Bruce A., 41n6
King, Jean, 243n17
Klaus, John, 241n3
Kliebard, Herbert M., 45n71, 94,
    131n1, 206n23, 207n33
Knox College, 2, 42n10, 62–4,
    210–24, 226, 228, 233, 236,
    238
knowledge code, 125, 128–130
knowledge frame, 125, 128–130
Komisar, B. Paul, 44n64, 166n1
Kuhn, Thomas S., 67, 69–71, 73,
    74, 77, 90n33, 91n55, 205n9

'the lads,' 115–18, 138
Laird, Susan, 241n3
Lasch, Christopher, 149, 168n30,
    169n42, 170n43
'laws of nature,' 52, 55, 57, 80–1
Lenzer, Gertrud 89n10
Lerner, Richard M., 89n16
*Learning to Labor: How Working Class
    Kids Get Working Class Jobs*,
    115–19, 138
Lee, Gordon C., 167n25
level of knowledge, 124, 126
liberal arts, 2, 3
liberal education, 4
lifestyle enclaves, 152–4
Liston, Daniel P., 242n10
The Long Revolution, 67, 74

Macdonald, James B., 98, 132n15
MacDonald, Madeline, 133n55

MacIntyre, Alasdair, 147, 168n28,
    169n36
MacNaughton, R., 207n30
Madsen, Richard, 168n29
Mann, Horace, 121, 122, 144
Martin, Jane Roland, 43n47, 243n14
Martin, Rich, 241n3
Marvin, F. S., 89n19
Marx, Karl, 158
marxism, marxist, 20, 140, 143, 144
McClellan, James E., 43n47, 44n64,
    166n1
McLaren, Peter, 166n4
mechanical solidarity, 110
medical knowledge, 105–6
Meiklejohn, Alexander, 6, 7, 42n16
mental and manual labour, 84, 117
Mill, John Stuart, 42n20, 68, 157
moral judgment, 137–44
Morril, Richard L., 169n34
Morrill Act, 8
Muelder, Hermann R., 42n10, 62,
    90n22

Nasaw, David, 207n34
A Nation at Risk, 27
National Board for Professional
    Teaching Standards, 28–9
National Commission on Excellence
    in Education, 24, 27, 44n62,
    144, 167n25
National Commission for Excellence
    in Teacher Education, 32, 34–5
Nevins. Allan, 42n23
new sociology of education, 97, 104
Newman, John Henry (Cardinal), 4,
    5, 41n5, 42n9
The Nicomachean Ethics, 179
Noble, David 89n20
Noble, Douglas D., 205n2
Noddings, Nel, 91n75, 171n70
normative frameworks, 13, 137,
    144, 155–60, 173, 189
Nozick, Robert, 158, 170n65
Nyberg, David, 43n43

objectivity, 52, 62, 71, 81, 83, 85,
    96, 120, 177, 184

O'Connor, James, 89n20
Olson, Lynn, 206n26
On What Is Learned in School, 95
organic solidarity, 110

Pagano, Jo Anne, 167n23
The Paideia Proposal, 139
paradigm, 70, 73, 74, 78
Pateman, Carole, 154, 170n54
Paul, Jeffrey, 170n67
Peters, Charles C., 206n15
Peters, Richard S., 18, 19, 43n37,
     43n40, 199
Phenix, Philip H., 45n88
Philosophy and Education, 20–3
philosophy of education, 16–24, 27
phronesis, 179–80
Piaget, Jean, 82
Pinar, William F., 45n71, 131n1,
     132n16, 206n24, 207n33
Plato, 13–5, 43n31, 49–50, 52,
     88n1
Popkewitz, Thomas, 44n55, 141,
     205n6
Popp, Jerome A., 17, 43n34
positivism, 52–62, 66, 67, 69, 70,
     75, 77, 79–82, 86, 87, 95, 135,
     136, 142, 144, 159, 176, 180,
     181, 186
practical philosophy/wisdom, 77,
     178–80
praxis, 48, 93, 137, 144, 166, 173,
     182, 185, 187, 188–91, 194,
     196, 197, 202, 204, 205n1,
     209, 235, 236, 238, 239, 241n2
Presley, C. F., 89n17
professionalism, 95, 174, 184–5,
     237, 240

Quantz, Richard, 205n8

The Reflective Practitioner, 94
Republic, 13
revisionist history of education,
     121–4
Rogus, J., 207n30
Rorty, Richard, 71, 72, 73, 74, 78,
     79, 90n41, 91n48

Ross, Earle E., 42n25
Rousseau, Jean Jacques, 157, 199
Rudman, Masha Kabakow, 171n77
Rugg, Harold, 98, 132n17
Ryan, William, 156, 170n59

Sacks, Susan Riemer, 241n1
Saint-Simon, 53
Scheffler, Israel, 18, 43n36
Schon, Donald A., 94–5, 132n6
Schooling in Capitalist America, 99,
     102, 140
The Science Question in Feminism, 84
scope of knowledge, 124–6
selective tradition, 113
Shea, Christine M., 243n15
Shearer, Derek, 170n62
Sheffield Scientific School, 5
Siegel, Harvey, 44n50
Singer, Marcus 167n18
Sirotnik, Kenneth A., 139, 167n12,
     206n18
Skinner, B. F., 59
Smith, B. Othanel, 9, 10, 24, 26,
     27, 42n29, 44n59, 44n64,
     166n1
social control, 110, 112, 115
social reproduction, 93, 103, 112,
     117, 119, 124, 129–30, 135–7,
     140, 144, 176, 182, 183, 189
socialization, 10, 22, 34, 36, 95, 96,
     97, 99, 101, 103, 110, 174,
     194, 239, 241
sociology of education, 97, 103,
     104, 187, 196
Socrates, 15, 199
Sola, Peter A., 243n15
Soltis, Jonas F., 20, 27, 43n41,
     169n37
Spodek, Bernard, 44n56
Spring, Joel, 158, 170n66
Stanley, Manfred, 168n32
Steedman, Philip H., 166n3
Strom, Bruce, 241n3
structural functionalism, 93, 96, 97,
     99, 103, 187
The Structure of Scientific Revolutions,
     67, 71

'structure of the disciplines,' 41, 49, 52, 176–8
Sullivan, William M., 168n29, 179, 205n11
Swidler, Ann, 168n29

Tabachnick, B. Robert, 44n55
Tabakin, Geoffrey, 205n4
Tanner, Daniel, 89n18, 166n4
Tanner, Laurel N., 89n18, 166n4
Taxel, Joel, 112–3, 115, 118, 133n47
Taylor, Frederick Winslow, 45n71
teacher training, 10, 173–7
technical rationality, 95, 98, 99, 101, 150–1, 159, 160, 174, 175
theory and practice, 1–3, 22–4, 27, 34, 39, 135–7, 146, 173, 177, 185, 186, 193, 209, 231–2
Thorndike, Edward L., 39, 59, 60, 181, 182, 238
Tipton, Steven M., 168n29
Tom, Alan R., 206n17
Tomorrow's Teachers, 35, 36, 39, 237, 238
Toulmin, Stephen, 50, 89n2
Travers, Eva Foldes, 241n1
Tyack, David, 134n65, 207n34

Understanding Education, 119, 125, 131, 189
University of Chicago, 64, 65

Valli, Linda, 114–5, 118, 133n50
Verba, S., 170n63

Violas, Paul, 121, 133n64, 207n34

Waller, Willard, 132n8
Watanuki, Joji, 170n53
Watson, John B., 59
Wegener, Charles, 90n29
Ways With Words, 126
Weis, Lois, 43n30, 133n46, 170n68, 206n19
Wellman, Carl, 167n22
When the World's on Fire, 113
Whitty, Geoff, 170n68
Williams, Raymond, 67, 74–6, 90n32, 91n50, 136, 144, 166n2, 167n24
Willis, Paul, 115–19, 133n54, 138–40, 167n7
Wilson, E. O., 92n76
Winch, Peter, 67–9, 74, 80, 90n31
Wirth, Arthur, 170n62
Wittengstein, Ludwig, 73
Women's Studies Program at Cornell College, 242n11
Wood, George H., 92n85, 134n86, 168n31, 170n67
workplace ot teaching, 22–3, 35, 183, 202–4, 218, 239

Yale University, 5

Young, Michael F. D., 44n60, 103–6, 111, 118, 132n27, 170n68

Zeichner, Kenneth M., 44n54, 131n3, 132n9, 242n10